Gens 1 : 26-31
2: 7/2;15-
25

The Co

Positive

The Coming of Lilith

reimagine story

Essays on Feminism, Judaism, and Sexual Ethics, 1972–2003

Judith Plaskow

Edited with Donna Berman

Beacon Press
Boston

Beacon Press
25 Beacon Street
Boston, Massachusetts 02108-2892
www.beacon.org

Beacon Press books
are published under the auspices of
the Unitarian Universalist Association of Congregations.

08 07 06 05 8 7 6 5 4 3 2 1

This book is printed on acid-free paper that meets the uncoated paper
ANSI/NISO specifications for permanence as revised in 1992.

Text design by Bob Kosturko
Composition by Wilsted & Taylor Publishing Services

Library of Congress Cataloging-in-Publication Data

Plaskow, Judith.
  The coming of Lilith : essays on feminism, Judaism, and sexual ethics, 1972–2003 /
Judith Plaskow ; edited with Donna Berman.
     p. cm.
  Includes bibliographical references.
  ISBN 0-8070-3623-4 (pbk. : alk. paper)
  1. Women in Judaism. 2. Feminism—Religious aspects—Judaism. 3. Sex—Religious aspects—
Judaism. 4. Sexual ethics. 5. Judaism—20th century. I. Berman, Donna. II. Title.

BM729.W6P54 2005
296'.082—dc22   2004027039

To Martha,
who was there from the beginning

CONTENTS

IV. SEXUALITY, AUTHORITY, AND TRADITION

Foreword

I first met Judith Plaskow in the spring of 1989, when I interviewed her for a wonderful, now defunct, feminist newspaper called *New Directions for Women*. I had pestered the editors relentlessly until they agreed to let me do it. They told me outright that interviews were not their usual genre. I knew it would probably never get published (and it never did), but I didn't care. I had just wanted an excuse to talk with this woman who was changing the face of Judaism.

Since 1972, as a graduate student at Yale, Judith had been writing essays that were clear articulations of what had previously been amorphous rumblings, glimpses of truths that were hard to name and, more than that, difficult to admit. Judith continually laid bare the real issues, the hard questions, the rot under the veneer that requires full, often painful, excavation in order for true healing to take place. For many women longing for a Judaism that spoke to them, and more importantly, *heard* them, Judith's work evoked what she calls the "yeah, yeah experience" of connection, sisterhood, and hope.

As a young rabbi and burgeoning feminist, I had been deeply influenced by Judith's thought. She was among those who first opened my eyes to the fact that (as naïve as it now sounds) women's entry into the rabbinate did not signal the end of Judaism's life-or-death struggle with patriarchy, but rather the beginning, and that I—and every woman rabbi—had a vital role to play in that struggle.

From reconceptualizing the triad of Jewish thought—God, Torah, and Israel—to exposing the very concrete impact of sexist God-language on women's lives, to making clear the connections between various forms of oppression, Judith's thought was a blueprint for a rabbinate that was a tool for change both within and beyond the Jewish community. For me, this meant that during my twelve years as rabbi of Port Jewish Center in Port Washington, New York, I felt empowered, indeed compelled, to constantly expose and speak out against what I saw as unjust in Jewish tradition. I wanted my congregants and my students to feel equally empowered and compelled to wrestle openly with their faith. I sought to ignite in them, as Judith had helped ignite in me, a burning passion for justice that would become a primary lens through which to view and evaluate both their secular and Jewish worlds. I bring this passion for justice to my current work as the director of the Charter Oak Cultural Center, a multicultural arts center in one of Hartford, Connecticut's poorest neighborhoods. My rabbinate has taken a different form as I continue to evolve as a Jewish feminist theologian.

But let me be blunt: Judith's work is not for the faint-hearted. She demands that we give up the safety of comfortable pretenses: the pretense of an objectivity that transcends our gender, race, socioeconomic location, and sexual orientation; the pretense that we have no presuppositions that determine which parts of a contradictory religious tradition we choose to pay attention to; the pretense that gay and lesbian rights are not ultimately about the dismantling of compulsory heterosexuality. Her work is hard-hitting, brutally honest, iconoclastic, and always rewarding and enlightening.

Mostly Judith complicates things. More accurately, she exposes the complexity we so assiduously attempt to avoid in our search for quick and easy answers and solutions. As early as 1973 she was cautioning us that there isn't one simple entity called "women's experience." Women's experience is as diverse and varied and rich as the lives and histories of the real women it encompasses. To privilege and universalize *some* women's experience, Judith reminds us, is to echo one of the most tragic flaws of patriarchy—the universalization of male experience. Moreover, Judith teaches us that just as women's experience cannot be neatly distilled, so Judaism cannot be thought of as one uniform belief system. In her articles on Christian anti-Judaism, she implores Christian feminists to resist the notion of a monolithic, normative Judaism that is entirely misogynist. Judaism, she stresses, is a complex, multivalent hodgepodge of a tradition with many competing strands, a tradition that must be seen in its entirety to be fairly judged. "Can we learn to listen to each other in our complexity?" she asks.

In these essays, Judith builds a powerful case for her contention that Jewish feminists will make limited progress in securing women's rights and privileges in Judaism if we focus exclusively on changing *halakhah* (Jewish law). Not surprisingly, Judith believes that creating real change in Judaism is more complicated than that. It is, she argues, a matter of confronting the notion of the Otherness of women that undergirds Jewish law. She urges Jewish feminists to question "the fundamental presuppositions of the legal system" so that we may, to use her metaphor, not just get a piece of the Jewish pie but begin baking an entirely new one.

Judith also brings into relief what she calls the "complexity of oppression," a reality that makes it possible, perhaps inescapable, for one to be both oppressed and oppressor. The fact that none of us is immune from being a victimizer just because we are or have been a victim is a sobering, important, and ultimately empowering truth if we are to see ourselves clearly and act with integrity. She writes, "to be a Jew and not a Nazi is, in a sense, a moral privilege, but it guarantees nothing about who the Jew will be when s/he comes to power."

Most recently, it is to the issue of authority that Judith turns her attention. The Bible, she reminds us, was written and continues to be interpreted by people with particular biases. Bringing our unique perspectives to bear on what we encounter is unavoidable, but Judith insists that the criteria we use for picking and choosing among conflicting texts must be openly acknowledged, lest we make our own preferences seem "Jewishly inevitable."

And, she argues, authority is key to the issue of gay and lesbian rights. The essential questions are not who is gay and why, but rather how, by whom, and for what purpose heterosexuality "comes to be constructed and accepted as normative." She claims that these questions have "the potential to begin a conversation that addresses the complexity of people's lives . . . that might lead to a new understanding of the nature of eroticism and its relationship to the holy." Judith teaches us that gay rights, like women's rights in Judaism, are about far more than changing the law. Each demands nothing less than a rethinking of our world. This, of course, helps explain why opponents of gay marriage feel so deeply threatened by something so seemingly benign; it is not marriage, but a worldview and its power structure that they are defending.

For me, one of the most powerful elements of Judith's thought is her contention that we need to honestly confront and acknowledge that which is difficult and painful to see in ourselves, in our tradition, and in God. If we do not confront the rejected parts of ourselves, we will almost inevitably project them onto those around us, seeing them and treating them as Other. If we do not confront the unjust aspects of our tradition, we will deprive ourselves of "places to name and explore the contours and causes of our pain." If we do not confront the troubling aspects of our tradition's depiction of God then, she argues, we are left with a "theology that would close off huge areas of our [own] experience and declare them devoid of sacred power." These disturbing, humbling, powerful insights again serve to complicate things, bringing into focus the simplistic post-9/11 worldview of us versus them, good versus evil, in which we now find ourselves immersed.

Fifteen years after that interview, Judith Plaskow's thought continues to stand as a beacon, illuminating the challenging terrain of some of the most difficult questions we face as a society. Her work is so layered with mind-bending ideas that you might find yourself, as I often do, needing to come up for air. This reaction makes sense. Judith traces the circuitous, insidious patterns and pathways of patriarchy, making the connections between interlocking oppressions and between abstract theological concepts and their impact on the real world. One feels like coming up for air partly because the stultifying nature of patriarchy is being so methodically and artfully exposed, but also because there is a sense that, at long last, there is again air to breathe.

DONNA BERMAN
Bloomfield, Connecticut

Intersections

An Introduction

Publication of *The Coming of Lilith* provides me with an opportunity to look back on my evolution as a Jewish feminist theologian and to examine the intertwining personal, intellectual, and spiritual threads in my development. Because I am a person who is excited by ideas and persuaded of their reality and power, I cannot separate my intellectual journey from my personal history. My story has too many strands to weave into a strictly chronological narrative, but I can best introduce the essays in this volume by connecting them to my emerging concerns as a feminist, a theologian, and a feminist Jew. Many of the essays have been somewhat shortened for this setting, but I believe they all retain their original substance and spirit.

I came to feminism with an inchoate sense of difference, oppression, and power that was clarified and transformed by my feminist experiences. I grew up Jewish in the 1950s in a Long Island town where Jews were a large minority, and I was both comfortable in my surroundings and aware of not being part of the dominant culture. In the classical Reform Jewish congregation in which I was raised, Judaism was defined as "ethical monotheism." Jews, we were taught, had given the world the purifying vision of belief in one universal God. It was our obligation to manifest this belief in the realm of human relations through fair dealings with others on an interpersonal level and through commitment to the vision of social justice central to the prophets. I fully embraced this version of Judaism without worrying about either its internal coherence or whether it really distinguished Jews from anyone around us.

An important part of my Jewish self-understanding as a young person, and a central source of the ethical awareness that fed my commitment to "ethical monotheism," was my fascination with the Holocaust. From about age twelve through my college years, I read obsessively about the extermination of European Jewry. This reading fed an interest in theological questions that had attracted me from my earliest childhood: Was there a God? Could God be said to be good? How could the deaths camps have been built in the middle of the twentieth century? What did they say about God's relationship to the Jewish people? What did they reveal about the nature of human beings? My preoccupation with the Holocaust meant that my Jewish identity was closely tied to a sense of victimhood. I experienced being a victim as a moral privilege that exempted me from having to know whether the evil perpetrated by the Nazis was also inside me. The question of whether Jews could have been Nazis, whether it was a historical accident or some real moral difference that cast Jews in the role of victims, has haunted me for as long as I can remember. I felt the painfulness of the Jewish historical experience; yet I was grateful for the privilege of the outsider's consciousness that led me to contemplate difficult ethical issues from the time I was a young girl.

My sense of Jews as victims led me to identify with other victims of oppression, especially African Americans. My introduction to social justice issues came in 1957 when my father explained a newspaper article about Governor Orval Faubus blocking the entry of black students into a high school in Little Rock. His voice shook with conviction as he insisted that all people were equal, regardless of the color of their skin. Ten years old at the time, I had never seen my father so earnest and vehement, and his words made a profound impression on me. When I was in seventh grade, I won second place in the junior high speech contest, talking about the relationship between apartheid in South Africa and segregation in the American South. In 1963, I went with a substantial contingent from our temple to the March on Washington for Jobs and Freedom. This event was my first experience of the power of transformative vision and the importance of collective action as a vehicle for social change. I can still feel the extraordinary exhilaration of standing at the foot of the Washington Monument, hearing Martin Luther King deliver his "I have a dream" speech, and feeling that, in that all-too-brief moment, the dream was a reality.

I became a feminist in the fall of 1969, my second year as a graduate student in religious studies at Yale, and the year Yale admitted women to the undergraduate college. When the *New York Times* ran a front-page story on the entry of women, and Yale prepared for women's education by hiring a gynecologist and putting full-length mirrors in the bathrooms, two female graduate students called an open meeting to discuss how it was that we had been at Yale for eighty years and no one had noticed. I went to the meeting out of curiosity and found myself in a room with about fifty other women. Very few of us were feminists; I certainly wasn't. We were at Yale because doors had been opened to us, and probably most of us assumed that they were open to any woman who was "good enough." Most of us had never before experienced the combination of suspicion, dismissal, surveillance, and condescending courtliness we met at Yale. We began meeting weekly and talking about our lives, at Yale and beyond. We called ourselves the Yale Women's Alliance, and, as I recall, we spent roughly half our time on consciousness-raising and half on activist issues connected to life at the university.

The process of our meetings that fall was life-changing for me; indeed, it constituted a conversion. As I began to connect my own personal history as a girl who had always been "too smart" with my new understandings of women's socialization and social roles, my whole way of looking at the world began to shift. In February of 1970, psychologist Naomi Weisstein spoke at Yale Law School about the importance of building a feminist movement. Describing with breathtaking precision the painfulness of being a female graduate student at an elite institution, she stressed over and over that changes in social structures require a social movement. She talked about women who wanted to be doctors, lawyers, and ministers, and ended up doctors' wives, lawyers' wives, and ministers' wives. As a rabbi's wife who had wanted to be a rabbi, I went home and spent half the night weeping, feeling at age twenty-two that I had wasted my life.

Since I was a graduate student in religious studies at the time I became a feminist, it was a small step to begin to apply my new insights to religion. Carol P. Christ was one of the other women at the initial gathering of the Yale Women's Alliance, and we fairly quickly began to relate our growing feminist awareness to our studies in theology. We began to *notice,* for example, that we had never been assigned a single book or article by a woman. We began to *notice* the dreadful things said about women by virtually every theologian we were studying. Carol wrote a short seminar paper on Karl Barth in which she connected his statement that women are ontologically subordinate to men with his hierarchical understanding of God and creation. In linking specific attitudes toward women with fundamental theological categories, she helped launch both of us on our way to becoming feminist theologians.

In the spring of 1972, I decided that, despite the opposition or nonsupport of almost everyone on the faculty, I would write a feminist dissertation. I wanted to start with Valerie Saiving's early critique (1960) of Protestant doctrines of sin and grace and root it in a nonbiological (in today's terms, nonessentialist) understanding of women's experience.[1] My choice to write a feminist thesis—I think perhaps the second in religious studies in the United States—was an important turning point for me in that it marked the beginning of my involvement in the creation of women's studies in religion.

In the summer of 1972, I attended the conference of Women Exploring Theology at Grailville, where I first experienced the excitement of women creating theology together. The process of the conference, the extraordinary images of God it generated, and the power of women's bonding that was a central part of the week remained theological reference points for me for many years afterward. The wonderful small group in which I participated tried to capture the significance of feminist community by focusing on consciousness-raising as a religious experience. At my suggestion, we then looked at the relationship between Eve and Lilith as a possible paradigm of sisterhood. The title essay in this volume, "The Coming of Lilith" (1972), reflects on the group's discussions in a way that I hope captures the intense optimism and exhilaration of those first forays into doing theology as feminists. The Lilith *midrash* (a classic Jewish mode of biblical interpretation and exposition) can be read as a metaphor for the unfolding of feminist work over the last thirty-plus years: when Eve and Lilith—indeed, many different Eves and Liliths—join together, theology, the world, and God must change. "The Coming of Lilith" was my first theological essay, and although, as I point out in "Lilith Revisited" (1995), it remains tethered to the Protestant categories of my graduate education, it also represents my first, albeit semi-unconscious, attempt to use traditional Jewish modes of expression.

The early 1970s continued to be years of important feminist theological exploration for me. In the fall of 1972, I became co-chair with Joan Arnold Romero of the Women and Religion Group of the American Academy of Religion, during the second and third years of its existence. I will never forget the excitement of those early sessions as we squeezed into rooms far too small to contain either the numbers or energy of those who gathered, knowing we were off to explore uncharted continents. In 1973, I was a research associate in women's studies at Harvard Divinity School during the first year of the program. I did not have much success in my assigned task—getting the theology department to change its curriculum—but my time at Harvard forced me to clarify my feminist critique of theology and provided me with another important experience of feminist community. Then, in 1974, I moved to New York and had the privilege of participating in the early conversations of the New York Area Feminist Scholars in Religion. It was there that I first was challenged by Goddess thealogy, heard original versions of ideas that became important books in women's studies in religion, and thrashed out issues in an emerging field with many remarkable women.

"Male Theology and the Experience of Women" (1978), which appears here in English for the first time, reflects my efforts during this period to formulate a substantive yet fluid definition of women's (and men's) experience and explore its implications for theology. The essay draws on ideas I developed in my dissertation, *Sex, Sin, and Grace: Women's Experience and the Theologies of Reinhold Niebuhr and Paul Tillich.*[2] Although today, the whole notion of women's experience is often dismissed as essentialist, I see myself as grappling in the early 1970s with questions that became central to feminist discussion only in the 1980s. How is it possible to talk about the exclusion of women's perspectives from theological discourse, and the possible impact of women doing theology, without assuming a static and monolithic understanding of women or women's experience? It was partly my Jewishness that led me to seek a definition of women's experience that could take account of cultural particularity.

During the period that I was becoming a feminist academic, I was undergoing a parallel, though in many ways more difficult, process of awakening as a feminist Jew. I entered a graduate program in Protestant theology because I wanted to be a theologian, and in the late 1960s there was nowhere in the country to study Jewish theology. My Jewish identity was only strengthened by my experience in a Christian-dominated institution, however, and, ironically, I discovered feminism at precisely a moment in my personal life when I was also exploring traditional Judaism. While I was attending Yale Women's Alliance meetings during the week, I was spending Saturday mornings sitting in the back of a chapel, a nonmember of a *minyan* (a quorum for prayer traditionally composed of ten men) consisting mainly of male undergraduates. One Sabbath, as my new husband and I were standing outside the chapel, chatting with a friend, a student came out and urged my husband to come in immediately to make the minyan. I suddenly realized that, although I had been attending services regularly for over a year and he was a relative newcomer, only his presence was relevant to the purpose for which we were gathered. That was an enormously important CLICK moment for me that redefined my relationship to Judaism. It made it impossible for me to attend either a traditional synagogue or a liberal synagogue, like the one in which I grew up, that paid lip service to equality but treated women as second-class citizens.

My conflicted relationship to Judaism for much of the 1970s is reflected in "The Jewish Feminist: Conflict in Identities," the talk I gave at the first Jewish feminist conference in 1973. There I argued that the identity of Jewish feminists "lies somewhere in the conflict between being a woman and being a Jew and in the necessity of combining the two in as yet unknown ways.... We are here," I said—and the assertion clearly struck a chord as I remember being interrupted by applause at this point—"because a secular movement for the liberation of women has made it imperative to raise certain Jewish issues now, because we will not let ourselves be defined as Jewish women in ways in which we cannot allow ourselves to be defined as women."[3] I was speaking as someone who had discovered a new source of community and identity in feminism and who desperately wanted to help bring its energy and transformative insights into the Jewish community. But the difficulty of finding a comfortable Jewish place for myself was brought home to me even by the wonderful Sabbath service at the same conference. As five hundred women prayed together, I was deeply moved to hear women's voices chanting Torah and to witness women who had been engaged Jews their entire lives look into a Torah for the first time. I was also furious, however, that I should have to be moved by watching women do things that men of the same commitment and education had been doing regularly from age thirteen.

Throughout the 1970s, there was a certain disconnection and even tension between my academic life and my life as a Jewish feminist. By the mid-

1970s, I had a wonderful group of feminist colleagues in the American Academy of Religion with whom I had developed a fairly nuanced scholarly understanding of the role of women in Western religion. We analyzed women's exclusion from public religious roles and the absence of women's experiences and perspectives from theology and religious symbolism. We also realized that this exclusion was not the whole truth, that women had found ways to express ourselves religiously within and against traditional frameworks. In the Jewish context, however, the realities of women's subordination and exclusion were far more real to me than the ways we had carved —or might someday carve—a niche for ourselves within this patriarchal tradition.

The early 1980s marked another period of intense transformation in my life that led me in the direction of an integrated Jewish feminist identity, changed my religious and scholarly commitments, and complicated my understandings of power, victimization, and difference. In the summer of 1980, I decided to teach a course on Jewish feminist theology at the first National Havurah Summer Institute—essentially an adult-learning camp for countercultural Jews. It was my first opportunity to raise in a Jewish context the theological questions that most excited me, and, although I had no idea whether anyone would be interested in taking such a class, in fact several people came to the Institute precisely because it was offered. The seriousness with which the women and two men present discussed the subordination of women in the Jewish community and grappled with the male-centeredness of Torah and traditional images of God gave me my first taste of Jewish feminist community. It was an incredibly exhilarating teaching experience, and a moment in which the separated aspects of my life began to come together. My essay "The Right Question Is Theological" (1982) grew out of that class. The Jewish counterpart of "Male Theology and Women's Experience," the essay sets out a systematic critique of tradition rather than focusing on particular problematic laws or texts. In calling for a new feminist understanding of Torah, God, and Israel, I was setting myself an agenda for the next decade and beyond. In articulating my developing theological perspective in the Jewish context, I was beginning to find a new voice.

Partly as a result of the excitement generated by several feminist courses at the Havurah Institute, a group of women decided to create a space in which we could explore feminist issues in an ongoing and more focused way. In May of 1981, sixteen Jewish feminists gathered at the Grail Retreat Center in Cornwall-on-Hudson with the modest goal of reconfiguring Judaism in four days. We felt we were coming together as a "new Yavneh," the founding moment of rabbinic Judaism. That weekend became the inaugural meeting of B'not Esh (daughters of fire), a feminist spirituality collective that has been meeting annually ever since. I now had a Jewish context within which to explore feminist questions and attempt to create a feminist Judaism. B'not Esh was not only a place to *talk* about feminism but also a space to *enact* some of the changes that we hoped might someday be incorporated into the larger Jewish community.

B'not Esh was founded in an era of identity politics, at a time when feminists of color, Jewish feminists, lesbians, and others were beginning to interrogate the "we" of a seemingly white, Christian, heterosexual feminism, and demanding that multiple realities be included in its self-definition and agenda. We gathered as Jewish feminists to explore the common issues that emerged from our standing on the boundaries of several different communities, hoping we had at last found the home that would welcome all of who we were. But one of the things the group had to confront our first weekend together was that, while we were all committed to creating a feminist Judaism, we were by no means agreed on the nature of that new beast. All of us had come to the weekend expecting finally to find the safe and completely like-minded community that had eluded us everywhere else in our lives; in fact, we were faced with profound differences in religious and feminist commitments that made us feel even more isolated. Over the course of the next several years, our religious differences—along with those of sexuality, class, Jewish ethnic identity and personal history—were to serve as important sources of strength for the group. Initially, however, they were upsetting and difficult to navigate.

In the end, it was B'not Esh among a confluence of factors that helped me to move from an angry sense of powerlessness to a vision of a transformed Judaism. On the academic side, the publication of Elisabeth Schüssler Fiorenza's *In Memory of Her* was a crucial intellectual turning point for me. Reading the book for a panel at the American Academy of Religion in 1983, I found myself struggling mightily against its fundamental premises. When

Elisabeth argued that women are fully part of the Christian past, and claimed that accepting androcentric texts as accurate depictions of reality meant colluding in women's oppression, I repeatedly scrawled in the margins: How do you know this? Isn't this an enormous assumption, indeed an a priori commitment? Then at some point, I realized I was resisting her thesis because it thrust me into a place of unaccustomed and frightening power. If I accepted the notion that religious history is the history of women, I would have to move beyond being a victim nursing my grievances to confront the huge task of reconstructing women's history. I would have to demand from the Jewish community that it integrate women's experience into every aspect of communal life.

Coincident with my beginning to make this internal shift was my coming out as a lesbian. This huge step could have added more fodder to my anger at Judaism, in that it threw into bold relief the relationship between its sexism and heterosexism. In the period I was struggling with whether to leave my marriage, I came to appreciate the enormous and pervasive nature of heterosexual privilege. But coming out did not, in fact, reinforce my sense of victimhood. Instead it freed me to claim my own emotional and spiritual power, just as *In Memory of Her* was encouraging me to claim my intellectual power. In part, I attribute this effect to a deep connection between sexuality, embodiment, and creativity that I experienced powerfully at this point in my life. But also, I think I discovered that, having walked through one closed door and survived, I could also walk through others.

A third pivotal event occurred in the early 1980s. Toward the end of our second retreat, B'not Esh resolved to stop seeking a common denominator in prayer that we would never be able to achieve. Instead of trying to reach consensus on how to worship together, we would empower individual women to take turns creating the liturgies that they wanted to experience, and we would agree to be present and try on things that might challenge our own proclivities and boundaries. This was a crucial decision that enacted in the realm of prayer an issue with which we were also struggling in our group discussions: how to use our differences as a source of power and growth, rather than seeing them as obstacles to community. Our Sabbath services offered a model for laying open our differences and learning from them, even where they might generate dissension or pain. The decision ushered in many years of exciting liturgical experimentation through which we all began to appreciate the various, sometimes radical, ways in which we could incorporate our voices as women into the liturgy and still maintain ties to the deep structures of tradition.

As I was taking power in these different areas of my life, I was also undergoing a shift in another important element of my Jewish identity. I have said that a sense of Jews as victims had always been central to my understanding of what it meant to be a Jew. Insofar as I was angry at "the tradition" for excluding women from Jewish religious participation and was waiting for someone with authority to bring about change, victimization was also central to my initial experience of Jewish feminism. Israel's invasion of Lebanon in 1982, however, forced me to reexamine my underlying beliefs about Jewish powerlessness on a deep existential level. I had been critical of Israeli policies before then, but my criticisms had not changed my internal sense of the meaning of my Jewishness. After 1982, I found myself compelled to explore the implications of Israel's power in the Middle East and to accept the fact that Jews could be victimizers as well as victims. Painfully relinquishing the sense of moral privilege that I had seen as adhering to suffering, I began to ask new questions about the responsibilities that come with wielding power.

From the 1980s on, I began to develop, in more self-critical directions, themes that were present earlier in my work. In 1978, I published the essay "Christian Feminism and Anti-Judaism," in which I examined the ways that Christian feminists had created new forms of old anti-Jewish arguments. Feminist consciousness, I pointed out, provides no inoculation against reproducing patterns of exclusion and domination. I returned to and embellished this argument a number of times, including at the European Society for Women in Theological Research in 1989, where I delivered the talk that became "Feminist Anti-Judaism and the Christian God" (1990). But Israel's invasion of Lebanon, along with the significant emergence of womanist and mujerista voices in the academy, led me to reflect more fully on the ways in which I stood on both sides of the supposed dichotomy between oppressed and oppressor. I realized that I had reproduced in relation to women of color many of the same forms of ignorance and stereotyping for which I chastised Christian feminists, just as Israel had recapitulated for Palestinians some of the traumas of the Jewish experience. From the mid-1980s on, I participated in many discussions in which I explored the experience of seeing myself from both sides of the marginalized/marginalizer divide. "Anti-Semitism: The Unacknowledged Racism" (1984) is the only example of this theme in my writing that stands as an independent essay.[4] It was originally part of a session on racism, pluralism, and bonding at the Women's Spirit Bonding conference at Grailville in 1982, but I later rewrote it so that it would make sense on its own. "Jewish Anti-Paganism" (1991) and "Dealing With the Hard Stuff" (1994) develop this complex perspective in my writing for a Jewish audience, laying out different ways in which Jews have created multiple "Others."

It was the confluence of these experiences and events that enabled me to begin writing my book *Standing Again at Sinai* in the mid-1980s. In working on that project, I was able to bring together the critical and constructive, academic, religious, feminist, and Jewish feminist commitments in my life. As I explored the implications of two decades of feminist work in religion for the Jewish context, I drew on many years of conversations with Christian and post-Christian colleagues in the academy, and at the same time tried to ground myself in B'not Esh as a very particular Jewish feminist community. Having spent most of my academic life in non-Jewish settings, I now attempted to find the appropriate categories for a Jewish feminist theology. "Jewish Theology in Feminist Perspective" (1994) is my fullest statement of the themes of Jewish feminism outside of *Standing Again at Sinai,* and my most mature. It responds to the challenge I posed for myself in "The Right Question Is Theological" in that it reframes the concepts of God, Torah, and Israel from a feminist perspective.

During the period that I was working on *Standing Again at Sinai*—and up to the present day—I had the privilege of lecturing and writing in a wide variety of settings about creating a feminist Judaism. I have never been interested in addressing only or primarily members of the academy; I have always wanted to share my ideas about feminism and the possibilities of religious transformation with as wide an audience as possible. The essays in the third section of this volume, "Creating a Feminist Judaism," are drawn largely but not entirely from the columns I wrote for *Tikkun* magazine in the 1990s. They address particular problems and questions involved in the feminist critique and transformation of Judaism, applying the methodology and perspective I develop in *Standing Again at Sinai* to specific feminist issues.

How is male God-language connected to the subordination of women, and how do feminists create new images and new conceptions of God? ("God: Some Feminist Questions," 1987.) Do feminists need a God who is loving and nurturing? ("Facing the Ambiguity of God," 1991.) Once feminists note the absence of women's voices from Jewish canonical texts, can those texts continue to function authoritatively? (" 'It Is Not in Heaven,' " 1990.) What do we do with texts that we find morally repellant? ("Preaching Against the Text," 1997; previously unpublished.) What are the goals of Jewish feminism? ("Beyond Egalitarianism," 1990.) Is Jewish feminism inherently separatist? ("The Continuing Value of Separatism," 2003); where do men fit in? ("About Men," 1992.)

One of the implicit themes of my work in the 1990s is the inseparability of theology and ethics. I consistently argue that seemingly abstract theological issues, like the nature of God or religious authority, have concrete implications for the ways communities are structured and the nature of the relationships within them. Conversely, ethical problems, such as the treatment of *agunot* ("chained women"; see "The Year of the Agunah" [1993]), always lead back to fundamental questions about the nature of Judaism. In repeatedly interweaving theological and ethical concerns, I was circling back to my early understanding of Judaism as ethical monotheism, but with a much more politicized understanding of ethics. Although the definition of Judaism that was so deeply meaningful to me as a girl came out of the prophetic commitment to social justice, it took me a long time to see my involvement in social change as related to my Judaism. When I returned from the 1963 March on Washington and my rabbi wanted me to address the Hebrew school on how I had gone to Washington *as a Jew,* I balked. I thought I had gone as a *person* who believed in justice. I felt the same way when, in college, I began to protest the war in Vietnam and later when I became a feminist. Working on *Standing Again at Sinai* made me aware of the absurdity of denying the Jewish roots of my ethical and political commitments—not because Jews are the only people who have such commitments, certainly, but because Judaism was the place *I* had learned them. It made me want to articulate the connections between a progressive Judaism and a broader progressive politics.

In the course of the 1990s, I also shifted the focus of much of my research, speaking, and writing to issues of sexuality. When I finished *Standing Again at Sinai,* the chapter of the book that I most wanted to develop further was "Toward a New Theology of Sexuality." I was not ready to come out in print as a lesbian when I wrote *Standing Again at Sinai,* and when I completed it, I felt the need to say more about gay and lesbian issues. I wanted to address the persistent liberal assumption that homosexuality is acceptable only because it is not chosen. I also wanted to develop a thoroughgoing critique of compulsory heterosexuality as a corrective to debates about whether gay, lesbian, bisexual, and transgendered people have a place in their religious communities. The 1990s were the decade in which Jewish denominational bodies began to issue statements on homosexuality and sexual ethics. I hoped to contribute to the emerging conversations about sexuality by reflecting on how they might include groups that had never been part of previous Jewish discussions. Issues of sexuality also interested me as vivid examples of one of my favorite topics—how to deal with aspects of tradition that seem morally unacceptable.

The essays in the last section of *The Coming of Lilith* reflect various elements of this agenda. "Sexuality and Teshuvah: Leviticus 18" (1997) addresses a Jewish text that is particularly problematic for contemporary sensibilities. It calls on local Jewish communities to form study groups to examine the sexual laws of Leviticus and think about how they might be rewritten. "Sexual Orientation and Human Rights" (1998) tries to move beyond liberal acceptance of homosexuality by beginning with the assumption of human sexual diversity and proceeding from there. "Authority, Resistance, and Transformation" (2000), which was written as part of a multireligious, multicultural volume on feminist perspectives on good sex, looks at compulsory heterosexuality as a block to women's sexual thriving. "Speaking of Sex" (2003), which is a new essay, analyzes recent denominational documents on sexuality through the lens of the crucial issue of authority. It began as one of a series of lectures on sexuality I delivered at the University of Manchester in England in the spring of 2000.

For a number of years, I thought I would develop these essays into a separate volume on sexuality, but then I realized that they say what I wanted to say about the subject. My work on sexuality represents an extension and concretization of issues I have addressed throughout my career, and it is best situated in that context. As I was wrestling with what to do with this material, my friend and then student Donna Berman began pestering me to publish a collection of my essays. Although I initially resisted her suggestion, she persisted and gradually won me over to the wisdom of the idea. When she offered to edit the volume herself, I could hold out no longer! I am deeply grateful to her for persuading and helping me to put together this volume at a historical moment when it seems very important to preserve and disseminate the accomplishments of the second wave of feminist work in religion. I am also grateful to Amy Caldwell, my editor at Beacon Press, who immediately shared Donna's enthusiasm for the project, and to her able assistant, Jennifer Yoon.

All the essays in this volume reflect a view of Judaism—and of Christianity—that I have been developing slowly over the last three decades: I see Judaism as a huge, often unwieldy and contradictory bundle of texts, traditions, laws, practices, folkways, and so on that constitute the past and establish the foundations for the future of the Jewish people. The subordination of women, sexual minorities, and non-Jewish Others is deeply woven into the fabric of those texts and traditions—so deeply that it can be difficult to separate out as a distinctive strand and even more difficult to extirpate. But just as individuals continually reevaluate, select, and reorder elements of our own personal histories as we move through our lives, so Jewish communities can sort, reconfigure, and add elements to the bundle that makes up Judaism, drawing on those parts that best serve our needs. The core of tradition is not a given but a subject of fierce and ever-renewed debate over where Judaism should be headed and who will have the power to decide. To be a Jewish feminist is to enter energetically into this debate, advocating on behalf of Jewish women and other marginalized groups within and outside of the Jewish community.

As I reflect on my participation in the process of trying to create a feminist Judaism, I am struck by the ways in which the different contexts of my feminist engagement have fed one another. My early experiences of consciousness-raising and of feminist community fostered both my critical awareness of the many forces constricting women's lives and a sense of the profound political and spiritual power of women uniting to bring about change. My involvement in the creation of women's studies in religion provided me with an important set of scholarly tools for developing a critical and constructive theology and repeatedly challenged me to grow intellectually as the landscape of the field expanded and changed. It also furnished me with companions on a journey that was at once intellectual and personal, academic, spiritual, and political. My participation in B'not Esh and in the wider grassroots Jewish feminist movement provided me with a religious context within which to "try on" feminist notions about the significance of women's history and the meaningfulness of female God-language. Jewish feminism gave me an appreciation of communities of identity, not as completely safe spaces or as resting places but as laboratories in which to create models of feminist practice that can be applied in a variety of spheres. My experience in all these arenas has strengthened my belief in women's power and responsibility to shape the future of our religious traditions as part of the broader project of repairing the world. Frail as this power often seems—especially at this frightening moment in history—I am nonetheless grateful for the profound adventure on which my feminism has propelled me. It is one I could never have imagined when I walked into the first meeting of the Yale Women's Alliance in 1969.

I

Formulating a Feminist Theology

The Coming of Lilith

Toward a Feminist Theology

The present questioning of theological language, premises, methods, and systems by women in every relation to religious life has critical and constructive sides. Women are both articulating the problems with traditional theology and struggling for ways to express their new relationships with their traditions and themselves. If the feminist theology,[1] which is just beginning to emerge from this struggle, has any one distinctive characteristic, it may well be its faithfulness to those experiences that engender it; content and process are inseparable. Since the felt need for such theology arises through the consciousness-raising experience, this theology constantly needs to measure itself against and recapture the richness of feeling and insight gained through consciousness-raising, finally becoming a continuation of it. Thus much feminist theology may be communal theology, for, in sharing the theological task, feminists can bring content and process together in a very real way. In this essay, I would like to share the results—fragmentary as they are—of one group's attempt to do theology communally[2] in the hopes that our questions will be taken up by other women and our process made part of an ongoing one.

It is not self-evident that theology must remain close to the experiences that generate it. Experience may provide the occasion for general, abstract reflection or argument. There are reasons why, in the case of feminist theology, the close relation between content and process seems imperative. Not surprisingly, these reasons have to do with the nature of consciousness-raising itself. Through consciousness-raising, I come to affirm the value of my experience as a woman and a person, the value of my whole, not only intellectual, self. I affirm my experience with and through other women in a process that is communal in essence. I cannot then write a theology that abstracts from my experience and ignores part of myself, or that abstracts from the community of which I am a part.

These considerations form the framework within which to see our group's work. Our group process reflected them, and the content of our discussions further developed them. The question with which we began was whether we could find in the women's movement a process, event, or experience that somehow expresses the essence of the movement and that might function as a central integrating symbol for a theology of liberation. Aware that such a symbol would have value only as it arises out of and remains close to the life of the movement, we proceeded to explore this question by sharing and reflecting on our experiences as women in the women's movement. We then discussed the ways in which these experiences are similar to or are religious experiences, and finally, attempted to reflect theologically on what we had done.[3]

The Women's Movement

Becoming involved in the women's movement means moving from isolation as a woman to community. Through telling my story, I reach out to other women. Through their hearing, which both affirms my story and makes it possible, they reach out to me. I am able to move, gradually, from defensiveness to openness, from fear of questioning to a deep and radical questioning of the premises from which I have lived my life. I experience relief; my anger has been heard, and I am not alone. But I am also frightened; I am undermining my own foundations. The walls come tumbling down.[4] *Anger, fear, rage, joy, celebration, rejoicing, high, flying, bursting forth, pregnant with newness, pregnant with possibility, hearing, wholeness*—these were the words we began with in attempting to describe our consciousness-raising experiences. What we wanted to do was to move from these words or experiences to one central word, symbol, or experience that captured them all. Mary Daly's "sisterhood of man"[5] was in our minds from the start of our discussion, but it was not quite what we were looking for. We felt that sisterhood happens between women because of something else happening to them—an individual process of coming-to-wholeness within community—and we wanted to try to get at that something else.

The "Yeah, Yeah Experience"

We arrived at a term for part of our experience quite spontaneously. One of us said something, and the others responded excitedly, "Yeah, yeah." Somehow, this triggered a double recognition. We saw ourselves in the experience to which we responded, and we also recognized ourselves as women come together, recognizing our common experience with other women. We spent the next hour trying to define the "yeah, yeah experience."

The "yeah, yeah experience" is, first of all, *the process through which we come to be sisters*. It may be the experience that brings me into the movement. I read an article by another woman, defending myself against it, and all of a sudden, undeniably, a piece of my life is there before me on the page. ("Yeah, yeah.") I attend a meeting, a lecture, "just to see what it's all about," and I am "converted," turned around, the pieces of my life fall together in a new way. ("Yeah, yeah.") The "yeah, yeah experience" is all the many individual moments of recognition and illumination through which I come to a new awareness of my situation and myself.[6] I talk to other women, and one describes as her hang-up something I thought was peculiar to me—and everyone else is nodding too. I read, I hear, I talk about the oppression of women, and all at once, it's *our* oppression.

Thus the affirmative, early Beatles sound of "yeah, yeah" is not meant to suggest that the "yeah, yeah experience" is always a joyful one. It can, of course, express deep joy—joy in sharing, joy in self-recognition, joy as I increase my freedom in relation to my past. But I can also say "yeah, yeah" as I put my finger on a hidden source of bitterness, as I hear my own anger spoken, or as I articulate my rage on behalf of my sisters' past and my own. In all cases, however, I express my conviction and my openness. I move forward; I respond toward a future where anything can happen.

My response, although sometimes an affirmation of only a limited area of agreement, is a response of my whole person. When I say "yeah, yeah," I am moved, and I move. I move physically, toward the one who spoke, and I move figuratively, into the consciousness-raising process. I affirm my sister and encourage her to go on while I myself enter the dialogue.

The "yeah, yeah experience" is thus a different way of thinking from our usual "yes, but" reasoning, which is inherently nondialogical and out of touch with its own basis in experience. "Yes, but" thinking focuses on the logic of the speaker or the argument advanced, to the exclusion of the aware-ness of being addressed by the speaker or argument. When I say "yeah, yeah," on the other hand, I do not forget logic or the fact that genuine disagreement may be, should be, part of the dialogue into which I have entered. But I com-mit my whole person to speak and to really hear. This true speaking and hear-ing is a possibility for all persons. The "yeah, yeah experience" is potentially universal.

Sisterhood

The value of my being with and for others that develops through the "yeah, yeah experience" finds its expression in sisterhood. But sisterhood is not only what evolves through the "yeah, yeah experience"; it is in some sense its pre-supposition. Sisterhood grows through my speaking and hearing, but were it not already partly there, I could not begin to speak and hear.

The experience of sisterhood is many-sided. It has, first of all, both a general and a specific dimension. In affirming my own womanhood—or personhood as woman—I affirm it in all women. But I also and particularly affirm those women with whom I share the experience of affirmation. (The other side of this—sisterhood as presupposition—would be that in affirming all women I affirm myself as a woman.) This does not mean that, in commu-nity, I acknowledge in myself the characteristics of the "eternal feminine" or make peace with my assigned role. On the contrary, what I proclaim is pre-cisely my freedom as a woman over these limited stereotypes.

Thus this experience is, secondly, both deeply personal and intensely po-litical. I affirm myself as a woman, but only as I enter into a new, and hitherto silent, community. In saying yes to myself, where I and my society had said only no, I open the possibility of seeing other women as persons and friends; I discover a source of energy for personal and social growth and change. I ac-quire a sense of freedom that is rooted in my new consciousness of personal integrity and wholeness; I express it by uniting with other women in the com-mon task of creating our future. I am freed to repossess or to try to free myself from parts of my past, but I can do this effectively only as I work for interper-sonal and institutional change in the present.

But sisterhood, more than an experience of community, *is* a community. It is a place where women can "get themselves together," begin to understand,

and thus begin to overcome, their common oppression. It is a place where women can begin to act out their new sense of wholeness, making their own decisions for their own lives. Thus the nonhierarchically structured women's movement refuses to replace one set of authorities with another. Instead, women who have rejected the myth of their own powerlessness create, in community, alternatives to a stunted past.

The Women's Movement as a Religious Experience

Throughout our discussion of the women's movement, we found ourselves both repeatedly seeing our experiences in the movement as religious experiences and repeatedly questioning the value of doing so. (See question 5 at the end of the essay.) While the words *grace, illumination, mission,* and *conversion* kept cropping up in our conversation, we recognized that women who do not think in religious categories, who would in fact reject them, share the experiences we expressed in this language. We did not wish imperialistically to insist that their experiences too are "really" religious despite their refusal to recognize the fact. Moreover, if we asked what we added to the "root" experiences by calling them *religious,* there was nothing specific we could identify. On the other hand, we did feel this was a valid way of looking at our experiences in the women's movement, a way that could enrich our understanding of both these experiences and of religious experience itself.

We began our discussion of the women's movement with the "yeah, yeah experience" rather than with sisterhood because we wanted to get more precisely at the experience of coming-to-wholeness that sisterhood presupposes. If our discussion of the "yeah, yeah experience" got at part of this process, our discussion of religious experience dealt with it from another angle. We saw the stages of consciousness-raising as analogous to the stages in a religious journey, culminating in the experience of full, related selfhood.

Again and again we came back to the word *graceful* to describe certain of our experiences with other women. At moments I can never plan or program, I am given to myself in a way I cannot account for by studying the organic progression of my past. Listening to another woman tell her story, I *concentrate* on words spoken and experienced as if our lives depended on them, and indeed they do. And yet I could not say what enables me to be really there, hearing, in a way that makes me feel that I had never really heard before—or been listened to as I am now.[7] Nor could I say why precisely at this moment I become aware of myself as a total person, why I feel myself as whole, integrated, free, fully human. Some of this feeling we hoped to convey through the "yeah, yeah experience." "Yeah, yeah" is my response to an illumination that includes the intellect but is more than intellectual. In this moment in which I transcend it, I feel sharply the limits of the taken-for-granted definition of myself and my capabilities.

This is where the experience of grace can also become the experience of conversion. Seeing myself in a new way, I am called to the transformation of myself. I must become the possibilities I already am in my moment of vision, for I am really not yet those possibilities. The call necessitates a decision, a response.

Here two factors come into play. The feeling of wholeness, which is also a call to self-transformation, is not continuous with my previous development. But this does not mean that I have skipped over a "stage" in my life. I must still decide whether and how to change myself and, having decided, work slowly through the difficulties and pain that my decision entails. My clear perception of the limits of my upbringing, of the lost opportunities and confining decisions of my past, does not relieve me of a lifetime of questioning and requestioning assumptions that I reject but cannot entirely overcome. On the other hand, there is a sense in which, once I have made a decision, I am already on the other side. At least I have overcome the fear that can only express itself in defensiveness. I have defined my goals and released the source of energy to achieve them.

Once again, the importance of sisterhood as a community comes into play. I make my decision for self-transformation in the context of a community whose support is ongoing. The continuing process of questioning, growth, and change remains collective. Thus, not only is my decision reinforced, but my energies for change are pooled with the group's energies. This expresses itself in a communal sense of mission. After a certain amount of time spent on consciousness-raising, a group generally feels the need to move outward, to become involved in projects that translate its goals into reality and that reach and bring in other women. Strengthened in themselves, its members feel ready and anxious to spread the good word to others.

This sense of community also expresses itself—and this is the last way in which we looked at the women's movement as a religious experience—in the formation of embryonic rituals and symbols. Telling our stories has become a ritualized way of getting into the consciousness-raising experience. Calling each other "sister," feeling a new freedom to touch and hug one another are concrete expressions of the new bonds between us. We have our heretics and our infidels; we have defined the "others" in a way that conditions behavior toward them: the token woman, the pussycat, and, of course, the male chauvinist pig. We have our political symbols: the woman symbol, the clenched fist. We indulge in ritual language corrections: we call all women "Ms." We are writing our songs, and we are beginning to find and define our peculiar forms of celebration.

Theological Process

With regard to this list of rituals, the first task we envisaged for theology in relation to the women's movement was a critical one. We needed a critical principle to act as a bulwark against the tendency to absolutize either particular issues in the movement or the movement itself. We needed to move beyond defining "others" and, instead, to find those others in ourselves. We saw the need to regard every center, every feminist goal, as only provisional. Beyond each of our "ultimate" perspectives is a still broader one from which ours is judged limited. (See question 4.)

With reference to our main, constructive task, we found it easier to discuss the women's movement and religious experience than to reflect theologically on either. (See question 1.) What is theology? What does it mean to apply a theological process? Is feminist theology the expression of a new religion? How can we relate ourselves to the old without destroying our new experiences through the attempt to understand them in terms of old forms? These were crucial questions we felt we had to, but could not, answer. There were times we found ourselves getting into some rather traditional discussions—the ambiguity of grace that is both fulfilled and "not yet" fulfilled; the question of which comes first, sisterhood or the "yeah, yeah experience," grace or the experience of grace. Many of the things we talked about set off old associations. There is a clear relation, for example, between the true speaking and hearing of the "yeah, yeah experience" and the I-Thou relation in Martin Buber. We considered what it would mean to write a systematic theology that affirmed the experiences we had been discussing—choosing a philosophical framework, our texts, our rabbis, or our saints. But we were worried about the disappearance of the four of us sitting there, our coming together, behind the framework we would create. We clearly needed a form that would grow out of the content and process of our time together.

Our Story: The Coming of Lilith

It was here that we realized that, although we had failed to come up with a single event or symbol that captured all of feminist experience, there had emerged out of our discussion many of the central elements of a myth. We had a journey to go on, an enemy (or enemies) to vanquish, salvation to be achieved both for ourselves and for humanity. If we found ourselves with a myth, moreover, this was particularly appropriate to our experience, for we had come together to do theology by beginning with our stories. It was no coincidence, then, that we arrived back at the story form.

We recognized the difficulties of "inventing" a myth, however, and so we wanted to tell a story that seemed to grow naturally out of our present history. We also felt the need for using older materials that would carry their own reverberations and significance, even if we departed freely from them. We chose, therefore, to begin with the story of Lilith, demon of the night, who, according to rabbinic legend, was Adam's first wife. Created equal to him, for some unexplained reason she found that she could not live with him, and flew away. Through her story, we could express not only our new image of ourselves, but our relation to certain of the elements of our religious traditions. Since stories are the heart of tradition, we could question and create tradition by telling a new story within the framework of an old one. (See question 3.) We took Lilith for our heroine, and yet, most important, not

Lilith alone. We try to express through our myth the process of our coming to do theology together. Lilith by herself is in exile and can do nothing. The real heroine of our story is sisterhood, and sisterhood is powerful.

———————•———————

IN THE BEGINNING, *the Lord God formed Adam and Lilith from the dust of the ground and breathed into their nostrils the breath of life. Created from the same source, both having been formed from the ground, they were equal in all ways. Adam, being a man, didn't like this situation, and he looked for ways to change it. He said, "I'll have my figs now, Lilith," ordering her to wait on him, and he tried to leave to her the daily tasks of life in the garden. But Lilith wasn't one to take any nonsense; she picked herself up, uttered God's holy name, and flew away. "Well now, Lord," complained Adam, "that uppity woman you sent me has gone and deserted me." The Lord, inclined to be sympathetic, sent his messengers after Lilith, telling her to shape up and return to Adam or face dire punishment. She, however, preferring anything to living with Adam, decided to stay where she was. And so God, after more careful consideration this time, caused a deep sleep to fall on Adam and out of one of his ribs created for him a second companion, Eve.*

For a time, Eve and Adam had a good thing going. Adam was happy now, and Eve, though she occasionally sensed capacities within herself that remained undeveloped, was basically satisfied with the role of Adam's wife and helper. The only thing that really disturbed her was the excluding closeness of the relationship between Adam and God. Adam and God just seemed to have more in common, both being men, and Adam came to identify with God more and more. After a while, that made God a bit uncomfortable too, and he started going over in his mind whether he may not have made a mistake letting Adam talk him into banishing Lilith and creating Eve, seeing the power that gave Adam.

Meanwhile Lilith, all alone, attempted from time to time to rejoin the human community in the garden. After her first fruitless attempt to breach its walls, Adam worked hard to build them stronger, even getting Eve to help him. He told her fearsome stories of the demon Lilith who threatens women in childbirth and steals children from their cradles in the middle of the night. The second time Lilith came, she stormed the garden's main gate, and a great battle ensued between her and Adam in which she was finally defeated. This time, however, before Lilith got away, Eve got a glimpse of her and saw she was a woman like herself.

After this encounter, seeds of curiosity and doubt began to grow in Eve's mind. Was Lilith indeed just another woman? Adam had said she was a demon. Another woman! The very idea attracted Eve. She had never seen another creature like herself before. And how beautiful and strong Lilith looked! How bravely she had fought! Slowly, slowly, Eve began to think about the limits of her own life within the garden.

One day, after many months of strange and disturbing thoughts, Eve, wandering around the edge of the garden, noticed a young apple tree she and Adam had planted, and saw that one of its branches stretched over the garden wall. Spontaneously, she tried to climb it, and struggling to the top, swung herself over the wall.

She did not wander long on the other side before she met the one she had come to find, for Lilith was waiting. At first sight of her, Eve remembered the tales of Adam and was frightened, but Lilith understood and greeted her kindly. "Who are you?" they asked each other, "What is your story?" And they sat and spoke together, of the past and then of the future. They talked for many hours, not once, but many times. They taught each other many things, and told each other stories, and laughed together, and cried, over and over, till the bond of sisterhood grew between them.

Meanwhile, back in the garden, Adam was puzzled by Eve's comings and goings, and disturbed by what he sensed to be her new attitude toward him. He talked to God about it, and God, having his own problems with Adam and a somewhat broader perspective, was able to help out a little—but he was confused, too. Something had failed to go according to plan. As in the days of Abraham, he needed counsel from his children. "I am who I am," thought God, "but I must become who I will become."

And God and Adam were expectant and afraid the day Eve and Lilith returned to the garden, bursting with possibilities, ready to rebuild it together.

Questions

1. Was the group's basic approach—beginning with the women's movement, then discussing religious experience, then reflecting on the two theologically—fundamentally misguided? Did we begin by assuming overly traditional notions of religion and theology, notions that would make it difficult to do anything really new? Had we understood theology as, say "the religious self-interpretation of [a] community," [8] we might have seen ourselves as theologizing already in discussing our experiences, and thus been able to enrich our understanding both of our experiences and theology. We could certainly have written our myth anyway, but we would not have seen it as an alternative to "doing theology."

2. There is a fundamental ambiguity in the term *feminist theology* that we never resolved. Is the expression "feminist theology" of the same sort as "Christian theology" or "Jewish theology," or are we always to understand it to mean "feminist (Jewish or Christian) theology"? Are we trying to create a new religion, reflecting on the experiences of a totally new community? Or are we trying to think in a new way within the boundaries of commitment to our own traditions?

3. If we do understand "feminist theology" to mean "feminist (Jewish or Christian) theology," what will be our relation to tradition? Critical? Will we see tradition as having fallen away from a truth to which the women's movement can return it? Will we attempt to extend or reinterpret tradition? (As our myth may be seen as doing.) Is our primary purpose to introduce a new style of theologizing, to replace, so to speak, the "yes, but" with the "yeah, yeah experience"?

4. Can the women's movement, in fact, function on its own as a religious community? It is certainly "a group of people who share a common vocabulary of images, concepts, gestures, who identify themselves with a common past and common hopes for the future," but does it have a sense of a "transcendent reality" by which it "believes itself constituted"?[9] Are these valid criteria of a religious community? Does the women's move-

ment lack criteria for self-judgment? Must these be imposed from without? Would it then need to be seen in a broader framework? What framework? A religious framework cut loose from any particular tradition? What does that mean?

5. Is our discussion of the women's movement as a religious experience in fact a discussion of the movement as a Christian religious experience? Grace, the call to self-transformation, being given to myself, the idea that decision puts me on "the other side"—these are all Christian conceptions. What we have charted is really the experience of individuals coming together to form a new church. Are there other religious frameworks that can be used to interpret feminist experience? Were we trapped in one model by our theological educations?

6. Certain of the experiences a feminist theology would want to affirm, for example, the importance of "total" as opposed to "head" thinking, are experiences that stereotypically have been assigned to women. This essay has dealt with the positive aspects of certain of these experiences. Clearly there are problems with them as well. The "yeah, yeah experience," for example, can be coercive, can lead to fuzzy thinking, and is simply inappropriate or impossible in certain situations. What would a feminist theology have to learn from reflecting on "women's experience" as a whole? What in women's experience do we want to adopt, reintegrate, affirm? What do we want to reject and why?

The Jewish Feminist

Conflict in Identities

This essay was originally delivered as a speech to the National Jewish Women's Conference in New York in February 1973.

I would like to discuss our identity as Jewish women. It seems to me that the identity of Jewish women—or rather of some of the Jewish women I know, including, first of all, myself—lies somewhere in the conflict between being a woman and being a Jew and in the necessity of combining the two in as yet unknown ways. So I want to speak about this conflict in two of its aspects.

I can best begin to explain what I mean by a conflict between being a woman and being a Jew by saying that it is not a coincidence that we are discussing the questions we are now discussing. We are not doing so due to some unfolding of the Jewish tradition, due to the fact that this is a Jewishly appropriate moment. We are here because a secular movement for the liberation of women has made it imperative that we raise certain Jewish issues now, because we will not let ourselves be defined as Jewish women in ways in which we cannot allow ourselves to be defined as women. This creates a conflict not just and not primarily because the women's movement is a secular movement whose principles we are attempting to apply to an ancient religious tradition, but because the women's movement is a different community around which we might center our lives. The conflict between communities is the first level on which I experience the conflict between being a woman and being a Jew.

Now of course we can belong to many different communities, and in fact we do. We identify as Jews, as women, as Americans, as students, as human beings. But it seems to me that, though we can belong to many communities, only one can be our organizing center through which we view and interpret and give room to others.

Since we are raising questions about the Jewish community because of it, it is clear that the women's movement makes some claim on us to be that organizing center. But it makes that claim not only because it forces us to raise new questions. For some of us—certainly for me—being involved in the women's movement has been one of the most important and exciting experiences of our lives. It has changed the eyes through which we see the world. Through it we have experienced sisterhood—a community far more vital than anything most of us have experienced through the traditional institutions of the Jewish "community."

Despite this, our relationship with our Jewishness would not need to be one of conflict were it not for a second problem—that the Jewish community will not let us, as feminists, feel at home. Every time I let myself be lulled into thinking that I as a whole person am a member of this community, some event lets me know in no uncertain terms that I am wrong.

This sense of exclusion arises partly from the fact that everything in our written tradition comes from the hands of men. The *halakhah* (Jewish law), most obviously, is the product of many generations of men. The same is true of the *aggada* (nonlegal material). The Bible was written by men. The myths from which the Bible borrowed and which it used and transformed were written by men. The liturgy was written by men. Jewish philosophy is the work of men. Modern Jewish theology is the work of men. It was men who wrote even the special books for women, and it was men who designated women's three *mitzvot* (commandments) and wrote the blessings.

Now my point is not that therefore all these things are irrelevant to us. That is simply not true. The Bible is very much our Bible. There are male-written Jewish stories that we love. There are prayers that express our feelings as well as the feelings of the men who wrote them.

My point is rather that all these things have a *question mark* over them. As Mary Daly has said, women have had our power of *naming* stolen from us. From the day that God brought the animals to Adam in the garden of Eden to see what *he* would call them, it has been through the words of men that we have known and addressed the world.[1] Although we do not know in advance that their words are not our words, neither do we know that they are. At a time when we are newly discovering and naming ourselves, we need to name anew the world around us.

If there are certain things that we will just call by their old names again, there are other words we will most definitely need to speak for the first time, for there are many times when the male power of naming has oppressed and excluded us. I needn't discuss this fact in relation to halakhah since it has been and will be a central topic of discussion here. I do want to say though that the exclusion of women intrudes itself into other, very different areas of Jewish life. I was recently reading Franz Rosenzweig's beautiful essay "The Builders," in which he talks about how the assimilated Jew can return to and reappropriate the tradition. One point he makes is that the demarcation between what is forbidden by Jewish law and what is outside the realm of law and therefore permitted must be broken down in order both that the law take on a positive character and that the realm of what is permitted become a Jewish realm. There I was, reading his essay, moved by it, trying to understand it as it was addressed to me, when all of a sudden, I came to an example of what he means by endowing the law with positive meaning. "In this united sphere of the doable lies, for instance," he says, "the legal exclusion of the woman from the religious congregation; but also in it lies with equal force her ruling rank in the home . . ." Thus what was one moment my essay the next moment was not. What I wanted to use as a gate back into the whole tradition became a door shut against me.

Let me give an example of another very different way in which our tradition excludes women. There is the fact that we address God as *he*. And it is not just that we use the masculine pronoun in the absence of neuter ones—we image *him* in male terms. Thus he is King, Lord, Shepherd, Father, etc. Aside from the fact that the exclusive use of male imagery is inaccurate—we know that God is not male—we are just beginning to explore the effects that this use has on the self-image and understanding of men and women. I recently read an article that quoted several church commission reports on the admission of women to the ministry.[2] Many of the arguments they came up with against the ordination of women were just incredible. One not atypical clergyman argued that the minister, whether he likes it or not, is a God figure, and that since in the Bible God is imaged in exclusively male terms, it is inappropriate for women to take this role. Just think what a statement like that says about its author's attitude toward women—and toward men! The Jewish community has not yet needed to resort to arguments like this to exclude women from the rabbinate,[3] but there is no reason to suppose that the psychological dynamic they evidence is foreign to Jews, or that we do not draw equally horrendous—if unexpressed—conclusions after calling God "he" all our lives.

The problems we as women face in relation to our tradition are deep and complex, involving almost every aspect of tradition. Where then are we going to find the new words, our words, which need to be spoken? How can we find the words that are our words and yet are Jewish words? Can we—how can we—assure ourselves in advance that if we are true to our own experiences we can remain in continuity with tradition?

I don't have a solution to these problems. The questions are much clearer to me than the answers, but I would like to conclude by saying something about the direction in which I think we need to look.

I know that when I pose the question to myself, "How can I find new words to express my experiences as a woman?" I have a tendency to mythol-ogize the notion of "women's experience." I unconsciously assume that there is something called "women's experience" that is separate from the lives and histories of real women and that we can discover only now that we have begun to question our traditional roles. In a way, this makes the lives of women who lived before us irrelevant. Only now are we going to find out who we really are, who we really have been. When I think about this objectively, however, I realize that this mythologizing process is also a falsifying one. There is no such thing as "women's experience" apart from what have been the experiences of real women, and that means experiences always in relation to what men have said being a woman means. This is the first clue to where our answers might be found.

The second is that in belonging to different communities that shape and feed our lives, and despite the conflicts between them and the division of our loyalties, there are points in time in which our histories as Jews and our histories as women intersect—in Sarah's laughter at the idea of bearing a child in her old age, for example, in Miriam's song at the Red Sea, in Hannah's prayer at the dedication of Samuel, in Deborah's battle hymn, in Beruriah's learning. I think that if we want to speak words as women that will also be Jewish words, we need to try to recover and reappropriate the histories of Jewish women who managed to be persons within the boundaries allotted to them. If "women's experience" and the actual experiences of women are the same thing, we have to begin looking for "women's experience" in the experiences of our foremothers. Can we know how they viewed their experiences? What in them do we want to appropriate? Are there things in their experiences that implicitly or explicitly judge the boundaries assigned to those experiences? What in them do we want to reject or to modify and why? It is not that through them we can say everything we want to say. But without them we might not even be able to begin.

I would like to conclude with a story that attempts to reappropriate two of the women in our tradition.[4]

The talk ended with "The Coming of Lilith," which is found on p. 31 of this volume.

Male Theology and Women's Experience

Throughout the long history of Western theology, the overwhelming majority of theologians have been men. This is a fact we have until recently taken for granted: Who else should be the theologians? Who else has been in a position to study, assimilate, and reflect on religious tradition? And what difference does it make, moreover? Surely the male theologian is capable of interpreting the insights of a particular faith for women as well as men? Though these may once have been rhetorical questions, they are no longer. The growing women's movement, in fostering awareness of a hidden history of women's experience, has made it necessary to ask whether the male authorship of theology has resulted in a distorted understanding of tradition and human experience. In this essay, I want to suggest that it has. My argument is simple: much theology is the product of a specifically male experience and naming of reality and has produced a one-sided picture of the world. To pretend otherwise is to blind ourselves to the destructive personal, political, and theological effects such theological one-sidedness can have. It is also to lose the opportunity to humanize theology through the deliberate incorporation of women's experience.

Male Experience Defined

Clearly, to say that theology reflects male experience is to assume that male experience exists and can be defined. I will use the phrase to refer to our assimilation and acceptance of a male-defined sexual polarity that has been shaped by religion and philosophy, economics and social organization, biological givens and human longings. This polarity defines for men and women their nature and their tasks in the world. "This is a man's world," our stereotypes tell us; "woman's place is in the home."[1] Men are aggressive, independent, dominant, ambitious, self-confident, etc., while women are passive, dependent, submissive, unambitious, self-deprecating, etc. The Victorians, who gave us this polarity in its present form, actually reserved the male attributes for white, middle-class men and based the female list on the character of the Victorian lady. Since the polarity has mythic force, however, it is always stated in general terms.

But it is not only acceptance of this polarity that has shaped male and female experience. One side of it—the male side—has been taken as the human norm. One side has set the standard for what it means to be a person. Simone de Beauvoir states:

> Just as for the ancients there was an absolute vertical with reference to which the oblique was defined, so there is an absolute human type, the masculine. . . . The relation of the two sexes is not quite like that of two electrical poles, for the man represents both the positive and the neutral, as is indicated by the common use of *man* to designate human beings in general; whereas woman represents only the negative, defined by limiting criteria, without reciprocity.[2]

The normative character of maleness was accepted by Thomas Aquinas when he defined females as "misbegotten males" and by Freud when he described female sexuality in terms of "penis envy." Apparently, it was also alive in the thinking of seventy-nine trained therapists who—in 1970—were asked to describe a healthy adult male, a healthy adult female, and a healthy adult (sex unspecified). While their conceptions of a healthy adult male matched their descriptions of a healthy adult, their conceptions of a healthy adult woman differed considerably—and the differences paralleled the sex-role stereotypes prevalent in our society.[3]

Actual experience is far more complex, of course, than acceptance of this sexual polarity allows. The reality of our lived experience as men and women, while never free from sex-role stereotypes, is also not defined by them. Individuals may struggle with or against sex roles as well as compromise with or accept them. Often in the course of compromise and struggle, the roles are altered or enriched in ways that are significant for theology. And yet, when all is said and done, the "wisdom" the sexual polarity expresses arises out of and is reabsorbed into a general social mythology that is part of the cultural air we breathe. There is no direction in which we can turn without bumping into it. There is no experience in isolation or abstraction from it. It is a starting point to which we continually return.[4]

One can recognize the complexity of experience, therefore, and still say that when a theologian writes out of male experience, this means two things. First, he accepts the male-defined sexual polarity. Second, the theologian writes out of the male side of this polarity; his understanding of God and humanity is derived from it. (A woman theologian, to the extent she has internalized this polarity, will write out of the same assumptions.)

Statements About Women

If this is our definition of male experience, then theology is a product of male experience in at least three ways: in the specific things it says about women, in its understanding of the nature of God, and in its understanding of the nature of humanity.

First, the specific things that it says about women. At this point in the development of a feminist literature in religion, the history of theological images of and attitudes toward women has been thoroughly researched and documented.[5] It is not necessary to reproduce once again the long list of appalling statements about women that appear throughout Jewish and Christian history from ancient to modern times. Quotations from two significant modern thinkers will suffice to illustrate the dynamics of such statements and some of the problems they raise.

One passage is from Dietrich Bonhoeffer's "A Wedding Sermon from a Prison Cell."

> God establishes an ordinance in which you may live together as husband and wife.... You may order your home as you like, save in one particular: the woman must be subject to her husband, and the husband must love his wife.... The place God has assigned for the woman is the husband's home. Most people have forgotten nowa-

days what a home can mean....It is a kingdom of its own in the midst of the world, the place where peace, joy, love, purity, continence, respect, obedience, tradition, and, to crown them all, happiness may dwell, whatever else may pass away in the world.[6]

The second passage is taken from the *Church Dogmatics* of Karl Barth:

Man and woman are fully equal before God and therefore as men and therefore in respect of the meaning and determination, the imperiling, but also the promise of their human existence....Yet the fact remains—and in this respect there is no simple equality—that they are claimed and sanctified as man and woman....Woman does not come short of man in any way, nor renounce her right, dignity, and honor...when theoretically and practically she recognizes that in order she is woman, and therefore B, and therefore behind and subordinate to man....If she occupies and retains her proper place, she will not merely complain even when man...encroaches upon her rights....If there is a way of bringing man to repentance, it is the way of the woman who refuses to let herself be corrupted and made disobedient by his disobedience, but who in spite of his disobedience maintains her place in the order all the more firmly.[7]

These passages are striking in a number of respects, not the least of which is that they fully accept the sex-role polarity previously described. Men and women have clearly defined different places in the world order, and the place of women is subordinate to men. The Bonhoeffer text even calls to mind certain sections of John Ruskin's "Of Queens' Gardens," a nineteenth-century essay which gives definitive expression to the Victorian chivalrous attitude toward women in terms not far different from Bonhoeffer's. Just as Bonhoeffer depicts women as custodians of "peace, joy, love, and purity," for example, Ruskin pictured them as guardians of the order and beauty, peace and shelter of the home. Just as Bonhoeffer sees men as leaving the sanctuary of the family for "the shifting sands of outward or public life," Ruskin saw them as having to contend with the rough and wicked world of work. The Bonhoeffer passage, and the Barth for that matter, take up cultural attitudes toward women and incorporate them into religious tradition, giving them theological sanction.

Such passages do not simply accept the sex-role polarity and leave it at that. In both the Bonhoeffer and Barth quotations, the thought is added, "And God wants it that way." In both cases there is an explicit claim that the subordination of women is divinely ordained. This adds another dimension to the sex-role polarity as articulated by culture. Beliefs that are the product of thousands of years of social development are difficult enough to change. How much more difficult to change something that is the will of God! In sanctifying and divinely authorizing current male/female relations, theology not only accepts but powerfully reinforces the social subordination of women. Barth takes this reinforcement one step further when he demands that women accept subordination even when men abuse their power. Women are to wait for the repentance of the oppressor, seeking to convert men by their good example. This notoriously slow way of bringing about change benefits only the oppressor and cannot help but look like special pleading on his part.[8]

Specific statements about women, then, reflect male experience in a clear and simple way: they explicitly affirm the male-defined sexual polarity and sanctify the maintenance of male superordination. This is obvious. Yet the very obviousness of passages like these represents a danger. One can read such selections and think, "I don't agree with what Barth has to say about women," and then bracket them and go on, as if it were possible to distrust Barth on women yet accept his views on much more abstruse theological questions. It is therefore important to recognize that such passages may indicate more complex anti-female bias in an individual's thought. Theology has more subtle ways of reflecting male experience.

God-language

A very significant way in which theology reflects male experience is through the use of male God-language. Even though we all know that God "really" transcends sexual differentiation, we talk about *him* in male terms. And it is not just that we use masculine pronouns because we lack gender-neutral ones. We also image God in terms taken from the male side of the stereotypic masculine/feminine sexual polarity. Thus God is Father, Lord, King, Shepherd, but never Mother, Lady, or Queen. While we *know* that these images are "only" symbolic, they are nevertheless more basic than our efforts to specify and control them through conceptualization. They function for us imaginatively with tremendous power. In fact, this is why we use them. The notion of kingship, for example, conjures up associations of golden scepters and royal purple that are not evoked by the statement, "God is very powerful." It is therefore absurd to imagine that we can break the hold of images by intellectually acknowledging that God is not what our every image of *him* says *he* is.

The problems with male God-language are manifold. First of all, like specific negative statements about women, male images can be used directly to authorize the subordination of women. A concrete example of this use of male God-language is provided by the debate over the ordination of women to the Episcopal priesthood. Bishop C. Kilmer Myers of California opposed the ordination of women on these grounds:

> A priest is a "God symbol" whether he likes it or not. In the imagery of both the Old and New Testament God is represented in masculine imagery. The father begets the son. This is essential to the *givenness* of the Christian Faith and to tamper with this imagery is to change that Faith into something else. Of course, this does not mean that God is male. The Biblical language is the language of analogy. It is imperfect. Nevertheless, it has meaning. The male image about God pertains to the divine initiative in creation. Initiative is in itself a male rather than a female attribute.[9]

The syllogism operating in this argument is clear. "Initiative" is a symbol taken from the male side of the stereotypic sexual polarity and attributed to God. The priest is a God symbol. Therefore, the priest must be male. Male God-language thus becomes an explicit legitimation for the exclusion of women from church leadership.

This is only the most obvious way in which male God-language functions to enforce female subordination, however. Such language also undergirds male authority in a more general manner. God was originally imaged (primarily) as male in Biblical culture because human models of power, authority, and majesty were primarily male. But thinking of God as male reinforces the notion that authority *should* be male. The New Testament Epistle to the Ephesians draws this connection quite explicitly: "Wives, be subject to your husbands, as to the Lord. For the husband is the head of the wife as Christ is the head of the church, his body, and is himself its Savior" (5:22, 23).

This verse enables us to see a clear relationship between male God-language and the specific passages concerning women with which we began. Women are to remain subordinate within the home and within creation because men represent the superior divine authority in relation to them. Individual negative statements about women may be taken as surface indications of a whole philosophy of divine/human relations.

Not surprisingly, Barth's thought provides an excellent illustration of these connections. It turns out that for Barth, the male/female relationship is a reflection or image of the divine/human relation and the relationship between Christ and the church. Barth's specific remarks about the subordination of women offer important clues to the structures of super- and subordination at work throughout his theology.[10] In his exposition of 1 Corinthians 11:3—"But I want you to understand that the head of every man is Christ, the head of a woman is her husband, and the head of Christ is God"—as well as the Ephesians passage mentioned above, Barth argues that women, through their subordinate role, are to represent the human community before Christ. Men, on the other hand, through their superordinate role, are to represent the majesty and lowliness of Christ before the human community. This does not mean anything so crude as that women achieve salvation through men. It simply means that women, in subordinating themselves to their husbands, represent the subordination of the community to Christ. There is no better place to be, Barth says, than "listening, obedient, and subordinate" to the one for whom the community exists. Indeed, women are privileged to be in this place, since their call to subordination is really only a particular form of the admonition to the whole community (including husbands) to subordinate itself to Christ.[11]

Barth is curiously ambivalent on this last point, however. Women are the models for the community; husbands are to learn subordination from their wives—but not too much, he seems to say! For elsewhere Barth writes:

"In regard to the theological, philosophical, and psychological thinking of Schleiermacher one might wonder among other things whether he was sufficiently aware of his male existence. Ought a male to have defined religion as the feeling of sheer dependence?"[12] Husbands ought to follow their wives in subordinating themselves to Christ, in other words, but not so much that they fail to reflect the majesty and lowliness of Christ in relation to the community. They must not flee their place as men in the created order—an order which, so far from having been overcome in Christ, has its meaning and origin in him.

The relationship between the subordination of women and male God-language emerges quite clearly within the context of particular theological works. But it remains extremely difficult to document the effects of this language on female identity and female participation in society generally. For one thing, masculine language appears obvious to us: we cannot imagine any other. For another, we have no neutral place to stand in order to measure the impact of male God-language on our lives.

Perhaps the best way to gauge the effects of this language on women is to read arguments for female subordination backwards. Bishop Myers's discussion of the ordination of women, for example, despite all its protestations to the contrary, very firmly identifies deity with maleness. This identification has obvious political implications, and in this context it is being used for political purposes. But it may also have consequences for personal identity formation. Thus one of the implications of Bishop Myers's comments is that in relating to God as a Christian, he feels his male identity affirmed. This suggests that the female Christian relating to God, though she may be affirmed in general as God's child, is not affirmed in her specific identity as female. It is not difficult to see why this lack of affirmation might be destructive in principle, but there may also be specific dangers for women in relating to a deity imaged as male. Psychologist Erich Neumann, in a paper on the stages of feminine development, points out that a woman who worships a "Spirit Father" who is wholly Other for her—in a way that *he* is not wholly Other for a man—may be tempted to spend her life in service to some male Other, never realizing her own personal identity. Whether this Other be God or some human "great man," her own identity as a woman is not as important as that of the male she serves.[13]

In a somewhat different vein, historical studies also give us possible clues as to the effects of male God-language on women. In her article, "What Became of God the Mother?" Elaine Pagels discusses ancient Gnostic use of feminine imagery for God.[14] The divine Mother, Pagels says, was represented by Gnostics as the eternal, mystical Silence, the Holy Spirit (the trinity was thus Father, Mother, and Son), and Wisdom. What is particularly interesting about this feminine imagery is that it did not remain purely theoretical; heretical groups seem to have derived concrete social implications from it. Orthodox Christian contemporaries of the Gnostics note with dismay that women were attracted to Gnosticism in large numbers and functioned as equals of men within certain Gnostic communities. Women were prophets, teachers, healers, priests, and even bishops. There is no proof, of course, that this equality in religious community was a direct outgrowth of female God-language. It may have had independent sources. But the connection certainly is suggestive. It raises in a particularly pointed way the question of the origins, purpose, and effects of orthodox language.

Human Nature

Pagel's article does more than raise questions about the social functions of male God-language. It also suggests that there is a definite relationship between a community's view of God and its view of human nature. Those groups that view God as male and female see the spirit and the gifts of God in male and female human beings. Those that see God as male find greater value in maleness. This brings us to the third way in which theology is a product of male experience: it privileges that experience. It takes as normative the experience of one side—the male side—of the stereotypic sexual polarity.

Valerie Saiving pointed out this imbalance seventeen years ago, and it has since been described numerous times in the literature of women and religion.

It is my contention [she wrote] that there are significant differences between masculine and feminine experience and that feminine experience reveals in a more emphatic fashion certain aspects of the human situation which are present but less obvious in the experience of men. Contemporary theological doctrines of love have, I believe, been constructed primarily upon the basis of masculine experience and thus view the human situation from a male standpoint. Consequently, these doctrines do not provide an adequate interpretation of the situation of women—nor, for that matter, of men.[15]

Her argument was aimed at Reinhold Niebuhr and Anders Nygren, but it called into question Christian theology's long history of identifying sin with pride and self-centeredness. These terms might accurately describe male sin, Saiving claimed, but they have little to do with the sins fostered by women's situation. In fact, a one-sided emphasis on pride has, if anything, reinforced the tendency to self-negation which might be described as "women's sin."

The problems of identifying sin with pride, while hardly limited to Reinhold Niebuhr, can be clearly illustrated through his thought. The power of human pridefulness is a recurrent theme, perhaps *the* theme, in Niebuhr's theology. While much of his work is devoted to exploring the destructive effects of pride in the world, he is also concerned with finding its source in human nature. The occasion for sin, according to Niebuhr, is nothing less than the peculiar doubleness of human nature as finite freedom. At the same time that we are creatures—finite, weak, dependent, thoroughly embedded in and bound up with the natural order—we can also transcend ourselves and this order. We have a unique ability to stand outside ourselves and look at ourselves and the world to which we belong. But this ability, while it makes us human, is also anxiety producing. The transcendent character of human consciousness enables us to envision limitless possibilities that, as creatures, we are not capable of realizing. Involved as we are in the natural order, limited by it in every respect, in our freedom we know ourselves as bound and limited. We try to escape the anxiety this causes either by identifying ourselves with the possibilities we apprehend in the reaches of freedom (pride), or by seeking to escape our freedom by identifying ourselves with some aspect of the world's vitalities (sensuality).[16]

While Niebuhr's account of human nature would seem to suggest that pride and sensuality are equally tempting and significant sorts of sin, in fact, he follows the mainstream Christian tradition in arguing that pride is the basic sin and sensuality a secondary phenomenon derived from it.[17] It is at this point that Niebuhr completely disregards women's experience. The socialization process that shapes "women" and "men" does not encourage women to explore the boundaries of human freedom, claiming for themselves achievements that are possible only in the sinful imagination. On the contrary, it limits women's sights to what is supposedly theirs by virtue of having a "female nature": to marriage and motherhood with their myriad demands. Since women are steered to these functions from the day they are born, it is not surprising if "women's sin" is less aptly described as pride than as the internalization of society's demands to the detriment of freedom. As Saiving puts it:

> The temptations of woman *as woman* are not the same as the temptations of man *as man,* and the specifically feminine forms of sin have a quality which can never be encompassed by such terms as "pride" and "will to power." They are better suggested by such terms as triviality, distractibility, and diffuseness; lack of an organizing center or focus; dependence on others for one's self-definition; tolerance at the expense of standards of excellence … in short, underdevelopment or negation of the self.[18]

It is ironic that in *The Nature and Destiny of Man,* Niebuhr seeks to relate his doctrine of sin to the "observable behavior of *men*" [emphasis mine] and that all his examples of sinful pride are either individual men or male-governed nations. His concern is with private and national claims to unlimited power, knowledge, or righteousness.[19] He is not concerned with timidity, with the failure to realize such power and knowledge as are appropriate to human freedom. The point is not that women are incapable of pride; this is obviously not true. But it may be that in women's experience, we can discern certain features of the human situation that theology needs to explore more fully. Women's tendency to become lost in the demands and details of everyday existence is analogous to broader trends toward conformity and abdication of responsibility in modern culture. Niebuhr does not illumine these either. He, and a good many other Christian theologians, single out the sin of pride because they have cast their eyes in one direction—the direction of powerful men.

If Niebuhr's insistence on the primacy of the sin of pride is inadequate, it follows that a doctrine of grace correlated with his doctrine of sin must be equally inadequate.[20] Indeed, when Niebuhr repeatedly describes grace as a "crucifixion," a "shattering," or a "destruction" of the prideful self, or when he describes the fruits of grace as growth toward the norm of sacrificial love, he reinforces precisely what is already destructive in women's experience.[21] As Mary Daly says, the norm of sacrificial love is in part a reaction to the behavioral excesses of a stereotypically male culture.[22] It represents a projection of the shadow side of the male psyche. Unfortunately, the people who have taken this norm to heart, those who are "divinely ordained" to represent the community in its subordination to God, are those who are already suffering from underdevelopment of the self—women.

The destructiveness of sacrificial love as the sole norm of the life of grace is well illustrated by Doris Lessing's novel *The Summer Before the Dark*. The book is about a middle-aged woman, Kate Brown, whose children are grown and who is spending the summer thinking about her past and her future. One of her recollections is of a morning three years earlier when, pausing to compare the faces of young and middle-aged women on a busy street, she is struck by the freedom and confidence on the faces of one and the trapped, fearful look on the faces of the other. "The faces and movements of most middle-aged women are those of prisoners and slaves," she thinks. Then she recalls her own metamorphosis from the one condition to the other. "With three small children and then four, she had had to fight for qualities that had not even been in her vocabulary. Patience. Self-discipline. Self-control. Self-abnegation. Chastity. Adaptability to others—this above all." If these were really virtues, she thinks, "if so, they had turned on her, had become enemies. ... At one end of some long, totally involving experience, steps a young, confident, courageous girl; at the other, a middle-aged woman—herself."[23] Kate Brown is aware of the necessity for self-sacrifice, but through her experience, she also becomes aware that the self must continually be replenished through mutuality; otherwise, it can give and give until it is depleted. Self-sacrifice then leads not to "new life" and "new selfhood"[24] but obsession with the innumerable demands of everyday.[25]

If we examine the conceptions of sin and grace Niebuhr represents in relation to the God-language discussed above, it emerges that both areas of theology are formulated primarily with reference to male experience. But the correlation between them is deeper than this: the content of this conception of human life also follows from the use of male imagery to describe God. As Barth points out, the relationship between humanity and God echoes or is a model for the culturally sanctioned relation of male and female in society, and this means that humanity plays an essentially feminine role before God. Once God is depicted in terms borrowed from the male side of the stereotypic masculine/feminine sexual polarity, the primary characteristic of the proper human attitude toward God must be sacrificial obedience. Such a God cannot help but resent invasions of his territory. He cannot help but find pride more damnable than self-abnegation when either appears in his subjects and children. He is simply playing the role of jealous patriarch, guarding his male prerogatives in relation to his female worshippers.

Theology and Women's Experience

In summary, then, it can be argued that theology draws on male experience in three ways that are thoroughly interrelated. Specific negative statements about women are not isolated phenomena but are set in a context of androcentric models of God and humanity. Since God is imaged as male, women are put in the position of representing, in their relationships with men, the obedience and humility of the human community before God. Since humility and obedience are in turn seen as *the* Christian virtues, there is no way for women to criticize these traits, and thus women's subordination is reinforced further. Theology is inattentive to women's experience of the destructive aspects of self-sacrifice as a model for human relations and the human relationship to God. Not only does it therefore fail to do justice to the reality of women's situation, it also fails to illuminate the human situation in all its complexity and to develop an adequate image of God. The question arises as to how theology may address itself to human experience in a richer and more rounded fashion.

It will be able to do so, I would argue, only as feminist theologians begin to write out of the depths of their experiences as women. There is no contradiction here. While it may seem that calling for theology's integration of women's experiences is just repeating the error of theological one-sidedness in a new form, this is the only way theology can humanize itself. While neglect of women's experience always involves neglect of some aspect of human experience, this does not mean that theology can move directly from preoccupation with male experience to concern for "universal human experience." For one thing, maleness and humanity have too long been identified for "the feminine" and for women's experience to be incorporated in the doctrine of God and theological anthropology other than deliberately. But we may also ask whether there *is* any "universal human experience" and, if there is, to what extent it can be the subject of theology.

In fact, it seems as if any individual theological work maintains a tension between the universal and particular in human experience. There are structures (or presuppositions) of experience that may be universal, but they are actualized in different ways by different cultures and different groups within a single culture. The theologian gives content to the universal structures of human experience through drawing on his or her own personal, cultural, and historical experiences. Thus categories in Niebuhr's analysis of human nature that might be considered universal take on meaning not through abstract discourse but through discussion of particular features of human experience. Finite freedom, for example, may be a universal, but as soon as Niebuhr begins to consider the dangers of finite freedom, he is no longer describing general features of human nature but the characteristics of particular human beings.

This is not in itself a criticism of Niebuhr's theology. If he does not succeed in showing that pride is *the* human sin, he does establish it as an important temptation of human finitude, and in such a way that it can be recognized and named wherever it is found. He accomplishes this, moreover, precisely through the detail with which he describes current manifestations of pride. The specificity of his account is not in conflict with breadth; rather, breadth emerges through specificity. The capacity of the theologian to illuminate significant aspects of human experience depends "not on an impossible horizontal impartiality...but on the human depth of a particular commitment."[26]

The problem with much theology, then, is not that it speaks from male experience—it must speak from some experience—but that it claims universality for its particular perspective. And while the attempt to take account of women's experience will undoubtedly result in new false claims to universality, these can be avoided only through vigilance, not by avoiding the particularities of experience. Theology cannot deal with "universal human experience" not simply because human reason is finite, but also because experience itself is so varied.

If what is common in human experience can be discerned only through the particularities of experience, it becomes the obligation of groups from which little has been heard to articulate their own experiences and contribute their perceptions to a multifaceted theological exploration of the human situation. Feminist theology must base its theological insights on the neglected experiences of half the human race. It must do this by taking seriously and exploring fully everything that is an authentic reflection of women's experiences—letters, diaries, artwork, dreams, literature by and about women—all of women's hidden history, anything that expresses women's experiences of themselves as opposed to male definitions of women's experience. The point of such explorations will be to recover images, metaphors, and stories that resonate with and express women's experiences and that contribute to a widened and enriched vocabulary of religious experience upon which theology can reflect and draw.[27]

If feminist theology is not to repeat the universalizing pattern of much theology, however, it must perform this task fully cognizant of the fact that women's experience is as diverse and complex as the experiences of the human race. The more deeply feminist theology delves into the experiences of all kinds of women—black women and white women, middle-class women and working-class women, Jewish women and Christian women—the more fully it will illuminate elements of our common human experience that have remained unsung or undiscovered. It is not yet clear how radical the theological implications of this delving will be. When we call into question the male naming of all our basic theological concepts, when we conjure up the lost or hidden stories of women's experience, we set in motion a process that has its own momentum and that may take us in unexpected directions.

One thing is clear. The theological implications of exploration of women's experience are not simply negative or critical. There is no area in which criticism from the perspective of women's experience does not also lead to construction. If it is humanly and theologically inadequate to image God solely in male terms, then drawing images from women's experience adds depth and breadth to our concept of divinity. If it is inadequate to view pride as *the* human sin, then in the light of women's experience we come to see other failings as equally firmly rooted in human nature. The submerged perspective of women's experience, once brought to expression, precisely in its particularity has the power to direct our attention to previously unexplored aspects of reality. God may dwell, sin may flourish, and grace abound where they have not yet been suspected.

The Right Question
Is Theological

In an article on the situation of Jewish women, Cynthia Ozick offers fourteen "meditations" pointing to the sociological status of the woman question in Judaism.[1] The subordination of women, she argues, is not deeply rooted in Torah but is the result of historical custom and practice, which can be halakhically (legally) repaired. Only in her last meditation does she raise the great "what if?": What if the Otherness of women is not simply a matter of Jewish incorporation of surrounding social attitudes but is in part created and sustained by Torah itself? What if the subordination of women in Judaism is rooted in theology, in the very foundations of the Jewish tradition?

The fact that Ozick postpones this question to the end of her paper places her in the mainstream of Jewish feminism. The Jewish women's movement of the past decade has been and remains a civil rights movement rather than a movement for "women's liberation."[2] It has been a movement concerned with the images and status of women in Jewish religious and communal life, and with halakhic and institutional change. It has been less concerned with analysis of the origins and bases of women's oppression that render change necessary. It has focused on getting women a piece of the Jewish pie; it has not wanted to bake a new one!

There are undoubtedly many reasons for Jewish feminism's practical bent: absence of a strong Jewish theological tradition, the minority status of Jews in American culture, the existence of laws (e.g., divorce) that have the power to destroy women's lives and thus require immediate remedy. But such emphasis is no less dangerous for being comprehensible. If the Jewish women's movement addresses itself only to the fruits but not the bases of discrimination, it is apt to settle for too little in the way of change. It may find that the full participation of women in Jewish life—should it come—will only bring to light deeper contradictions in Jewish imagery and symbolism. And most likely, far-reaching change will not come until these contradictions are examined and exorcised. It is time, therefore, to confront the full extent of our disability as Jewish women in order that we may understand the full implications of our struggle.

Of the issues that present themselves for our attention, halakhah (Jewish law) has been at the center of feminist agitation for religious change, and it is to halakhah that Ozick turns in the hope of altering women's situation. But while this issue has been considered and debated frequently in the last ten years, it is specific *halakhot* that have been questioned and not the fundamental presuppositions of the legal system. The fact that women are not counted in a *minyan* (quorum for prayer), that we are not called to the Torah, that we are silent in the marriage ceremony and shackled when it comes to divorce—these disabilities have been recognized, deplored, and in non-Orthodox Judaism, somewhat alleviated. The *implications* of such laws, their essentially nonarbitrary character, has received less attention, however. Underlying specific halakhot, and *outlasting their amelioration or rejection,* is an assumption of women's Otherness far more basic than the laws in which it finds expression. If women are not part of the congregation, if we stand passively under the *huppah* (marriage canopy), if, even in the Reform movement, we have become rabbis only in the last ten years, this is because men—and not women with them—define Jewish humanity. Men are the actors in religious and communal life because they are the normative Jews. Women are "other than" the norm; we are less than fully human.[3]

This Otherness of women functions as a presupposition of Jewish law in its most central formulations. In the last section of her article on Jewish women, finally turning to the sacral nature of women's status, Ozick points out that the biblical passion for justice does not extend to women. Women's position in biblical law as "part of the web of ownership" is taken as simply the way things are; it is not perceived as or named "injustice." One great "Thou shalt not"—"Thou shalt not lessen the humanity of women"—is absent from the Torah.[4] The Otherness of women basic to the written law also underlies the Mishnaic treatment of women. Jacob Neusner points out that the Mishnah's Division of Women deals with women in states of transition, whose uncertain status threatens the stasis of the community. The woman who is about to enter into a marriage or who has just left one requires close attention. The law must regularize her irregularity, facilitate her transition to the normal state of wife and motherhood, at which point she no longer poses a problem.[5] The concerns of the division, and even the fact of its existence, assume a view of women as "abnormal" or "irregular" and therefore requiring special sanctification. While the mechanisms of sanctification are elaborated extensively, the need for it is never questioned. It is simply presupposed.

The fact of women's "special" status is underlined by another point: all reasons given for women's legal disabilities—e.g., they are exempt from positive time-bound commandments because of household responsibilities; they are closer to God and therefore do not need as many commands—presuppose the sex-role division they seek to explain.[6] But while the origins of this division are thus hidden from us—they remain part of the broader historical question of the roots of female subordination—the division itself is imaged and elaborated in clear and specific terms. As in the Christian tradition, in which the Otherness of women is expressed in the language of mind/body dualism, Judaism tenders a similar distinction between *rukhniut* (spirituality) and *gashmiut* (physicality), men and women.[7] The need to regulate women is articulated not as a general problem but as the need to control their unruly female sexuality because of its threat to the spirituality of men.

This fear of women as sexual beings finds expression in both halakhic and aggadic (nonlegal) sources. Neusner suggests that it lies just under the surface of the Mishnah's whole treatment of women. Even where a text's explicit topic is the economics of property transfer, it is the anomaly of female sexuality, with its "dreadful threat of uncontrolled shifts in personal status and material possession," that is the motive of legislation.[8] Moreover, rabbinic concern with female sexuality need not always be deduced from discussion of other matters. The rabbinic laws concerning modesty, with their one-sided emphasis on the modesty of women, make clear that it is women who endanger public morality through their ability to tempt men. These careful regulations of dress and exposure lack any sense of reciprocity, any sense that men tempt women and may therefore also be defined as tempters. Woman may be a "bag of filth"; "it [may be] better to walk behind a lion than behind a woman,"[9] but apparently men are different since there is no danger in a woman's walking behind a man!

The concepts of woman as Other and as temptress are certainly not new to Jewish feminism. They were articulated by Rachel Adler in her classic essay on women and halakhah, elaborated by others,[10] and recently reiterated by Ozick. These writers seem not to have fully understood the implications of their own categories, however, for they tend to assume that the Otherness of women will disappear if only the community is flexible enough to rectify halakhic injustices.[11] Would this were true! But the issue is far deeper than is suggested by this assumption.

Indeed, the situation of the Jewish woman might well be compared to the situation of the Jew in non-Jewish culture. The Gentile projection of the Jew as Other—the stranger, the demon, the human-not-quite-human[12]—is repeated in—or should one say partly *modelled on?*—the Jewish understanding of the Jewish woman. She too is the stranger whose life is lived parallel to man's, the demoness who stirs him, the partner whose humanity is different from his own. And just as legal changes have ameliorated the situation of the Jews without ever lifting the suspicion of our humanity, so legal change will not restore the full humanity of the Jewish woman. Our legal disabilities are a *symptom* of a pattern of projection that lies deep in Jewish thinking. They express and reflect a fundamental stance toward women that must be confronted, addressed, and rooted out at its core. While it is Jewish to hope that changes in halakhah might bring about changes in underlying attitudes, it is folly to think that justice for women can be achieved simply through halakhic mechanisms when women's plight is not primarily a product of halakhah.

But this is just one issue. The Otherness of women is also given dramatic expression in our language about God. Here, we confront a great scandal: the God who supposedly transcends sexuality is known to us through language that is highly selective and partial. The images we use to describe God, the qualities we attribute to God, draw on male pronouns and male experience and convey a sense of power and authority that is clearly male in character. The God at the surface of Jewish consciousness is a God with a voice of thunder, a God who as Lord and King rules his people and leads them into battle, a God who forgives like a father when we turn to him. The female images that exist in the Bible and (particularly the mystical) tradition form an underground stream that reminds us of the inadequacy of our imagery without, however, transforming its overwhelmingly male nature. The hand that takes us out of Egypt is a male hand—both in the Bible and in our contemporary imaginations.

Perceiving the predominance of male language is not the same as understanding its importance, however. Ozick, for instance, begins her article with the question of God and dismisses it quickly. She does not deny the dominance of male imagery, but argues that reflection on the absence of female anthropomorphisms "can only take us to quibbles about the incompetence of pronouns."[13] If the Jewish-woman question is unrelated to theology, theological questions can only lead to dead ends. But as with Ozick's treatment of halakhah, this position seriously underestimates the depth of the issue. Religious symbols are significant and powerful communications. Through them, a community expresses its sense and experience of the world. The maleness of God is not arbitrary—nor is it simply a matter of pronouns. It leads us to the central question, the question of the Otherness of women, just as the Otherness of women leads to the maleness of God.

Anthropologist Clifford Geertz offers us important insights into the function of religious language. In an essay on "Religion as a Cultural System," Geertz argues that religious symbols express both the sensibility and moral character of a people and the way in which it understands and structures the world. Symbols are simultaneously *models of* a community's sense of ultimate reality and *models for* human behavior and the social order. The Sabbath, for example, as a model of God's action in creating the world, is also a model for the Jewish community which, like God, rests on the seventh day. The double reference of symbols, up and down, enforces a community's sense of its symbols' factuality and appropriateness.[14] If God rested on the seventh day, can we fail to do so, and how can our doing so not bring us closer to God?

If we apply Geertz's analysis to the issue of male God-language, it is clear that such language also functions as a model-of and model-for. This language both tells us about God's nature (it is, after all, the only way we know God) and justifies a human community that reserves power and authority to men. When Mortimer Ostow used the maleness of God as an argument against the ordination of women rabbis, he made the connection between language and authority painfully clear.[15] But we do not need Ostow's honesty to grasp the implications of our language; language speaks for itself. If God is male, and we are in God's image, how can maleness *not* be the norm of Jewish humanity? If maleness is normative, how can women not be Other? And if women are Other, how can we not speak of God in language drawn from the male norm?

One consequence of the nature of male God-imagery as a model for community is that the prayer book becomes testimony against the participation of women in Jewish religious life. Women's greater access to Jewish learning and our increased leadership in synagogue ritual only bring to the surface deep contradictions between equality for women and the tradition's fundamental symbols and images for God. While the active presence of women in congregations should bespeak our full membership in the Jewish community, the language of the service conveys a different message. It impugns the humanity of women and ignores our experience, rendering that experience invisible, even in the face of our presence. But since language is not a halakhic issue, we cannot change this situation through halakhic repair. It is not "simply" that halakhah presupposes the Otherness of women but that this Otherness reflects and is reflected in our speech about God. The equality of women in the Jewish community requires the radical transformation of our religious language in the form of recognition of the feminine aspects of God.

Here we encounter a problem; for it is impossible to mention the subject of female language without the specter of paganism being raised. For critics of (this aspect of) Jewish feminism, introducing female God-language means reintroducing polytheism into the tradition and abdicating all that made Judaism distinctive in the ancient world.[16] While, on the one hand, cries of "paganism" couch the question of language in dishonest and hysterical terms, they also make clear that the issue evokes deep emotional resonances. Rationally, it seems contradictory to argue that the Jewish God transcends sexuality—that anthropomorphism, while necessitated by the limits of our thought, is not to be taken literally— and at the same time to insist that broadening anthropomorphic language will destroy the tradition. As Rita Gross asks in her article on Jewish God-language: "If we do not mean that God is male when we use masculine pronouns and imagery, then why should there be any objections to using female imagery and pronouns as well?"[17] Use of sexually dimorphic images may be the best way to acknowledge the limits of language and God's fullness, so that the inclusion of women becomes, at the same time, an enrichment of our concept of God.

But the issue of female God-language touches chords that are not reached or responded to by rational discussion, and so such arguments do not do. The exclusive worship of Yahweh was the result of a long, drawn-out struggle, not simply with the people of the land, but with the many within Israel who wanted to maintain Goddess-worship alongside the worship of God. The victory of Yahwehism entailed suppression of the female side of divinity (and of women as members of the cult), almost as if any recognition the feminine was accorded might overwhelm the precarious ascendancy of God. The gods could seemingly be superseded, their qualities included in the many-named God and recognized as aspects of himself. But the goddesses were apparently too real and too vital for their attributes to be incorporated in this way.[18]

It might seem we are now distant enough from paganism to understand the historical context of suppression of the Goddess without feeling the need to refight this struggle. But if Ba'al is impotent and voiceless, an object of purely theoretical condemnation, the Goddess still evokes resistance which is vehement and deeply felt. Albeit through the lens of our monotheistic tradition, she seems to speak to us as powerfully as ever. Yet this is itself a strong argument for the incorporation of female language into the tradition. It is precisely because she is not distant that the Goddess must be recognized as a part of God. For the God who does not include her is an idol made in man's image, a God over against a female Other—not the Creator, source of maleness and femaleness, not the relativizer of all gods and goddesses who nonetheless includes them as part of God's self. Acknowledging the many aspects of the Goddess among the names of God becomes a measure of our ability to incorporate the feminine and women into a monotheistic religious framework. At the same time, naming women's experience as part of the nature of the deity brings the suppressed experience of women into the Jewish fold.

This brings us to our last issue, one that is closely related to the other two. As Ozick points out in a particularly eloquent meditation, the Jewish tradition is not the product of the entire Jewish people, but of Jewish men alone.[19] Of course women have lived Jewish history and carried its burdens, shaped our experience to history and history to ourselves. But ours is not the history passed down and recorded; the texts committed to memory or the documents studied; the arguments fought, refought, and finely honed. Women have not contributed to the formation of the written tradition, and thus tradition does not reflect the specific realities of women's lives.

This fact, which marks so great a loss to tradition and to women, is cause and reflection both of the Otherness of women and the maleness of God. Women are not educated as creators of tradition because we are Other, but of course we remain Other when we are seen through the filter of male experience without ever speaking for ourselves. The maleness of God calls for the silence of women as shapers of the holy, but our silence in turn enforces our Otherness and a communal sense of the "rightness" of the male image of God. There is a "fit" in other words, a tragic coherence between the role of women in the community, and its symbolism, law, and teaching. The Otherness of women is part of the fabric of Jewish life.

Once again, and now most clearly, we are brought up against the impotence of halakhic change. For halakhah is part of the system that women have not had a hand in creating, neither in its foundations, nor as it was developed and refined. Not only is this absence reflected in the content of halakhah, it may also be reflected in its very form. How can we presume that if women add our voices to the tradition, halakhah will be our medium of expression and repair? How can we determine in advance the channels through which the tradition will become wholly Jewish, i.e., a product of the whole Jewish people, when women are only beginning consciously to explore the particularities of our own Jewishness? To settle on halakhah as the source of justice for women is to foreclose the question of women's experience when it has scarcely begun to be raised.

Clearly, the implications of Jewish feminism, while they include halakhic restructuring, reach beyond halakhah to transform the bases of Jewish life. Feminism demands a new understanding of Torah, God, and Israel: an understanding of Torah that begins with acknowledgment of the profound injustice of Torah itself. The assumption of the lesser humanity of women has poisoned the content and structure of the law, undergirding women's legal disabilities and our subordination in the broader tradition. This assumption is not amenable to piecemeal change. It must be utterly eradicated by the withdrawal of projection from women—the discovery that the negative traits attributed to women are also in the men who attribute them, while the positive qualities reserved for men are also in women. Feminism demands a new understanding of God that reflects and supports the redefinition of Jewish humanity. The long-suppressed femaleness of God, acknowledged in the mystical tradition, but even here shaped and articulated by men, must be recovered and reexplored and reintegrated into the Godhead. Lastly, feminism assumes that these changes will be possible only when we come to a new understanding of the community of Israel which includes the whole of Israel and which therefore allows women to speak and name our experiences for ourselves. The outcome of these new understandings is difficult to see in advance of our turning. It is clear, however, that the courage, concern, and creativity necessary for a feminist transformation of Judaism will not be mustered by evading the magnitude of the required change.

Jewish Theology in Feminist Perspective

It is often claimed that theology is not Jewish or that Jewish theology does not exist. Christianity, it is asserted, rests on a common faith that makes one a Christian, but Judaism is about *behaviors,* and these are elaborated through Jewish law, not through theology.[1] As Arthur A. Cohen and Paul Mendes-Flohr point out in the introduction to their *Contemporary Jewish Religious Thought,* however, "Theology is the discipline that Jews eschew while nonetheless pursuing it with covert avidity."[2] The practices that are central to Judaism are grounded in a series of theological claims: that God gave the law to Moses on Sinai, that revealed law is both written and oral, that the law constitutes part of the obligation of the covenant, that there is a special covenantal relationship between God and Israel, and so forth. All Jewish observance rests on some relation to these fundamental claims, however they are interpreted, modified, or even rejected. What would be the meaning of a Jewish identity that had no relation to any set of beliefs about the nature of Jewishness?

Given the precarious place of theology within Judaism, Jewish feminist theology is a double outsider to Jewish discourse. Feminist theology deals with questions of the meaning and purpose of Jewish and human existence that are central to all Jewish theologies, but it also subjects other theologies to searching criticism. It asks fundamental questions about the origins, nature, and function of theological discourse. It is concerned with the foundations of central Jewish ideas, the groups that generated them, and the interests they serve.

Jewish Feminist Theology as Critique and Recovery

Jewish feminist theology has its roots in the Jewish community and is also part of the larger context of feminist scholarship as a critical and constructive enterprise. Like feminist scholarship in many disciplines, it has gone through a number of stages that began with a critique of male writings and then moved to a process of redefinition and transformation.

The first feminist works in many areas were criticisms of canonical male texts, theories, presuppositions, and images. They attempted to show the particularity of what had been accepted as universal perspectives, to expose the androcentrism of traditional scholarship, and to highlight the absence of the voices of women and other oppressed groups. This critique of male sources was often followed by an emphasis on the recovery of lost women, by efforts to show that certain disciplines, movements, and historical periods were not defined solely by men, but that women made important contributions that had been forgotten or passed over. Often in this second phase, feminist scholars accepted prevailing definitions of historical importance and sought to locate women in contexts deemed important by reigning norms. The third or constructive phase of feminist scholarship is characterized by radical questioning of such norms, by redefinitions of "importance" from the perspective of women's experience, and by the creation of theory from a feminist point of view. These phases were consecutive in terms of a shift in emphasis over the past twenty years, but they are also concurrent in that no stage has disappeared to make way for the others. Feminist scholarship remains critical scholarship and continues to insist on the ubiquity of women's historical agency.

These stages provide a useful structure for discussing Jewish feminist theology, and for seeing how its development has been affected by the subordinate role of theology within Judaism. It is striking, especially in contrast to Christian feminist theology, that virtually no work has been done by Jewish feminists that criticizes earlier Jewish theologians. Although Christian (and non-Christian) feminists have analyzed the thought of Augustine, Aquinas, Paul Tillich, Reinhold Niebuhr, and numerous other thinkers, no parallel body of work exists that discusses Saadia, Maimonides, Franz Rosenzweig, Martin Buber, or other Jewish figures.[3] There is little specifically intratheological dialogue within Jewish feminism. This is probably owing in part to the absence of an institutional base for such studies. The paucity of graduate programs in Jewish theology means that there are few places that might generate or encourage such work. Perhaps Jewish feminists, however, also have the sense that theology is not sufficiently central to Judaism to be worth criticizing.

The transformative and communal bent of Jewish feminist theology makes it unlikely that theological critiques will ever constitute a major part of Jewish feminist discourse. Yet there is interesting scholarly work to be done in this area. Lauren Granite has pointed out, for example, that the centrality of relation in Martin Buber's work has led feminists uncritically to adopt aspects of his thought without thinking to analyze it from the perspective of gender.[4] Buber's I-You theology, however, rests on the assumption that we human beings spend most of our lives in the It-world, only occasionally experiencing moments of I-You connection. Granite suggests that "while relation is key both to Buber's philosophy and feminist theory, it seems that it enters their experience from opposite ends: Buber works toward relation, while feminists begin with relation."[5] The relevance of a gender analysis to Buber's work becomes especially clear in connection with his discussion of the emergence of the two modes of I-You and I-It relation. Here Buber focuses on the experience of the child and its gradual acquisition of self-consciousness without ever naming the mother as the one with whom the child is in relation or looking at the mother-child relationship from the mother's side.[6] Were the child's development seen from the perspective of the mother, a third mode of relation might be required to capture her experience. The child is not characteristically an object to the mother—as in the I-It mode—but neither does she necessarily experience a perpetual reciprocity of relation. Her experience of care and connection even when mutuality is absent may constitute a third sort of relation insufficiently accounted for in Buber's theology.[7]

If theological criticism in the narrow sense awaits the attention of a new generation of Jewish feminist thinkers, criticism on a broader scale is absolutely central to Jewish feminist theology. Starting from Jewish religious practice and the communal exclusion of women, Jewish feminists have examined the theological presuppositions embedded in the Bible, halakhah (Jewish law), and liturgical texts and have called into question a range of basic assumptions, from the normative character of maleness to the holiness of separation.

As I argued in my article "The Right Question Is Theological"—the first sustained theological critique of Jewish women's subordination—the nor-

mative character of maleness is the basic principle of Jewish theological anthropology. Women's Otherness is not simply a sociological fact but a fundamental assumption that underlies both the details of halakhah and a larger
discourse about the nature of Israel as a people.[8] Israel, in both the narrative
and legislative portions of the Bible and in the basic categories of the Mishnah, is defined as male heads of households. If one asks within Judaism, What
is a Jew? What is a person? What are the responsibilities of a Jew? the questions are impossible to answer in any but the most abstract way without re-
course to gender differentiation and hierarchy. This is the starting point of
the feminist critique of Judaism: that a woman is not simply a Jew but always
a female Jew (as in "a *woman* rabbi")—always perceived as Other in relation
to a male norm.

Drorah Setel makes the further point that maleness-femaleness is not the
only hierarchy within Judaism, but rather one of a host of dualistic separations that together are taken to constitute holiness.[9] From the very beginnings of its history, Israel saw itself as called on to separate or differentiate
itself from the surrounding peoples. This differentiation was made manifest
both in the theological claim to chosenness and in many internal separations
that were to mark the life of a holy nation: Shabbat and week, kosher and *treif,*
male and female.[10] Since a critique of hierarchical dualisms has been central
to the entire feminist project from its beginnings, Setel locates the central
tension between Judaism and feminism at this point: in separative versus re-
lational modes of understanding. Her critique raises a series of fascinating
questions for Jewish theology: Why the centrality of separation as a mark of
holiness, especially in those cases where separation seems to have no moral
significance (as in the separation of linen and wool or different kinds of
cattle)? How closely identified are separation and holiness within Judaism?
Is separation itself problematic for feminism, or only hierarchical modes of
separation?[11]

Seen in the context of these other issues, the image of God as male in Judaism is not the only locus of feminist theological criticism but one important aspect of a larger pattern. Jewish feminists have pointed out that the
overwhelming preponderance of male images for God in biblical and rabbinic texts and in the traditional liturgy correlates with the normative status
of maleness. Since God in the fullness of God's reality is ultimately unknow-

able, our images tell us more about our social arrangements—in this case the subordinate status of women—than they do about God.[12] Moreover, the image of God as a being outside ourselves ruling over and controlling the world fits into the pattern of hierarchical dualisms that Setel identifies as central to Judaism. God as the locus of holiness, meaning, and value is infinitely more than the world "he" created. The idea that this God has chosen Israel supports the dualistic separation between Israel and other people. The idea that this God is male supports the normative character of maleness.[13]

These points do not exhaust the feminist theological critique of Judaism. The fundamental nature of women's Otherness, of hierarchical dualisms, and of the male image of God has implications for the concepts of revelation and Torah as well as for other issues. What is the source of Jewish understandings of self, world, and God? Why is it that these understandings seem so clearly to reflect a patriarchal social order? What is the source of Torah, and what are its parameters? If women's voices and experiences are excluded from Torah as it has been handed down, does it need to be expanded? Is there a "woman's Torah"? How do we recognize it, and what would it include? A full theological critique of Judaism is beyond my scope here, but even a brief outline of feminist criticism serves to suggest the range and significance of a feminist probing of Jewish theological foundations.

If we turn to the second stage of feminist scholarship, the recovery of women's history, we find that it has been similarly affected by the status of theology within Judaism. Although it may well be that time will turn up medieval or other women theologians whose names are as yet unknown to us, there is no dense history of theologizing among Jews in whose twists and tangles women can be easily lost. What feminists have attempted to recover, therefore, is not necessarily full-blown theologies, but the history of women's *spirituality*—understandings of God and Jewish life embedded in ritual and prayer, memoirs, and sermons—that may at some point be incorporated into theologies by contemporary Jewish women.

In seeking out the history of women's spirituality, feminist theologians are dependent on the work of women in other areas of Jewish studies who have examined ancient sources, studied archaeological remains, and searched for new documents in modern women's history. Since, particularly for the early periods of Jewish history, few sources are interested in the religious lives of women, hints concerning women's experiences must be carefully ferreted out from narratives, prophecies, and legal texts focused on other matters. Biblical scholars, for example, have argued that the scant sources concerning Miriam suggest that she was probably an important cultic leader in early Israel.[14] What exactly was the nature of her contribution and role? Or, in a different vein, Genesis 34:1 tells us, "Dinah ... went out to visit the women of the land." Does this bespeak some kind of connection on the part of Israelite women to Canaanite religion? Prophetic texts accusing women of worshiping the Queen of Heaven (Jer. 44) or bewailing Tammuz (Ezek. 8:14), son of the Goddess Ishtar, imply that women may have been more resistant than men to giving up the worship of female deities. What are the implications of this resistance for our understanding of both paganism and Israelite monotheism? From the rabbinic period, the stories about Beruriah in the Talmud suggest that a small number of women found pleasure and religious purpose in the study of rabbinic texts, in the same way that an elite group of men has.[15] Jewish women's spirituality apparently has both diverged from *and* flowed into the mainstream of Jewish spirituality.

As we get into the modern period, texts written by women provide evidence of both a distinct religious outlook and one shaped by the role of women within patriarchal Judaism. Chava Weissler, for example, has discussed the *tkhines,* or petitionary prayers of early modern eastern European Jewish women. These prayers, written for women and some by women, reflect a spirituality structured by private events and experiences. Unlike the public liturgy of the *siddur* (daily prayer book), the content of the *tkhines* revolves largely around women's special commandments (lighting the Sabbath candles, taking the hallah dough, and ritual immersion), women's biological experiences, and personal and intimate moments (a visit to the graves of the dead, the illness of a child, the desire to raise children well). Although these prayers connect women to the larger tradition and occasionally even subtly transform it, they most strikingly convey the emotionality and intimacy of women's piety and its relation to ordinary life. If the God of Jewish women was the "God of our fathers" and of Jewish history, God was also the God of the matriarchs, domestic routines, and biological experiences particular to women.[16]

Interestingly, these same themes of the importance of religious feeling and the presence of God in everyday life also come through in the work of those modern women who have the most claim to the title theologian, in that they developed a coherent religious vision that they shared with others. Ellen Umansky has examined the sermons and addresses of Lily Montagu, founder of liberal Judaism in England, and Tehilla Lichtenstein, cofounder and leader of the Society of Jewish Science, to see whether and how the religious visions of these women differed from those of the men they saw as their mentors and teachers. Umansky finds that, although the women understood themselves as simply promulgating the teachings of their mentors, in fact both saw religion as emotional and personal and grounded their sermons in their own life experience, feelings, and perceptions. Thus, although Claude Montefiore, Montagu's inspiration, preached about abstract concepts like beauty, truth, and justice, Montagu rooted her sermons in specific plays, movies, poems, books, and people that to her embodied the principles of liberal Judaism and allowed the discovery of these principles in everyday life. Similarly, although Lichtenstein's husband, Morris, spoke in general terms about human character and the capacities of the mind, she always tied her discussions of Jewish science to concrete examples, most drawn from her experiences of motherhood, marriage, and the home.[17] Whether this focus on the concrete comes from a specifically women's perspective or is simply the product of the restricted role of women in Judaism, there is an interesting continuity between the work of these modern women and the spirituality of more traditional women.

The search for the gaps and silences in traditional texts and for devotional and sermonic material by women suggests a broadening of the definition of Jewish spirituality. Spirituality is found not simply in the products of a male elite but in the experiences and testimonies of women and ordinary men whose religious lives and theological presuppositions have generally been neglected. One could even argue that to understand the range of women's spiritual expression in the modern era, it is necessary to move beyond the realm of texts altogether. The female social reformers of the late nineteenth century, the founders of religious schools, settlement houses, and Jewish women's organizations, as well as participants in Zionist and Bundist activities saw themselves as serving God through moral and social action. Sharing the wider nineteenth-century belief in the innate piety of women, they believed that this piety placed a special obligation on them to worship God by helping others.[18] Their activism came from a clear theological understanding that prefigured the insight of feminist liberation theology: that theological reflection must always be rooted and expressed in concrete actions.

Jewish Feminist Theology as Construction

The need to expand the definition of spirituality to incorporate women's experience begins to suggest the constructive and transformative nature of Jewish feminist theology. A repetition or contemporary restatement of traditional ideas is impossible for such a theology because it begins with the critical moment in which all Jewish texts and ideas are viewed with suspicion for their possible collusion with patriarchy in silencing women's voices. This is why the stage of criticism is never left behind in the move to construction. Rather, the transformative character of Jewish feminist theology is revealed in the back-and-forth movement between stages.

Insistence on the value of women's experience and its integration into the tradition has ramifications for every theological question. In the rest of this essay, I look at some of the implications of women's experience for the concepts of God and Torah, but a similar dialectic of critique and reconstruction would characterize a feminist discussion of any theological issue.

A Jewish feminist approach to Jewish God-language and Jewish concepts of God begins with the critique and process of recovery of women's spirituality I described earlier. The correlation between dominant images of God as male and Jewish social and institutional arrangements raises basic questions about the nature and purpose of God-language. What are Jews saying when we attribute particular qualities or characteristics to God? Are we describing God in words that God has revealed to us? Are we projecting our own wishes or social systems onto the cosmos? Are we responding to some special dimension of our experience using the concepts and vocabulary at our disposal? Although a theory of God-language is often more implicit than explicit in feminist theological constructions, by and large Jewish feminists insist on the socially shaped and created nature of religious language, but without reducing language about God to purely social projection. On the one hand, language about God is precisely that, *language* about God. Everything we say about God represents a human attempt to recapture or evoke experiences sustained within linguistic and cultural frameworks that already color our experience and interpretation.[19] On the other hand, language about God, if it is to move people and provide a sense of meaning, must come from genuine individual or communal experiences. It cannot be a product of individual fiat or scholarly consensus, nor can it be a mechanical response to a diagnosed ailment in Jewish God-language of the past.

For an increasing number of Jewish women and men, images of God as a male Other no longer work. This is the communal, nonacademic basis of the feminist theological quest. The search for the God of Jewish feminism is a search for a God experienced in women's new sense of empowerment and presence within the context of the Jewish tradition. Although feminist images of God draw on many sources, I see a fundamental experience out of which the new naming of God arises as the discovery of women's agency in the Jewish past and present in relation to a greater power that grounds and sustains it. Women's sense of coming to full selfhood in community—which to me is the fundamental feminist experience—is not simply self-referential but leads to a sense of participation in a reality and energy that finally enfold the cosmos and to which both the individual and community must respond.

The sense of women's power and agency that has propelled the Jewish feminist movement and its attempts at new God-language constitutes a new Jewish situation in discontinuity with much of the spirituality of Jewish women of the past. Gluckel of Hameln, whose memoir captures a segment of Jewish life and faith in seventeenth-century northern Germany,[20] the women who wrote or recited the *tkhines,* even as bold a figure as Montagu, were all trying to define their own religious lives within the context of a male-defined Judaism, be it traditional or Reform. Where they departed from tradition —or in Montagu's case, the Reform theology of Montefiore—they did so unselfconsciously. Contemporary Jewish feminists, by way of contrast, are deliberately claiming power as women to criticize the oppressive aspects of tradition and to reshape our relation to it. This means that although the history of women's spirituality is an important resource in that it reminds us that women always have been agents within Judaism and that Jewish religious belief and practice have always been broader than male elite texts would have us believe, women's history cannot simply be taken over whole. The relation between a self-consciously *feminist* spirituality and traditional *women's* spirituality remains an open question that feminist theology needs to explore.

Thus, although earlier generations of Jewish women spoke to the God of Jewish tradition as a God present in the details of their daily lives, for the most part they spoke to "him" using traditional images. Contemporary Jewish feminists also seek God in messy, embodied, everyday reality, but they have tried to translate this sense of God's immanence into the very language of metaphors for God. Feminist God-language, moreover, seeks to give expression not simply to God's presence in ordinary events and situations, but more specifically to the amazing discovery of God's presence moving in and among women. Rita Gross's article on female God-language, the first to raise the issue in a Jewish context, argued that if we want to reflect and affirm the "becoming" of women within the Jewish community, then everything we say about "God-He" we must be equally willing to say about "God-She."[21] Although on one level Gross's text reads like a simple political prescription for the disease of Jewish sexism, it also clearly represents an attempt to give concreteness to the image of God as present in women. At the time Gross wrote her article, Naomi Janowitz and Maggie Wenig were compiling a Sabbath prayer book for women that not only used female pronouns for God but also experimented with female metaphors. God was not simply the traditional deity in female form, but a mother birthing the world and protecting it with her womb. The accumulation of female pronouns and images in both their prayers and those of later innovators provides a wonderful celebration of women's sexuality and power rare in the culture and still rarer in a religious context.[22]

Important as such language was and is as an affirmation of female selfhood in relation to the sacred, there is also a certain naïveté in the assumption that the insertion of female pronouns or images into traditional prayers provides a solution to women's invisibility. Rather, insofar as male images of God are part of a larger pattern of hierarchical dualisms, female language introduces a contradiction into the pattern that begins to reveal and disrupt it but does not in itself dislodge the larger system of dualisms. God-She can also be the supreme Other in a hierarchical system. Jewish feminist God-language has therefore also tried to address the notion of God as wholly Other, a notion that persists even in female imagery, by more radically challenging traditional metaphors and blessing formulas.

Lynn Gottlieb, for example, has drawn on images from various religious traditions to create a litany of names and metaphors for God that evoke the infinite, changing, and flowing depths of God's nature. Gottlieb is much interested in female metaphors, which she borrows from ancient Goddess traditions and develops from the feminine resonances and associations of many Hebrew terms. What characterizes her use of God-language above all, however, is not just its female imagery but its fluidity, movement, and multiplicity, its evocation of a God within and without, in women and in all that lives.[23] Marcia Falk works in a different way to dislodge the traditional conception of God and male images. Focusing on the blessing formula that is so central in Jewish life, she challenges not simply its maleness but its anthropocentrism. Her blessing over bread, for example, changes "Blessed art thou Lord our God king of the universe," to "Let us bless the source or wellspring of life" that "brings forth bread from the earth." The Hebrew word for source *(ayin)* is feminine; adding the feminine ending "ah" *(ha-motziah)* to the verb "bringing forth" displaces the ubiquitous masculine. Beyond this, the image of wellspring or source is both natural and nonhierarchical, shifting our sense of direction from a God in the high heavens ruling over us to a God present in the very ground beneath our feet, nourishing and sustaining us.[24]

In some ways, it is easier to articulate the new conception of God that lurks behind this abundance of imagery than it is to find the images that express the conception. The effort to create new metaphors for God bespeaks an understanding of monotheism that rejects the worship of a single image of God in favor of a new and inclusive notion of unity. Many Jewish feminists have pointed out that the inability of most Jews to imagine God as anything but male is a form of idolatry in that it identifies a finite image with the reality of God. Jews are used to thinking of idols as stones and carved figures, but verbal images can be equally idolatrous in their fixedness—indeed, can actually be more dangerous for being invisible.[25] Underlying feminist metaphors, by way of contrast, is a conception of monotheism, not as a single image of God, but, in Falk's phrase, as "an embracing *unity* of a *multiplicity of images*."[26] Since the divine totality is all-embracing, every aspect of creation provides a clue to some dimension of God's reality. Every image of God is part of the divine reality that includes the diversity of an infinite community of human and nonhuman life. A true monotheism is able to discern the One in and through the changing forms of the many, to glimpse the whole in and through its infinite images.[27]

The nature of this divine totality is developed in feminist discourse through both what is denied and what is affirmed. God is not male. God is not a lord and king. God is not a being outside us, over against us, who manipulates and controls us and raises some people over others. God is not the dualistic Other who authorizes all other dualisms. God is the source and wellspring of life in its infinite diversity. God—as our foremothers seem to have known—is present in all aspects of life, but present not just as father and protector but as one who empowers us to act creatively ourselves. God, to use Nelle Morton's image, is the great hearing one at the center of the universe, the one who hears us to speech and is altered by the hearing.[28] God is inside and outside us. God is transcendent in the way that community transcends the individuals within it. God is known in community, encountered by the Jewish people at Sinai at the same time they became a community. But God embraces the inexhaustible particularities of all communities and is named fully by none.

A second important focus of feminist theological discussion is the nature and meaning of Torah. Obviously, there is a connection between the concept of Torah and the concept of God, for the assertion that God is the giver of Torah is central to Jewish theology and, like many important theological assertions, justifies itself through its circularity. Because God is the giver of Torah, it reliably testifies to the nature of God, and the faithfulness of God is warrant for the believability of Torah. But if feminists are suspicious of traditional metaphors for God because they reinforce larger patterns of male domination, this suspicion in turn implies a critique of Torah as itself in bondage to patriarchy.

Feminist suspicion of Torah does not stem specifically from its male God-language, but as I suggested earlier, from the normative character of maleness Torah assumes. Whether understood in the narrow sense as the five books of Moses or the wider sense as all Jewish teaching and learning, Torah defines the male as the normative Jew and perceives women as Other in relation to men. Torah is male texts—not simply in the sense of authorship, but in the sense that its concerns are defined and circumscribed from a male perspective. Women are often absent—"You shall not covet your neighbor's wife" (Exod. 20:14)—or nameless—Jephthah's daughter (Judg. 11) and Samson's mother (Judg. 13). Women's religious experiences are passed over in silence. (What was Miriam's true role in the Exodus community?) Women's sexuality is strictly controlled in the interests of male heads of household.

Torah constructs a world that orders and makes sense of Jewish experience, but the world it constructs places men at the center. It is the written record of those with the power to keep records and to interpret and define the meaning of Jewish existence. In creating a particular vision of reality, it disguises alternative Jewish realities that may have coexisted alongside it. It understands the imperatives of Jewish life from the perspective of those at the center: the prophets rather than the common people, who for centuries "whored after false gods," and the rabbis who said that only men could write a bill of divorce, rather than the individual women who gave themselves that power.[29] The feminist relation to Torah thus begins in suspicion, critique, and the refusal to assign revelatory status to the establishment and reinforcement of patriarchy.

This insistence on suspicion does not mean, however, that Jewish feminists view Torah as just a series of historical texts, interesting for what they reveal about the past but of no enduring significance. The decisions to struggle with Torah, to criticize it, to remain in relation to it, all presuppose a more complex attitude. Elsewhere, I have called Torah a "partial record of the 'God-wrestling' of part of the Jewish people."[30] In using the term *Godwrestling*, I am trying to encapsulate several assumptions about the theological status of Torah. First, I suggest that Torah is, at least in part, a record of response to some genuine encounter. To be sure, it is an interpretation of encounter encoded in patriarchal language, but still, it tries to remember and to actualize in the life of a concrete historical community the workings of a God understood to be guiding and calling a particular people to their destiny. It testifies to moments of profound experience, illumination, and also mystery, when the curtain was pulled back from the endless chain of historical circumstance and some underlying meaning and presence were traced and read from the events of Jewish history.

The word suggests that Torah is incomplete because it is the nature of religious experience that no oral or written record can either exhaust it or spring entirely free from historical context. "Revelation" can challenge those who receive it and open up perspectives that are genuinely new, but Israel reached its understanding of God and its own destiny at a time when patriarchy was being consolidated throughout the ancient Near East. Its self-understanding helped to institute, support, and reinforce this historical development; it rarely disputed it. My characterization of Torah suggests, moreover, that it is the record of only part of the Jewish people because we do not know how women experienced the large and small events of Jewish history. We do not have Sinai seen through their eyes, their double enslavement, or their wanderings in the desert. We have the names of some of their prophets but not their prophecies. We do not know how women wrestled with God, or even whether, like Jacob, they would have named their experience wrestling.

Although some feminists would argue that reading the traditional Torah from a new angle of vision can provide women with the history we need, others seek to expand Torah, to redefine what Jews consider revelatory and normative.[31] On the one hand, there is no question that Torah as traditionally understood can be sifted and mined for more information about women. Read through feminist lenses, it can provide fragmentary evidence of women's religious leadership, of changing patterns of family and gender relations, of women's lives in and outside normative religious institutions. On the other hand, if we begin with the assumption that Judaism is constituted by women and men, then we must be open to finding Torah far outside the traditional canon. Archaeological evidence that challenges written sources, the writings of nonrabbinic groups, the history of women's spirituality, literature by Jewish women dealing with religious themes, *midrash* (a classic Jewish mode of biblical interpretation and exposition) "received" by contemporary women —all these become Torah in that they are parts of the record of the Jewish religious experience, of what Jews have found holy and meaningful in their lives, and of the Jewish attempt to give order to existence.[32]

This new content of Torah is discovered and created in a number of ways. In part, the findings of feminist historiography, when appropriated as normative, themselves come to have the status of Torah. If the *tkhines,* for example, were taught or recited alongside other Jewish liturgy as equally valid forms of Jewish liturgical expression, their understanding of God would eventually become part of the Jewish imagination much like the God of the synagogue service. If divorce documents written by women had the same status in Jewish legal history as the Mishnah's view that women cannot initiate divorce, the halakhic precedents for contemporary divorce law would be greatly expanded and thereby transformed. If ancient inscriptions describing women as presidents and leaders of synagogues were taken as seriously as the absence of women from the rabbinate, discussion of the ordination of women in the Orthodox community might take on a different complexion. In each of these cases, historical evidence is given *theological* weight that serves to shift and enlarge the meaning of Torah.

Yet historiography is not the only nor the best source for the feminist expansion of Torah. Jews have traditionally used midrash to broaden or alter the meanings of texts. The midrashic process of bringing contemporary questions to traditional sources and elaborating on the sources in response to questions easily lends itself to feminist use. Lacking adequate information on Miriam's role in Israelite religion, we can fill in the gaps with midrash; lacking texts on what women experienced at Sinai, we can recreate them through midrash. Such midrash can then become part of the content of Torah, both through study and through incorporation into liturgy. Indeed, just as the structure of feminist liturgy conveys something of the feminist understanding of God, so the content of feminist liturgy is an important vehicle for communicating an expanded Torah.

Such extension of the content of Torah necessarily opens and challenges traditionally normative texts *and* the theological conclusions we might draw from them. Insofar as traditional texts become part of a larger Torah, their authority is relativized and their claims to normativeness are shaken. Including and valuing women's religious experience as Torah precipitates a new critical moment in feminist theology. It leads us to examine the process by which particular texts become normative, the interests they represent, and the kind of social order they support and undergird. What is more important from a theological perspective, broadening Torah broadens the historical and textual basis of Jewish theological discourse. Highlighting aspects of Jewish experience that had previously been obscured and neglected, and valuing these as Torah, offers a richer and more diverse Judaism on which to reflect theologically. The Jewish God is not simply the God of the patriarchs and rabbis, but the God of the matriarchs, the *tkhines,* and women who interpret and create Torah today. Any attempt to articulate a Jewish understanding of God must take account of all these sources, exploring the concepts and images of God in women's Torah as part of the heritage that a contemporary theology reworks or transforms. The same must be said of any theological concept. It must be grounded in a history and present that is wholly Jewish, one that represents the Jewishness of the whole community rather than the religious experience of a male elite.

The importance of Jewish feminist theology should by now be obvious. Such theology calls into question our basic understandings of Jewishness, Jewish texts, history, and literature. It also moves beyond critical questions to ask what Judaism looks like when we take seriously the perspectives and experiences of women as they try to understand and construct their own visions of the world. It pursues the task of shaping meaning, of making sense of being a Jewish woman and person in the world today. Like all Jewish theologies, it encourages the development of a personal worldview accountable to the needs of a larger community.

Lilith Revisited

Writing "The Coming of Lilith" was one of the few experiences I have ever had of serving as a medium for words and images beyond my own conscious powers. I wrote the Lilith story in 1972 at the Grailville conference on Women Exploring Theology. I had spent the week in a morning group with Karen Bloomquist, Margaret Early, and Elizabeth Farians, exploring and analyzing the early feminist consciousness-raising process as a religious experience. As we repeatedly returned to and shared our own most powerful moments of feminist transformation, we struggled to find a theological vocabulary for expressing those experiences. At the end of our time together, we realized that, although we could not formulate a "feminist theology" apart from particular religious frameworks, we did have a tale we wanted to tell. While the rest of the group was happy to discuss the elements of our journey and leave it at that, I sat down after our last session to see whether I could actually write a story. Rather to my surprise, the words came pouring out of me, and "The Coming of Lilith" was born.

As I read the tale at the final large group gathering at Grailville that night, and as I have reheard or reread it many times since, I repeatedly have been struck by two things: the power of the story to capture a very particular moment in the history of feminism, and the complexity of the issues and feelings it raises and evokes. The spontaneous applause at the first reading, the immediate decision of Rosemary Ruether to publish "The Coming of Lilith" as the epilogue to *Religion and Sexism,* the feelings of delighted recognition numerous women have expressed to me over the years, testify to the extent to which the story has touched a chord in many readers. It is clear to me that my ability to write a story that has evoked such a response was rooted in my having spent a week in the Grailville group, immersing myself in the process and content of feminist consciousness-raising. "The Coming of Lilith" works because its method and message are the same: it is a tale of sisterhood that came out of a powerful experience of sisterhood.

While the success of the piece was not accidental, then, in the sense that I and the group at Grailville were trying to articulate experiences that we knew were shared by a much larger community of women, many of the issues the story raises I was not aware of at the time of writing. Thus Rosemary Ruether's discussion of "The Coming of Lilith" in the preface to *Religion and Sexism* quite amazed me when I first read it. She wrote that the "parable turns male misogynist theology upside down, revealing it for what it is, a projection of male insecurity and demand for dominance." She also commented that "the fearsomeness of Lilith in the male imagination preserves a recognition of suppressed power and creativity in women."[1] While I agreed that these things were there in the story, I certainly had not had such profundities in mind when I wrote it! It was only afterward that I came to see Lilith as a classic example of male projection. Lilith is not a demon; rather she is a woman named a demon by a tradition that does not know what to do with strong women. In a somewhat different vein, it was only when I came out as a lesbian more than a decade after writing the story that I first was struck by the potentially sexual nature of the energy between Eve and Lilith. The erotic possibilities in the intensity of their encounter and their care for each other seem so clear to me now that I am astonished I didn't see them earlier.

One of the elements of "The Coming of Lilith" that I often have been challenged on over the years is the maleness of God in the story. Some women have argued that, in making God male, I adopted and reinforced the patriarchal perspective that I was simultaneously criticizing. This was a deliberate decision on my part, and I still completely stand by it. The story is not saying that God in God's reality is actually male. It is playing with our perceptions of God at a particular point in history. The God of the original medieval Lilith midrash is certainly male. He sides with Adam in the struggle with Lilith for reasons that are utterly mysterious. In 1972, also, God was male! Feminists were beginning to raise questions about male images of God but were moving only in the most tentative ways toward alternative concepts and metaphors. It was the process of consciousness-raising and the long, slow experimentation with new images and liturgies that were gradually to make possible a new understanding of the sacred. In this sense, the coming together of Eve and Lilith precipitates a change in (our perceptions of) God. In depicting God as reflecting on that change I was drawing on what has always been one of my favorite aspects of the Jewish tradition: the fact that God is understood as growing through interaction with and challenge from human beings. In alluding to Abraham's argument with God over Sodom and Gomorrah, I was trying to place the feminist challenge in the larger context of fateful divine/human dialogues within Judaism.

I continue to be proud of "The Coming of Lilith" then, and even were I to want to change it, I do not feel it is quite fully mine to do so. I think it still stands as an expression of the original, heady round of consciousness-raising, an expression that perhaps provides a taste of the moment to those who were not part of it. But if the story as story seems to have had a life of its own apart from me, such is not the case with the theoretical and theological context in which it was originally embedded.[2] My understanding of Lilith as a Jewish story is entirely different from what it was when I first wrote it, and I would now describe its theological meaning and import entirely differently.

Today, when I look at the larger framework in which "The Coming of Lilith" was initially presented, I am shocked by the Christianness of the religious language that we/I chose to impose on our feminist experiences, describing them in terms of "conversion," "grace," and "mission." I do not think that my willingness to use this language stemmed simply from the fact that I was working with three Christian women. Especially since the language is heavily Protestant and two of the women were Catholics, I assume these terms were as much a product of my own immersion in Protestant theology in graduate school as of the influence of the group. I was certainly aware at the time of the tension between this vocabulary and my own Jewish identity, but there was as yet no Jewish feminist discussion of theological issues offering an alternative language and conceptual framework.

Were I reflecting today on the religious dimension of feminism, I would try to remain close to the experiences being described rather than impose on them the foreign vocabulary of any particular tradition. When I think back to the larger conference at Grailville, for example, and especially the contributions of a group that was working on images of God, I see that in coming to a new sense of ourselves as agents in the world with power to shape our destinies, many feminists also experienced a sense of connection to larger currents of power and energy in the universe.[3] One can talk about the relationship of such experiences to specific theological concepts, but one does not *need* the concepts to authorize the experiences, and using traditional language may serve to mask the freshness and iconoclasm of the consciousness-raising process.

Were I interested in using traditional language to interpret feminist experience, however, I now see a much closer fit between the shared communal self-understandings of feminism and Judaism than I do between feminism and an individualistic Protestantism. Central both to our group reflections and the Lilith story is the notion that insight and empowerment emerge from the experience of community. Eve and Lilith by themselves are each isolated and powerless. Their ability to transform the garden and God results from their coming together; it is sisterhood that grows them into consciousness and action. This notion that human personhood is fundamentally social, that one stands in relation to God always as a member of a people, is also central to Judaism.[4] Moreover, rather than using the term "mission" to describe the expansive dimension of feminism, I would now talk about Eve and Lilith's transformation of the garden in terms of *tikkun olam* (repair of the world). While mission to me implies a somewhat condescending "I know better than you what is good for you," *tikkun olam* refers to the obligation and project of healing the world from the ontological and social brokenness that has marked it from creation. In contemporary usage, the concept of *tikkun olam* brings together mystical and social understandings of repair within Judaism in a way that fuses spirituality with a commitment to social justice.[5] By creating a more just social order, either through the liberation of women or commitment to other issues, one is also healing the alienation and separation within God. This, of course, is precisely what Eve and Lilith are doing at the end of the story.

What is most striking to me in revisiting Lilith, however, and most glaringly absent in terms of Jewish categories and analysis, is any understanding of the story as midrash. In referring to "The Coming of Lilith" in the framing material, I consistently label it a myth.[6] This points to a rather interesting paradox. On the one hand, for all that I was willing to adopt a Protestant vocabulary, when our group's convoluted theological discussion was over and done, I/we returned to the old Jewish mode of storytelling to capture the truths we had arrived at. On the other hand, in doing so, I had no conscious awareness of standing in a long Jewish tradition of using midrash as a way of expressing religious insight and grappling with religious questions.

Judaism, unlike Christianity, has no continuous history of systematic theological discourse. A tradition in which deed is more central than creed, it deals with theological issues not through the elaboration of doctrine but through engagement with biblical narratives. Midrash is a form of biblical interpretation that often begins from a question, silence, gap, or contradiction in a biblical story and writes the story forward in response to the interpreter's questions. Thus the original Lilith midrash emerged from the contradiction between the creation narratives in Genesis 1 and Genesis 2. Because in Genesis 1 the man and woman are created simultaneously and apparently equally, while in Genesis 2 Eve is created from Adam's rib, the rabbis wondered whether the stories might not describe two different events in the history of creation. Their response was that, indeed, Adam did have a first wife named Lilith, who fled the garden when Adam tried to subordinate her. God sent three angels after her to bring her back, at which point in the midrash Lilith turns into a demon, killing new babies in retaliation for the deaths of her own children.[7] Midrash as a major technique of interpretation is not limited to this particular narrative, of course. Rabbinic midrash on countless biblical characters and texts functions as a vehicle for exploring religious questions in a way that makes room for disagreement, ambiguity, and complexity.

In the last decade or so, Jewish feminists have begun to use midrash as an important way of both reconnecting with and transforming tradition. Just as rabbinic midrash often begins from some gap or silence in the biblical text, Jewish feminists are using midrash to explore and fill in the great silence that surrounds women's history and experience. Just as the rabbis brought their own questions to the Bible and found there answers that supported their religious worldview, so Jewish women are asking new questions of biblical narratives and, in the process of responding, recreating tradition.

My story, "The Coming of Lilith," both does and does not fit into this recent explosion of feminist midrash. First of all, unlike most examples of the genre, it is a midrash on a midrash, and not on a biblical text. In beginning from the Lilith story in the *Alphabet of Ben Sira* rather than from Genesis, I comment on the biblical creation narrative only indirectly. Second, and more significantly, I did not intend to write an interpretation of the traditional midrash but to capture the experience of consciousness-raising within a religious framework. I cannot remember now how I had even heard of Lilith, but I borrowed her tale because it fit my contemporary need. I did not realize that in retelling her story, I was doing for the traditional midrash what it had already done for the biblical text. And yet, once the story was completed, it *read* as a midrash on a midrash of creation, and to that extent stands in the stream of Jewish feminist midrash that was to follow.

I find it interesting that, in beginning from consciousness-raising as a religious experience and moving from there into Protestant theological categories, I nonetheless ended up with a story that, in content and form, reflects important aspects of Jewish tradition. Insofar as "The Coming of Lilith" has spoken to a generation of readers about the transformative implications of feminism, it testifies to the power of story and the power of midrash to create and communicate religious meaning.

II

The Complexity of Interlocking Oppressions

Christian Feminism
and Anti-Judaism

There is a new myth developing in Christian feminist circles. It is a myth that tells us that the ancient Hebrews invented patriarchy: that before them the goddess reigned in matriarchal glory, and that after them Jesus tried to restore egalitarianism but was foiled by the persistence of Jewish attitudes within the Christian tradition.[1] It is a myth, in other words, that perpetuates traditional Christianity's negative picture of Judaism by attributing sexist attitudes to Christianity's Jewish origins, at the same time maintaining that Christianity's distinctive contributions to the "woman question" are largely positive. The consequence of this myth is that feminism is turned into another weapon in the Christian anti-Judaic arsenal. Christian feminism gives a new slant to the old theme of Christian superiority, a theme rooted in the New Testament and since reiterated by countless Christian theologians.[2]

Invidious comparisons between Judaism and Christianity most often appear in one particular context in feminist work. Writers exploring the Jewish background of Jesus's attitudes toward women frequently exaggerate the plight of women in Judaism in order to make Jesus's position stand out more positively in contrast. If Jewish women are unclean chattels, then Jesus's treatment of them must be revolutionary. "Jesus was a feminist," as Leonard Swidler puts it.[3] Understanding Jesus's relations with women in the historical context of contemporary Judaism is surely a legitimate and important task. But many feminist accounts of Jesus's Jewish milieu suffer from three serious scholarly errors or oversights which are rooted in biased views of Jesus's Jewish origins.

First of all, a number of discussions of Jewish attitudes toward women use the Talmud or passages from it to establish the role of Jewish women in Jesus's time.[4] The Talmud, however, is a compilation of Jewish law and argument that was not given final form until the *sixth century*. Passages in it may be much older or at least reflect reworkings of earlier material. But this can be determined only on the basis of painstaking scholarly sifting of individual original texts. Such sifting clearly has not been done by authors who can blithely refer to the whole Talmudic tractate Shabbat as contemporary with Christ[5] or who can say that certain taboos against women were incorporated into the Talmud "and from there passed on into Christianity."[6] Similarly, references to rabbinic customs or sayings as contemporary with Jesus also reflect a misunderstanding of the development of Judaism.[7] The rabbinate emerged as an institution only after the fall of the Temple in 70 CE, and it then took considerable time before rabbinic authority was consolidated and came to represent more than a minority opinion within the Jewish community.

Secondly, it is deceptive to speak of rabbinic opinion, customs, or sayings as monolithic. Even if one assumes that the Talmud gives an accurate picture of Jesus's Jewish background, the Talmud is at least as ambivalent as the New Testament on the subject of women. Yet writers dealing with Jewish attitudes toward women often select only the most negative rabbinic passages on the topic. Their treatment of Judaism is analogous to conservative Christian arguments for the subordination of women which quote only certain verses from Paul. Perhaps the most egregious instance of this type of distortion of Jewish tradition is Virginia Mollenkott's statement that "the Rabbis" would have been shocked and alienated by Christian belief in the mutual love and service of husband and wife.[8] Is she speaking of "the Rabbis" who said "Love your wife as yourself, honor her more than yourself," or "If your wife is small, stoop and whisper in her ear?"[9] Certainly, there are many dreadful rabbinic sayings about the relationship between husband and wife, but there are also a large number of precepts celebrating the joys of a loving match. And if the negative statements influenced Jesus and the New Testament authors (a questionable assumption!), then the positive ones must have as well.

The third error frequently made by feminist scholars is more subtle. It lies in comparing the words and attitudes of an itinerant preacher with laws and sayings formulated in the rarefied atmosphere of rabbinic academies.[10] Many discrepancies between Jesus and "the Rabbis" on the subject of women can be explained by the fact that Jesus was constantly in contact with real women, speaking to and about them in the context of concrete situations. Rabbinic discussions about women, on the other hand, were often largely theoretical, taking place in institutions where there were no women present. Where we do have rabbinic stories of actual male/female interaction, we find that rabbis too—whatever their ideological statements—were capable of re-acting to women as persons. The often-quoted story of Jesus's compassion for the woman taken in adultery (John 7:53–8:11), for example, finds a parallel in a rabbinic anecdote told of Rabbi Meir. A man became so angry at his wife for staying out late attending Meir's sermons that he vowed to bar her from the house unless she spat in Meir's face. Meir, hearing of this, sent for the woman and told her that his eyes were sore and could be cured only if a woman spat on them. The woman was then able to go home and tell her husband that she had spit on Meir seven times.[11] The theological point of this story is not the same as the New Testament one. But it is not very different in showing a rabbi react with concern and sympathy for the trials of an ordinary woman.

These deficiencies in feminist scholarship are serious, and they suggest the need for major revisions in treatment of Jesus's Jewish background. Re-quired, first of all, is honest, balanced, nonpolemical discussion of those texts that are in fact contemporary with Jesus. Such discussion should take into ac-count variations in Jewish practice in different areas of the ancient world as well as differences in the setting and audience of Jewish and Christian mate-rial. Only when Christian feminists have deepened their understanding of Ju-daism can they honestly evaluate the uniqueness or non-uniqueness of Jesus's attitudes toward women.

At the same time that Jesus's milieu is being reevaluated, the Talmudic rabbis ought to be compared with their true contemporaries—the Church Fathers. Admittedly, this task is less rewarding than comparison of the Talmud with Jesus: examination of rabbinic and patristic attitudes toward women leaves neither Christians nor Jews much room for self-congratulation. Rather, what is immediately striking is the similarity between the two tradi-tions—in both, the developing association of women with sexuality and the fear of woman as temptress. Christianity compensates for the image of the temptress with that of virgin; Judaism, with the good wife with whom sex is permitted and even encouraged. But while these images saddle women with different disabilities and provide them with different opportunities, it would be difficult, and certainly pointless, to label one superior to the other.

The persistence of biased presentations of Judaism in feminist work is disturbing. But were sloppy scholarship the only issue at stake in feminist anti-Judaism, it could easily be corrected. Much more important, the popularity of such research indicates a profound failure of the feminist ethic. The morality of patriarchy, Mary Daly argues, is characterized by "a failure to lay claim to that part of the psyche that is then projected onto 'the Other.'"[12] Throughout the history of Western thought, women, blacks, and other oppressed groups have had attributed to them as their nature human traits that men could or would not acknowledge in themselves. Sexuality, bodiliness, dependence, moral and intellectual failure were all peculiarities that belonged to everyone except ruling-class males. The feminist ethic, in contrast to this, is supposedly an ethic of wholeness, an ethic based on the withdrawal of projection and the recognition that the full humanity of each of us embraces those despised characteristics patriarchy ascribed to a host of Others.

Christian feminist anti-Judaism, however, represents precisely the continuation of a patriarchal ethic of projection. Feminist research projects onto Judaism the failure of the Christian tradition unambiguously to renounce sexism. It projects onto Judaism the "backsliding" of a tradition which was to develop sexism in new and virulent directions. It thus allows the Christian feminist to avoid confronting the failures of her/his own tradition. This is the real motive behind biased presentations of Jesus's Jewish background: to allow the feminist to present the "true" Christian tradition as uniquely free from sexism. Otherwise, why not present positive Jewish sayings about women along with the negative ones? The former are just as conspicuous as the latter in English anthologies of rabbinic thought. And why not compare the Talmud with the Fathers instead of Jesus? Clearly, because that would not permit as dramatic a contrast between the two traditions.

The Other who is the recipient of these projections is, of course, the same Other who has received the shadow side of the Christian self since the beginnings of the Christian tradition. Feminists should know better! During the period when witch persecutions were at their peak, witches and Jews were the Church's interchangeable enemies. When the Inquisition ran out of Jews, it persecuted witches—and vice versa.[13] This fact alone should alert feminists to the need to examine and exorcise a form of projection that bears close resemblances to misogyny. But besides this, what Other is more truly a part of the Christian than the Jew? Where should the withdrawal of projection *begin* other than with Judaism? Yet women who are concerned with the relation between feminism and every other form of oppression are content mindlessly to echo traditional Christian attitudes toward Judaism.

The purpose of these criticisms of feminist scholarship is not to suggest that traditional Jewish attitudes toward women are praiseworthy. Of course, they are not. But Christian attitudes are in no way essentially different. They are different in detail, and these differences are extremely interesting and worthy of study. But weighed in the feminist balance, both traditions must be found wanting—and more or less to the same degree. The real tragedy is that the feminist revolution has furnished one more occasion for the projection of Christian failure onto Judaism. It ought to provide the opportunity for transcending ancient differences in the common battle against sexism.

Anti-Semitism

The Unacknowledged Racism

The subject of anti-Semitism frightens me, both because anti-Semitism is frightening and because even discussion of it threatens to separate me from other women. It reminds me of our differences rather than our similarities. It reminds me that the women's movement, in appealing to women as women, frequently erases important cultural differences among us. It reminds me that sisterhood, while powerful, is not powerful enough to eradicate deeply seated prejudice. The very process of trying to write this essay reminds me that I belong to different communities. As a feminist addressing other feminists, I want to be honest about the contradictions I see in Judaism and Jewishness. As a Jew, I do not want to be misheard or provide ammunition to the anti-Semite in my Christian feminist sisters.

Perhaps these conflicts are appropriate to my subject: complexity. As feminists, we are learning to acknowledge the complexity of oppression. We are becoming aware that race, class, and sex oppression are interstructured in the lives of many women.[1] We are recognizing that the complexity of oppression makes it possible for the same person to be both oppressed and oppressor and that as American feminists, many of us are in both categories. The situation of Jewish women in America illustrates many aspects of this complexity.

It is necessary to say at the outset that Jews hardly appear oppressed in the United States today. Anti-Semitism in the United States, never as virulent as in Europe, declined in the decades after World War II to the point where many were predicting its complete disappearance.[2] While, contrary to all the stereotypes, there are many poor and working-class Jews, the majority of American Jewry is comfortably ensconced in the middle class. Indeed, it is unfortunate that the upward mobility of Jews has often been used against other minority groups.[3]

Moreover, since the vast majority of American Jews are white, we share white-skin privilege and have assimilated racism along with other American values. The many Jews involved in the 1960s civil rights movement never represented a majority of American Jewry. Most Jews' attitudes toward blacks are probably indistinguishable from the attitudes of other Americans.[4] More concretely, in the last fifteen years, the Jewish and black communities have come into conflict on a number of specific issues. The fact that Jews have sometimes been the last group out of an area before blacks moved in has meant that in certain black neighborhoods, a disproportionate number of storekeepers and landlords are Jews. This makes Jews the buffer group, the representatives of the exploitative white community to the black community. In New York City, the underlying tensions created by this situation were exacerbated by the school crisis of 1968. In the fall of that year, a struggle between the largely black Ocean Hill school board and the United Federation of Teachers, with its many Jewish members, quickly acquired racial overtones. Jews who had "made it" in American society through the school system perceived black insistence on community control of assignment of teachers as a threat to their livelihood and place in society. For many blacks, on the other hand, the teachers' strike seemed to mark the Jewish community's backing away from commitment to quality education for blacks and thus to racial justice. Jews suddenly found themselves cast in the role of oppressor rather than oppressed.

Yet to be a Jew in the United States is to know that acceptance comes in many shades. It is perhaps to have the money that would enable you to live in certain parts of town or to join certain clubs, and yet not be permitted to live there or join anyway. It is to have a cousin or uncle or sister who went to an inferior medical school or did not get to go at all because of anti-Jewish discrimination. I recall being taught as a child never to ask people their religion, the hidden message being that they might ask me mine in return! While I would never deny my Jewishness, I was uncomfortable acknowledging it. This discomfort explains the unwillingness of many Jews to press their own Jewish concerns, and it gives rise to the more subtle forms of self-contempt that come with not living up to particular standards of beauty, manners, or discretion. Such concerns and self-censoring are signs of internalized oppression, the process through which oppressed groups adopt the standards of the dominant culture and turn them against themselves.

While there are many ways internalized oppression affects all Jews, there are also ways it takes special forms in Jewish women. Other Jewish feminists have written of attempts to iron their dark, kinky hair so different from the American blonde ideal, or to stop being "pushy" or shooting off their big mouths.[5] The epithet "pushy" need not be explicitly accompanied by "Jew" for the message to be conveyed that Jewish ethnic mannerisms do not conform to American norms, particularly norms of femininity. This message is proclaimed most clearly through a range of popular "Jewish woman" stereotypes, especially the image of the powerful, intrusive, devouring Jewish mother. She epitomizes all that the culture fears in women and all that Jewish women fear to be. When this stereotype, and others—the spoiled, whining "JAP" (Jewish American Princess), the overbearing "equal," the sexual neurotic—are perpetuated and popularized by Jewish men, one sees their own self-hatred being projected onto and turned against Jewish women. Jewish women then bear the double burden of nonconformity to the rules of the wider culture and the contempt of Jewish men who have internalized the culture's norms.

The broader and more profound determinants of the American Jewish experience, however, fall on men and women more equally. To be a Jew in the United States is to live in an overwhelmingly and often unselfconsciously Christian country. It is to have one's school vacations scheduled around Christian holidays, to learn Christmas carols and participate in Easter egg hunts, all the while being assured that these customs and holidays are not really Christian but American, "that they belong to everybody." Like other oppressed groups, Jews must know about the dominant culture, but members of the dominant culture need know nothing about them.[6] Ironic as this is given the Jewish roots of Christianity, American Jews necessarily acquire a surface knowledge of major Christian beliefs and celebrations, while particularly outside of New York City, Christians are often totally ignorant of Jewish holy days and their meaning.

It is not surprising, given Christian dominance, that to be a Jew in America is to meet anti-Semitism in its particularly Christian formulations. It is to learn that one is a Christ-killer, and perhaps to be beaten for being one. It is to be asked repeatedly why Jews reject Christ. From the Jewish perspective, this makes almost as little sense as the idea that the essence of Buddhism is rejection of Christ. Judaism has nothing to do with Christ. It is an independent tradition that did not end with the Old Testament, but that, in its mainstream rabbinic form, *began* in the same period that Christianity did.[7] This fundamental misunderstanding of Judaism denies its integrity and legitimacy as a living religion at the same time that it supports a Christian interpretation of reality.

To be a Jew in the United States is to know as a fundamental part of one's identity that in this century, a third of world Jewry was exterminated simply because they were Jews. To be a Jew in the United States is often to know that one *is* a Jew in the United States because parents and grandparents came here fleeing pogroms at the turn of the century. Had they not come fleeing other persecutions, they would have been part of the statistics of the Holocaust. Therefore, to be a Jew in the United States is to be a survivor. Jews are sometimes accused of seeing anti-Semitism where it does not exist and bringing it into being by their expectations. I do not doubt that this is sometimes true. But it is all too easy for non-Jews to discount or tire of the scars that come with knowing even thirdhand the impassioned hate directed at one's people within or almost within one's lifetime.

This is all just background, however, to what many Jews perceive as a new escalation of anti-Semitism in this country as part of the right-wing backlash of the last few years. Reports of anti-Semitic incidents such as vandalism and cross burnings have recently risen dramatically. And whether this is new or not, the women's movement has had its share of anti-Semitic incidents and feelings. Indeed, it is ironic that women who had abandoned their Judaism because it was sexist, seeking community in the women's movement, are now being forced back to Judaism because of feminist anti-Semitism.[8] As Sartre said in his book *Anti-Semite and Jew,* "The Jew is one whom other men [*sic*] consider a Jew."[9] Jewish women are learning the truth of this in a very painful way.

Certain forms of Christian cultural and linguistic imperialism in the women's movement cannot really be called anti-Semitism. When feminist events are scheduled on Jewish holidays, this can be understood simply as everyday thoughtlessness. Other reports coming out of the women's movement are more disturbing, however. Jewish feminists have reported having to listen to anti-Semitic jokes. Their concerns have been trivialized and treated as "Jewish paranoia" in contexts where every other form of oppression is taken seriously. Anti-Semitic stereotypes have been used to silence or discount feminist Jews: she's just a Princess/Jewish intellectual/rich Jew/pushy Jew/cunning Jew, etc. Most upsetting are stories about the women's conference at Copenhagen where American delegates found the anti-Semitism overt and intense.[10]

An important element in the anti-Semitism at Copenhagen, and in the American feminist movement, is anti-Semitism in its new and acceptable form of anti-Zionism. I do not consider criticism of the Israeli government anti-Semitism. The war in Lebanon horrifies me, and I deplore Israel's West Bank policies as strongly as anyone. But when the Jewish people are denied the right to decide *for ourselves* whether we are a nation, how to define ourselves, and how to shape our destiny, that is anti-Semitism whatever other names one chooses to put on it. Jews can raise their voices against Israeli policy and still ask themselves why, when other peoples kill, lie, maim, or steal, the world closes its eyes or legitimates their deeds in the name of self-defense or national liberation. When the Jews behave as a "normal" nation, however, the moral outrage of the world is focused upon them. From this I can only conclude that the world wants to see the Jews remain victims.

But I learn something else from Israel which brings me back to my initial point: to be oppressed does not protect one from being an oppressor. The bodies of Sabra and Shatila proclaim that to be a Jew and not a Nazi is a moral privilege, but it guarantees nothing about who the Jew will be when s/he comes to power.

A number of years ago, I wrote an article on anti-Judaism in Christian feminist treatments of Jesus.[11] Several months later, I read an article by Alice Walker on racism in white feminist writing.[12] Essentially, she was saying about white feminists exactly what I had said about Christian feminists, and every point she made applied to me. The article frightened me because it made me wonder whether we are all locked into our own experiences of oppression, wanting other people to hear and know us, but unwilling to undertake the difficult process of trying to know others. How can we use our experiences of oppression, I wondered, not to wall ourselves in but to build bridges to one another?

This question sends me back to a basic affirmation of the Jewish tradition, its insistence on remembering that "we were slaves in the land of Egypt." Every Passover, the telling of the story of the Jewish people begins here. Several years ago, in an anthology on Jewish feminism, Esther Ticktin suggested that the knowledge that we were slaves in the land of Egypt should become the basis of a new Jewish law governing the relationships between Jewish women and men. Just as Jews have the right to expect that a decent Gentile will not join a club that excludes Jews, so Jewish women have the right to expect that decent Jewish men will not participate in any Jewish institution or ritual that excludes Jewish women.[13]

But as women from many different backgrounds, each of us in her own way has been a stranger or slave in the land of Egypt. Could not Esther's sensitizing and consciousness-raising device become the basis for our ethical dealings with each other? As Cherrie Moraga put it, "We don't have to be the same to have a movement, but we *do* have to be accountable for our ignorance. In the end, finally, we must refuse to give up on each other."[14] Can we learn to listen to each other in our complexity? Can we learn to value our differences instead of being threatened by them? Isn't this part of what it should mean to be a feminist? Isn't this part of what it should mean to be a Jew?

Feminist Anti-Judaism
and the Christian God

The issue of Christian feminist anti-Judaism is just one piece of a larger question of how we as feminists, and as members of various religious, national, and international communities, can learn to see diversity not as a threat but as a source of enrichment and even a cause for celebration. The dream we had in the heady, early days of the feminist movement, that the bonds of sisterhood would annul or eradicate traditional divisions of religion, race, and class, and that we could formulate an analysis of women's situation and a program for action that would embrace all women, was based not on engagement with the particularities of women's experiences but on a wave of a magic wand that made differences invisible. Racial/ethnic feminists have increasingly made clear that feminist theory and priorities often have ignored the multiple communities that shape women's lives.[1] Assuming that male/female difference is the oldest and only important social difference, white middle-class—often heterosexual, often Christian—feminists have constructed accounts of women's experience that falsely universalize a particular cultural, religious, and class perspective. This bias is illustrated by the persistence of anti-Semitic stereotypes in feminist literature; the additive analyses of sex, race, and class that ignore their interpenetration in women's lives; and the exclusionary phrases "women and blacks" or "women and minorities" that appear and reappear in feminist writing. The message such work communicates to women rooted in dominated communities is that if we want to be part of the "women's movement," we should bring ourselves as women in the abstract (which is to say women of the dominant group), leaving aside the particular women we happen to be.

Confronting feminist anti-Judaism, as well as all other types of oppression, is part of a process through which we face the fact that *there is no reason* why becoming feminists should suddenly free us from the other forms of hatred that mark our world or the groups to which we belong; that without con-

tinual self-examination and vigilance we are as likely to use feminism to per-
petuate other forms of domination as to overcome them; and that feminism
at best commits us to struggle against traditional forms of dominance, but it
does not guarantee that we will be successful.

In the case of the relationship between Jewish and Christian feminists,
there are profound asymmetries that make it difficult for us to respect, and on
the Christian side, even to perceive, the differences between us. On the one
hand, there is the long history of Christian anti-Judaism, firmly rooted in the
New Testament, and expressing itself historically in social, economic, political, and religious sanctions against Judaism and Jews. Christians have had the
power to forbid Jews to practice Judaism, to herd Jews into ghettoes, to re-
strict Jews to certain professions, and to kill Jews. And in a continuing way,
they have had the more subtle power of any dominant group to impose their
own worldview without the slightest idea that they are doing so. Not surprisingly, this history makes it very difficult for Jews to take seriously Christian
claims—traditional or feminist—that Christianity is a religion of love, liberation, or right relation.

On the other hand, feeding anti-Judaism in a different way is the religious and psychological reality that Christians need Jews in a way that Jews do
not need Christians. Wondering what Jews think about Jesus or why Jews reject Jesus as the Messiah, Christians seem to find it almost impossible to hear
that Jews *don't* think about Jesus—except when Christian questions and a
Christian culture force them to do so—and that they do not reject Jesus, they
are simply not interested in him. The fundamental irrelevance on a religious
level of Christianity to Judaism means that Christians taking Judaism seriously as an independent, living tradition must rethink the self in a way that
is not true for Jews in relation to Christianity. What does it mean to affirm
Christian identity without defining it over against Judaism? This is a question
that the Christian tradition has never satisfactorily answered. And in large
measure, it still has not been resolved by Christian feminists, who have simply turned feminism into a new way of yet again defining Christian identity
at the expense of Judaism.

While there are a number of areas of feminist discourse I could turn to to
illustrate this point, the topic of images of God in many ways brings us to the
center of Christian feminist anti-Judaism. I would like to discuss, therefore,

three places where anti-Judaism asserts itself in relation to the subject of God: the contrast between the supposedly wrathful God of the "Old Testament" and the New Testament God of love, blaming Jews for the death of the Goddess, and the "Jesus was a feminist" theme as an aspect of the broader—and to my mind most difficult—subject of the specialness of Jesus. I will make no attempt to be exhaustive, but will simply cite some typical examples of feminist use of traditional anti-Jewish themes in order to open up some of the questions they raise.

The idea that the God of the "Old Testament" is a jealous, wrathful, and essentially tribal deity in contrast to the New Testament God of universal love is a well-established stereotype that long predates feminism. (I place the term "Old Testament" in quotation marks, for obviously it is not a Jewish term, and the contrast "Old Testament"/"New Testament" itself implies a supersession that can be applied to any of a host of issues: law/gospel, people of the flesh/people of the promise, God of wrath/God of love, and so on.) The idea of two contrasting natures of God has been seized by feminist mythmakers who, perhaps in an effort to free themselves from some of the more problematic aspects of God's nature, have depicted an internal development in the nature of God that amounts to a virtual dualism. Sheila Collins, for example, began her early feminist theology *A Different Heaven and Earth* with a story about the son of the great Queen of Heaven who one day inexplicably arrogates kingship to himself, turning against the Goddess who bore and nurtured him. Dictatorially protecting the illegitimate power he always fears to lose, he surrounds himself with fire and thunderbolts, and makes up ugly stories about the Queen to explain human suffering under his rule. In due time, however, the Queen has another son who teaches people gentleness and compassion and alerts them to the fact that the King's priorities are seriously distorted. "He taught them that wisdom was not found in learned books nor in secret ceremonies, but in the heart of the child and the simple justice of nature."[2] A similar feminist myth is retold nine years later as the preface to Rosemary Ruether's *Sexism and God-Talk*. In her version, God the Father bellowing "I am the Lord thy God" from his high throne is contrasted with the iconoclastic teacher who speaks of a kingdom for the poor and the meek.[3]

There are several problems with this dualistic depiction of two natures of God, the most serious of which is that it projects a tension that exists *within* both Judaism and Christianity as a conflict *between* Judaism and Christianity. In the so-called Old Testament, God is fully developed as a God of justice *and* a God of mercy, and both these aspects of God are elaborated by rabbinic Judaism which also considers and problematizes the relation between them. In the Rosh Hashanah and Yom Kippur liturgies, the thirteen attributes of God from Exodus 34 are repeated over and over again as the congregation prays for mercy on the (annual) day of judgment: "The Lord, the Lord is a merciful and gracious God, slow to anger and abounding in kindness and truth. He keeps kindness to the thousandth generation, forgiving iniquity and transgression and sin, and acquitting the penitent." The contrasting aspect of God, present in Exodus but dropped from the liturgy—"but who will by no means clear the guilty, visiting the iniquity of the fathers upon the children . . . "—appears indirectly in numerous rabbinic *midrashim* and discussions that seek to make sense of Jewish suffering in light of belief in a merciful God. Indeed, Rosemary Ruether, in her myth, acknowledges the complexity of the God of the Hebrew Bible when her jealous God the Father remembers other ways of being God, such as vindicating the oppressed and freeing captives.[4] But then, as a Christian conscious of the history of anti-Judaism, why does she not portray a liberating God who is tempted by dominance rather than playing off the traditional stereotypes while hinting that they don't fully apply?

If the God of mercy is present in the Hebrew Scriptures, then the God of wrath is also present in the New Testament, although often more as a background threat than as a vital presence. "He who believes and is baptised will be saved," says the risen Christ in the Gospel of Mark (16:16), "but he who does not believe will be condemned." Judgment as the left hand of conversion and repentance is fully developed in the book of Revelation, a book that Christians playing out the contrast between the God of love and the God of wrath conveniently ignore. Moreover, the later Christian notion of the eternal damnation of masses of humanity—and the vigorous depiction of that damnation in Christian sculpture and painting—has no parallel in Judaism, which can think of no worse fate for the wicked than that they will be forgotten.

Often linked to the image of the jealous and dominating God of the "Old Testament" is the notion that this God is responsible for the death of the Goddess. While this theme has been most fully elaborated by post-Christian feminists as an implicit assumption of their historical reconstructions, it also plays a role, interestingly enough, within Christian feminism. In Sheila Collins's myth, God becomes King of the universe by turning against his wife/ mother, the Queen of Heaven who is presumed to have reigned over the whole earth until overthrown by the God of the "Old Testament." God's need for absolute dominion is a product of both his guilty conscience and his continuing fear of the mother whose power he usurped, but who always impinges on the margins of his consciousness. In Ruether's myth too, God thinks, " 'The Queen of Heaven. Why does She still appear in my head? I crushed her rule a millennium ago.' "[5] Ruether's use of this theme is particularly surprising, given her insistence in other contexts that Goddess religions themselves were often patriarchal.

The feminist origin of the idea that biblical religion struck the deathblow to the Goddess is not difficult to see. As Carol Christ pointed out in her essay "Not Blaming the Jews for the Death of the Goddess,"[6] it must come as a shock to any feminist brought up reading the Bible that the "idols" repeatedly vilified by the prophets were not mere sticks and stones, but the gods and goddesses of another religion—among them goddesses whose images and histories feminists are trying to reclaim. The realization that the biblical writers helped to suppress female imagery comes with a sense of betrayal that easily attaches itself to traditional anti-Jewish themes. Now the Jews have not one deicide on their hands, but two. Their perfidy in betraying Christ, not a comfortable theme in feminist circles, echoes their earlier banishment of the Goddess whose rightful rule was usurped by Yahweh, the upstart son.

That this theme should find its way into Christian feminist mythmaking is ironic, given the role that Christianity played in the suppression of Goddess worship after the conversion of Constantine. It seems that in this case, as with the image of the wrathful God, it is easier for Christian feminists to point the finger at problematic aspects of the Christian tradition as they also appear within Judaism than it is to deal with them within Christianity itself. Beyond examining the anti-paganism in Christian history, however, feminists must also realize that it is not Judaism or Christianity, separately or together, that bear the whole guilt for the death of the Goddess. As scholars of the ancient Near East have pointed out, patriarchal societies and religions began to emerge throughout the Near East and Mediterranean worlds in the fourth through second millennia BCE. The struggle documented within the Hebrew Bible between advocates of exclusive worship of Yahweh and a larger population of Hebrew polytheists was just one facet of an older and much larger struggle between what some have depicted as Goddess-centered, matrifocal societies and emerging patriarchal societies with ascendant male gods.[7] As the evidence for such a wide-scale social transformation grows and becomes clearer, Jewish and Christian feminists will be able to locate the particular contributions of Hebrew and Christian patriarchy to this larger process.

The contrast between the God of love and the God of wrath and the condemnation of Jews for the death of the Goddess represent two areas in which feminist treatments of God continue traditional anti-Jewish themes. Anti-Judaism still seems most entrenched, however, in relation to the figure of Jesus, and, in particular, feminist attempts to articulate his uniqueness and significance. I find the persistence of anti-Judaism in this area especially significant, given the profound ambivalence of many Christian feminists about the nature and role of Jesus. In the U.S. context, Christian feminist anti-Judaism certainly does not take the traditional forms of reproaching the Jews for rejecting the Messiah or accusing Jews of deicide, for Christian feminists are not always sure who they want to say Jesus was and is. Indeed, the charge of deicide is much more comfortably made in the Goddess context, for the Goddess at least is a clear representation of the sacred, even if not one Christian feminists wish to adopt. Yet in wanting to hold on somehow to the centrality and specialness of Jesus without necessarily making ontological claims about his nature, feminists are forced to focus on his human uniqueness, and this uniqueness is most easily established by contrasting him with his Jewish context.

I first made this point many years ago in relation to the still-popular claim that Jesus was a feminist. As I argued then and still would insist, this claim depends on wrenching Jesus out of his Jewish context and depicting the Judaism of his period in unambiguously negative terms. As one writer on this topic put it, "At the historical moment when Jesus was born into the world, the status of Jewish women had never been lower.... By the time of Jesus's birth, many decades of rabbinic commentary and custom had surrounded Old Testament literature. And these rabbinic traditions considerably lowered the status of women."[8] The author then goes on to quote a series of misogynist Talmudic passages that may date anywhere from before the time of Jesus to five centuries later.

Such polemical use of rabbinic material to document Jesus's feminism shows no interest in the serious examination of Jesus's actual context. Aside from the fact that the Talmud is much more appropriately compared with the Church Fathers than with the sayings of Jesus, rabbinic literature is as varied as the New Testament in its comments about women and its legal treatment of women's issues. As Judith Wegner points out in her book *Chattel or Person? The Status of Women in the Mishnah*, the Mishnah, a second-century legal text that lays the basis for the Talmud, is perfectly comfortable treating women in some contexts as full legal persons with the rights and responsibilities of Jewish males, and in other contexts as virtual chattel.[9] To cite one side of this contradiction without the other is like quoting 1 Timothy 2 on women—"Let a woman learn in silence with full submission"—with the implication that it represents the entire New Testament.

Ignoring the complexities of rabbinic literature is just one problem with the Jesus-was-a-feminist argument, however. A more curious aspect of the strategy of contrasting Jesus with his Jewish background is that it simultaneously acknowledges and negates the fact that Jesus was Jew. He was a Jew sufficiently that his supposed difference from other Jews is significant and noteworthy, yet he was not a Jew in the sense that his behavior counts as evidence for the nature of first-century Judaism. If we acknowledge that the Jesus movement was a movement within Judaism, however, then whatever Jesus's attitudes toward women, they represent not a victory *over* Judaism but a possibility *within* early Judaism—a Judaism that was in fact so diverse and pluralistic that it is impossible to state its normative position on anything. The notion of a normative Judaism is a later rabbinic construct from which Jewish feminists are trying to free ourselves, and that we would urge Christian feminists not to adopt.

The argument that Jesus was a feminist is theologically very interesting for its simultaneous radicalness and conservatism. Obviously, its intent is to awaken the Christian tradition to self-transformation; yet it does so on the basis of an unnuanced and uncritical reading of the New Testament and early Judaism that focuses only on texts that support a particular feminist perspective. It assumes, to use Krister Stendahl's phrase, that contemporary Christians are called upon to "play 'First Century Bible-Land'" and to do as Jesus did, however Jesus's actions are understood.[10] Moreover, though the Jesus-was-a-feminist argument does not depend upon explicit claims about Jesus's unique ontological status, it leaves these traditional claims unexamined in the background as a buttress to the feminist cause. It is perhaps not surprising then that traditional anti-Jewish attitudes work their way into this argument, along with other traditional assumptions.

I find it especially disturbing, therefore, that the tendency to define Jesus as unique over against Judaism remains even in feminists who do not make use of the Jesus-was-a-feminist argument, who are quite aware of Christian anti-Judaism, who are freely critical of Christian sources, and who have gone very far in deconstructing notions of Jesus's divinity. Carter Heyward's view of Jesus, for example, as a man of passionate faith who shows Christians the way to live their own lives in relationship to God, but who cannot do it for them, seems to provide very little grounding for traditional anti-Jewish themes. And yet when Heyward tries to state the meaning of the "dynamic re-latedness we call Christ," she says that Jesus "seemed to perceive his own work would involve a radical shift in consciousness . . . from an emphasis on ritual to right-relationship; from salvation as 'deliverance-from-enemies' to salva-tion as 'right-relationship-with-God' which might involve deliverance into the hands of enemies."[11] Here we have the conventional law/gospel, carnal Jew/spiritual Christian dichotomies clearly stated in feminist form. This for-mulation is utterly astounding to me as a Jewish feminist, for what is Judaism about, if not right-relation?

It seems as if the feminist struggle with patriarchal Christologies itself generates a dilemma that leads back into the trap of Christian anti-Judaism. If Jesus is not the Messiah and the incarnate son of God on any traditional in-terpretation of these terms, then how does one articulate his uniqueness in a way that makes sense out of remaining a Christian? If one is unwilling to make statements about Jesus's ontological status or about God's work in and through him, then maybe it is necessary to make some claim about his spe-cialness as a human being—and how does one do that except by contrast-ing him with his Jewish context? This is why I said earlier that confronting anti-Judaism forces Christians to redefine the self. Must Jesus be different from every other human being who ever lived in order for Christianity to make sense? Can Christians value Jesus if he was just a Jew who chose to emphasize certain ideas and values in the Jewish tradition but did not invent or have a monopoly on them? If claims about Jesus's specialness are intrinsic to Christianity, then is there any way to make these claims that does not end up rejecting or disparaging Judaism as their left hand?

In discussing three loci of Christian anti-Judaism in relation to the question of God, I have tried to speak in a way that would not deny the kernel of truth in the issues concerning Judaism that Christian feminists have raised. The image of a dominating, angry father God is a problem for Jewish feminists as much as for Christian feminists. Jews *have* contributed to the suppression of the Goddess. The early Christian movement was open to women, whether we see that openness in contrast to Judaism or as part of it. Given these kernels of truth, even if Christian feminists engage in a continuing process of consciousness-raising and self-monitoring with regard to anti-Judaism, there always will remain gray areas in the anti-Judaism discussion that will need to be openly talked through with the utmost sensitivity. Christian and Jewish feminists need to be very aware of how we *talk about* and *hear* feminist criticism of Judaism and discussion of Jesus in light of the past and present history of Christian anti-Judaism.

This history, and efforts to begin grappling with it, raise very different dilemmas for Jewish and Christian feminists. On the one hand, it is very difficult for Jewish feminists to critique Judaism in a non-Jewish context when we know that what we say as internal criticism may appear against us in Christian work. On the other hand, it is obviously essential to our health and well-being as Jewish feminists that we do critique Judaism and seek to transform it. On the one hand, the Hebrew Bible *is* the Christian Old Testament, and Christian feminists have a right to explore and critique the Old Testament—including images of God in the Old Testament—as part of their tradition. On the other hand, Christianity has a history of using the Hebrew Bible in a way that belittles and discredits the people who wrote it, and Christian feminist criticism cannot but be read in that context. On the one hand, Christian feminists have every reason to explore and value Jesus's openness to women. On the other hand, in doing so, they need to take account of the difficulty of talking about Jesus's relations with women without evoking in the hearer negative comparisons with Judaism. On the one hand, I as a Jewish feminist could write a feminist critique of modern Protestant theology without ever having anyone suggest I was anti-Christian. On the other hand, a Christian feminist whose field is Judaism might well find herself in very uncomfortable waters if she chooses to do work on documenting the patriarchal character of Judaism.

I do not have answers to the questions of exactly when critique or historical research veers into anti-Judaism or exactly who should speak and when. I do find it helpful, however, to keep in mind a joke that addresses the sometimes delicate boundary between self-critique and something else. What is the difference, the joke asks, between an anti-Semite and a prophet? The answer: an anti-Semite says, "Jews are terrible," and a prophet says, "Jews are terrible, oy." This joke suggests to me that if Christian feminists want to say "Jews are terrible," they had better first have said the "oy" loudly and clearly in their work and in their lives. The absence of that "oy" is not simply a matter of a missing syllable. It is a matter of lending aid and comfort to those persons and institutions wedded to a society that excludes Jewish difference.

Finally, however, no awareness of feminist anti-Judaism and its relation to a long history, no effort to weed it out of one's thinking and writing, no sensitivity to the power imbalance in the relations between Jews and Christians can replace knowledge of Judaism as a living religion as the best antidote to anti-Judaism. Certainly, Jews have been oppressed. Certainly, Christianity's contribution to that oppression is something every Christian should be aware of. But Jews are not defined by our oppression. It is not what makes us Jews. It is not what makes our identity valuable and our difference worth asserting. To know Judaism primarily through anti-Judaism, to see anti-Judaism as the central issue confronting Jews, is itself another manifestation of anti-Judaism. If there is a role for Jewish-Christian dialogue in a feminist context, perhaps its most important function is this: to foster awareness of Judaism as defined by Jews—as a complex, varied, and evolving tradition.

Jewish Anti-Paganism

Beware of making a covenant with the inhabitants of the land against which you are advancing, lest they be a snare in your midst. No, you must tear down their altars, smash their pillars, and cut down their sacred posts; for you must not worship any other god.

—EXODUS 34:12–14

Perhaps because "some of my best friends are pagans," and perhaps because the charge of paganism has been easily and wantonly leveled at Jewish feminists, I find myself increasingly angry that biblical exhortations against paganism receive scant critical attention in the Jewish community. While I have been part of Torah discussions in which people struggle with the intolerance and virulence of such passages, criticism rarely extends to the Bible's basic image and understanding of Canaanite religion. Instead, Jews internalize and defend a set of stereotypes that lead to contempt for others and undermine our understanding of our own tradition.

There are two major components to the image Jews have of Canaanite religion, and paganism more generally. First, pagans worship concrete images —they cannot tell the difference between sticks and stones and the living God. This is a constant theme of biblical literature. "Their idols are silver and gold, the work of men's hands. They have mouths but cannot speak, eyes but cannot see.... Those who fashion them, all who trust in them, shall become like them" (Ps. 115:4–5, 8). This is the paganism Jewish children hear of in the often-told midrash in which Abraham destroys the idols in his father's shop, then tells his father that the largest idol smashed all the others.

Second, Judaism portrays pagan worship as licentious, revolving around forbidden sexual practices. The repeated characterization of Israelite apostasy as "whoring after other gods" (see, for example, Exod. 34:15, 16; Lev. 17:7; Deut. 31:16), combined with the Levitical injunction against the abhorrent sexual acts performed by the people of the land (Lev. 18:24–30), convey a picture of Canaanite worship as largely prostitution and Canaanite society as bereft of sexual morality or order.

I find Jewish willingness to accept the truth of these images deeply disturbing. We Jews have long been victimized by the propaganda of New Testament writers, yet we rarely stop to ask ourselves whether analogous processes are at work in our own sacred texts. We know that the New Testament portrait of the Pharisees is a caricature that emerged out of the competition between Judaism and early Christianity, and that was designed to prove the superiority of the new religion. But we do not ask whether a similar situation of religious competition produced an equally distorted portrait of Canaanite religion, a portrait designed to prove the superiority of biblical Judaism.

In fact, like the New Testament picture of the Pharisees, Jewish images of pagan religion cannot bear close scrutiny. If we look at ancient religious texts and living traditions that use plastic images in worship, we see that there never has been a tradition that identified the work of human hands with the essence and reality of the sacred. Images serve many functions: they are manifestations of the sacred, they reveal certain of its qualities, they provide foci for worship or meditation. But they are not the sacred itself. Moreover, the notion that Canaanite worship involved ritual prostitution and other forms of sexual immorality has drawn fire from scholars of ancient Near Eastern religion. Jo Ann Hackett recently suggested that the dominant scholarly construction of "fertility religion" is basically a projection of the fantasies of Protestant clergymen who, accepting the biblical invective against Canaanite religion at face value, combine fragmentary, controversial, and disparate evidence into a portrait of their own making.

I do not mean to suggest that New Testament anti-Judaism and Jewish anti-paganism have had the same destructive effects. For the last two thousand years Christian anti-Judaism has had worldly power and has claimed a great many victims; Jewish anti-paganism has not. But the fact that, until recently, there have been few pagans to suffer from anti-pagan attitudes does not mean that they have no consequences. Five in particular trouble me.

1. The Jewish caricature of paganism cuts us off from aspects of our own history. It disguises the important role that concrete artifacts played in

ancient Jewish practice. Cherubim, for example, covered the ark in the Holy of Holies, and the golden calf was not a unique example of apostasy in the desert but part of the cult of the Kingdom of Israel (1 Kings 12:25–33). Caricaturing paganism leads us to project the battle over paganism as a battle between "us" and "them" instead of a protracted struggle within Israel between those who advocated worship of Yahweh alone and the apparently far larger number who worshipped Yahweh along with the other deities.

2. It keeps us from asking what was gained and what was lost in the Jewish victory over paganism. Pagan traditions offered their followers a wide range of male and female images of the sacred and allowed women to serve as dancers and diviners, musicians and priestesses in the cult. The biblical polemic against paganism renders invisible the abolition of female images and the exclusion of women from religious leadership that accompanied the consolidation of monotheism.

3. Envisioning paganism as dangerous, licentious, and foolish prevents us from seeing that so-called pagan concerns find their way into contemporary Judaism. As Jo Ann Hackett remarked, once we rid ourselves of the stereotypes evoked by the phrase "fertility religion," we find that religious concern for fertility is everywhere, as much in the Bible as in the competing Canaanite cult. Howard Eilberg-Schwartz's recent book, *The Savage in Judaism,* argues convincingly that many themes and modes of thought dismissed as savage or pagan have striking parallels in biblical and rabbinic Judaism and continuing Jewish practice. Circumcision as the mark of the covenant, for example, symbolizes hope for a son's fertility and for his ability to propagate male descendants. Recognizing such parallels does not diminish Judaism but leads us to appreciate the extent to which diverse religious traditions respond to fundamental human dilemmas in similar ways.

4. Defining paganism as the worship of man-made objects affects our attitudes toward other traditions and prevents us from seeing our own idolatries. When we see a Hopi kachina ceremony, or a Hindu procession, or

a Christian kneeling before a statue of Mary, are we able to understand the complex conception of the sacred involved in the use of imagery? Or does the biblical caricature of pagan worship shape—consciously or un-consciously—our attitudes toward other religious practices? Conversely, because as Jews we see idols only in material terms, it is difficult to real-ize that the identification of particular verbal images (such as the image of God as male) with the reality of the sacred is just as much idolatry as the deification of sticks and stones.

5. Lastly, the use of the label "pagan" to attack Jewish feminism shows that the biblical projection of the pagan Other still evokes strong images and passionate feelings that can be wielded against modern enemies. Jewish feminists who use female or natural metaphors for God have repeatedly been accused of paganizing Judaism, as if women or nature were intrin-sically pagan symbols, and as if a variety of images were the same as a variety of gods. Feminist calls for reconsideration of Jewish attitudes toward sexuality have been countered by lurid portraits of pagan licen-tiousness, as if there were no moral alternative to a patriarchal sexual ethic. Such charges conjure and build on unexamined stereotypes in or-der to strike fear into the hearts of feminists and any who might listen to them. They also allow critics to dismiss serious feminist questions with-out considering the merits of the issues.

I suggest these are five good reasons to attend more closely and critically to the theme of anti-paganism when it appears in the Torah. Such projections left unquestioned and unexamined end up being used against real human be-ings, and distort our understanding of ourselves.

Dealing with the Hard Stuff

For many years, I had difficulty listening to the Megillah reading on Purim. I found the story morally repugnant. Vashti's banishment for refusing to display herself before a group of drunken revelers seemed to me an example of male chauvinism it was impossible to slide over. And I experienced chapter nine, in which the Jews slay their enemies, as dreadful and bloodthirsty. That Haman should be hanged was utterly fitting; he was the one who hatched the plot against the Jews. But why should that be an excuse for a general bloodletting in which Jews treated an unnamed enemy in precisely the way they feared to be treated themselves?

But a few years ago—I'm not sure how or why—I came to adopt the perspective certain friends had long been pressing on me. The story was Purim Torah—nonsense, parody. I suddenly heard the full absurdity of the line "for the fear of the Jews had fallen upon all peoples" (9:2), and my gestalt shifted. Ahasuerus was a complete fool, the story of Vashti obvious silliness, chapter nine the drunken fantasy of a powerless people. I thoroughly enjoyed the last several years of Megillah readings.

And then, in 1994, on the afternoon of Purim, I turned on my radio and heard that Baruch Goldstein had used the occasion of the holiday to mow down thirty Arabs praying in a mosque in Hebron. I realized that reading the story as Purim Torah had not banished or addressed the layer of poisonous objectification of the Other contained in chapter nine.

The massacre in Hebron raises a question posed many times in the course of the annual cycle of weekly and holiday readings: What do we do with hard texts? What do we do, when as individuals or communities, we find ourselves faced with texts that not only express values we no longer share, but that seem to support and encourage hatred, oppression, and violence in the world? For me, the end of the book of Esther is not the only or even the most egregious example of this problem. According to tradition, in avenging themselves against their enemies, the Jews were simply acting on a broader warrant for genocide: the commandment to exterminate Amalek (Deut. 25:19; Ex. 17:16). Numerous passages in the Torah call for the annihilation of the peoples and indigenous religious traditions of Canaan (e.g., Deut. 7:1–5). And others identify groups within Israel as fitting targets for destruction or dehumanization. A man who lies with a man as with a woman should be put to death (Lev. 20:13). Lot offers his virgin daughters to be gang-raped by the men of Sodom (Gen. 19:8), an act on which the Torah makes no comment.

I am not suggesting that there is a direct and simple connection between difficult texts and contemporary examples of intolerance or hatred. Baruch Goldstein did not kill thirty Arabs in cold blood because the Megillah told him to do so. Nor do I see a direct relationship between discrimination against gays and lesbians in the Jewish community and the injunctions of Leviticus. Not only have appeals to problematic passages been too selective to support such easy correlations, but also there are obviously complex social, historical, and political factors that shape religious attitudes toward particular communities. I am arguing, however, that these texts foster and support a process of objectification of people who are "not like us." We learn from the Torah that there are whole groups of human beings who are so evil, or so other than we are, that marginalizing or destroying them is not only thinkable but divinely ordained.

Despite my willingness to read the Megillah as Purim Torah, I have never been of the school that feels we can simply dismiss troubling passages as reflections of an earlier time period. Nor do I think we can interpret them away. In reading the Torah aloud each week as sacred text, we receive it ever again in the present, hearing it directly and unadorned. In this context, the fact that the midrashic tradition sees Lot as sharing in the sinfulness of Sodom cannot entirely eradicate the cruelty and violation of his readiness to sacrifice his daughters. There is no easy way to escape or ignore the hard places in Torah. Insofar as it has shaped our values, it necessarily has shaped them for good and for ill.

In dealing with hard texts, then, we have several possibilities. Sermons and Torah discussions constitute the most obvious context for grappling with the difficult passages in Torah. Their purpose is to provide occasions for interpretation and application of the weekly reading. But there may also be other creative ways to turn troubling passages into opportunities for communal conversation and learning. In an article on Leviticus and homosexuality, Rebecca Alpert suggests that all synagogues declare the weeks of *Parshiot Ahare Mot* and *Kedoshim* (the Torah portions that contain Leviticus 18 and 20) lesbian and gay awareness weeks.[1] Synagogues might set up panels and invite speakers, foster discussion, and formulate policy. One can imagine analogous events for other problematic passages. The week of *Ki Tetse*, when the injunction to exterminate Amalek is read, might serve—in the contemporary context—as the occasion for examining Jewish attitudes toward Palestinians. *Parashat Vayera*, when we read about Lot, might provide the opportunity to talk about sexual abuse in the Jewish community. And so on.

As another response in the aftermath of the Purim massacre in Hebron, Rivkah Walton has come up with a proposal for *liturgical* acknowledgment of the problematic nature of certain canonical sources. She suggests that when the Torah verses concerning Amalek are read, congregations read softly and rapidly, as they do for the curses at Gerizim and Ebal (Deut. 27:11–28). And she also proposes that Esther 9:1–16 be read in the *trop* (melody for chanting) traditionally used for Lamentations.[2] Varying *trop* is a classic way of expressing feelings and values surrounding the material being read, and it has the advantage of calling community attention to morally difficult texts in the very process of reading.

But if certain texts seem to call out for attention and action, confronting hard texts also has its dangers and even absurdities. If we extend the principle of expressing our distance or mourning through *trop*, or set up "awareness weeks" for every passage whose import is damaging, where does the process end? It is not always easy to separate the stories and values we want to affirm from those we find troubling or simply unacceptable. We run the risk of always and only using Torah against itself, ignoring its richness and flattening its ambiguities.

And there is an opposite danger as well. It is one thing for adults who have already been affected and formed by difficult texts to find ways publicly to struggle with them. But can we justify teaching such passages and passing them on to the next generation so that they also need to exorcise the objectification of the Other that the text teaches and supports?

I do not have any easy answers to these questions. When I think about what I will do next Purim, I hope to be able to read on two levels. I do not want to lose the level of Purim Torah—the fun and self-mockery that is an important part of the cycle of human celebration and that has helped a persecuted people to survive. But I also want to grapple in community with the dangers of the Purim story for a people with power, and with the criminal use to which this text has been put, partly in my name. I continue to search for ways of dealing with a complex and contradictory heritage, and for ways of wresting life and justice from even its hardest places.

III

Creating a Feminist Judaism

God

Some Feminist Questions

An extraordinary passage in *Pesikta Rabbati* (21.6) describes the many guises in which the one God has appeared to the children of Israel. God spoke to the Israelites on Mount Sinai not "face to face" (Deut. 5:4) but "face after face." "To one he appeared standing, and to one seated; to one as a young man and to one as an old man." Showing them a variety of aspects, God revealed a threatening face and a severe face, an angry face and a joyous face, a laughing face and a friendly face.

This midrash at once points the way out of the feminist dilemma of God-language and simultaneously illustrates its most trying aspect. It acknowledges the legitimacy, indeed the necessity, of plural ways of perceiving and speaking about the one God. It asserts that multiple images of God are not contradictions of monotheism but ways in which limited human beings apprehend and respond to the all-embracing divine reality. And yet while the passage authorizes theological and liturgical inventiveness, the many faces of God it describes are only male ones. God is an old man or a young man, a man of war or a man of wisdom, but never a woman.

This unyielding maleness of the dominant Jewish image of God is not the end of the feminist critique of God-language, but it is the beginning. The absence of female metaphors for God witnesses to and perpetuates the devaluation of femaleness in the Jewish tradition. The God-language of a religious community is drawn from the qualities and roles the community most values, and exclusively male imagery exalts and upholds maleness as the human standard. It belies the biblical insight that God created human beings, male and female, in God's image. It denigrates women's lives and experiences as resources for knowing the sacred.

As this language has become increasingly alienating to large numbers of women, those committed to shaping a living Jewish spirituality and theology have looked for ways to change it. They have sought a richer and wider range of images for speaking about and to the sacred. The *Pesikta Rabbati* passage seems to suggest that of those who saw God on Sinai "face after face," it was only the men who recorded and passed down their experiences. Feminists have taken on the task of recovering and forging a female language for God— female not simply in its metaphors but in its mode of religious apprehension and expression.

But if feminist attempts to find a new vocabulary for God began in the concern with gender, they have not resulted in a uniform response to the oppressiveness of traditional language. Rather, feminist explorations of God-language have gradually opened up deeper dimensions of the problem of God. Early feminist efforts to make God a mother and give her a womb, to praise her as birthgiver and nourisher, performed important functions. They validated women's sexuality and power as part of the sacred. They pressed worshippers to confront the maleness of a supposedly sex-neutral liturgy. Yet at the same time, these efforts often left intact images of dominance and power that were still deeply troubling. If the hand that drowned the Egyptians in the Red Sea was a female hand, did that make it any more a hand feminists wanted to worship?

The issue of the maleness of God-language has thus ineluctably moved to the question of the nature of the God to whom feminists want to pray. Where do Jewish women find God in our experience, and what do we find there? What images most powerfully evoke and express the reality of God in our lives?

While these questions lend themselves to unanimity even less than the issue of gender, there is a theme that seems to sound strongly through a range of feminist discussions of God-language: the need to articulate a new understanding of divine power. If the traditional God is a deity outside and above humanity, exercising power over us, women's coming to power in community has generated a counter-image of the power of God as empowerment. Many Jewish feminist arguments about and experiments with God-language can be understood to revolve around the issue of how to express this new image and experience of power in a way that is Jewishly/feministly authentic.

For some Jewish feminists, for example, it is nonpersonal imagery for God that most effectively captures a conception of divine power as that which moves through everything. Metaphors for God as source and fountain of life evoke the deity that is the wellspring of our action without tying us to gendered language that channels and confines. For other feminists, the question of divine power lends new interest to the continuing debate about the viability of the image of Shekhinah (in Jewish mysticism, the feminine presence of God in the world) in a feminist Judaism. This image, which at first seemed to promise such a clear Jewish way to incorporate female language into theology and liturgy, also has been resisted by many feminists as part of a system that links femaleness to immanence, physicality, and evil. In the context of the quest for new metaphors for power, however, this image of deity provides an interesting resource for feminist thinking about a God who dwells in the world and in the power of human relation. For still other feminists, it is incorporation of the names of goddesses into feminist liturgy that best conveys multiple images of female power, images that may have had power to our foremothers and that thus connect us in community to them. Use of these images does not constitute polytheism any more than do the multiple images of *Pesikta Rabbati*. Rather, these images fill out the traditional record, exploring and recovering faces of God that have been forgotten or expunged.

These forays into new imagery are experimental and tentative, and there are many Jews for whom some or all of them will seem shocking or foreign. Yet if we attend to the roots and intention of these lively experiments, we can find in feminist experience a potentially powerful resource for the revivification of Jewish religious language. The feminist experience is one of finding in community both a sense of personal identity and power and the power and knowledge of God. This experience may not be so different from that of the early Israelites who found together in community both a new national identity and connection with the God who gave it. From a feminist perspective, the problem with traditional Jewish God-language is that the initial experience of empowered community found expression in images that established hierarchy within the Jewish community and that marginalized or excluded half of its members. The challenge to women as we seek to name the God we have experienced "face after face," is to find a language that carries through the experience of divine power in community and that evokes the living presence of God in the whole Jewish people.

"It Is Not in Heaven"

Feminism and Religious Authority

The problem of authority plagues modern theology and ethics. Two centuries of biblical criticism combined with increasing awareness of the religious beliefs and practices of other peoples have undermined the secure foundations of written and oral revelation on which earlier thinkers grounded their philosophical reflections and legal decisions. Biblical criticism reminds us that the religious sources we look to for fundamental values are human creations, the culture-bound expressions of past societies. Recognition of global diversity weakens the claims of any specific tradition to divine authority or eternal truth so that it becomes impossible for the sophisticated modern to respond, as a student of one of my colleagues did when asked to describe the difference between parallel miracle stories in the Talmud and the New Testament, "the one in the New Testament is true."

The difficulty of grounding our actions and convictions in some absolute authority by no means reduces the hankering for certainty—witness the worldwide rise of fundamentalism. This hankering is very powerful in our individualistic North American culture. The fear is that, if we do not have the divine word, we are left with only our own fragile and individual words and desires.

Feminism can be very helpful in getting past the easy opposition of divine revelation and individual subjectivity—not because it has solved the problem of authority, but because it has had to confront it head on. The issue of authority is one area among many where feminism has embodied and focused larger dilemmas posed by modernity. Religious feminism has benefited from and contributed to the breakdown of traditional authority structures. Elizabeth Cady Stanton's *The Woman's Bible,* a feminist commentary published at the end of the nineteenth century, used the advent of biblical criticism to radically question the religious authority of the Bible, and in so doing set the tone for future generations of feminist critics. Yet while feminists have helped undermine biblical authority by pointing to the patriarchal origins and development of so-called normative texts, they have also tried to develop alternatives to patriarchal religion which are themselves in need of some authoritative grounding. Whether a particular feminist seeks to "prove" the fundamentally liberating nature of her own tradition or elaborate a new feminist spirituality, she still faces the issue of secure foundations which no constructive thinker can avoid.

Feminists have responded to this problem of authority in several ways. A number of Christian feminists, for example, have sought to find a "real" (that is, nonsexist) Paul or a "feminist" Jesus who can function as a model for Christians today. This nonsexist strand of Christianity is identified with "true" Christianity, while sexist Christianity is seen as a distortion of its own founders' vision and therefore in need of change. Other feminist thinkers have acknowledged the basic androcentrism of biblical thinking but have found in Scripture minority voices that submit the Bible to self-criticism. Themes like the prophets' passion for justice, the equality of man and woman in Genesis 1, and the presence of female God-language throughout the Bible, while not the statistical norm, may function as *normative* by providing a scriptural basis for feminist faith.

Such attempts to ground feminism in Scripture, however, point to the flaw in all attempts to base contemporary convictions on sure biblical foundations: *they disguise or deny the authority of the reader.* Since both feminists and antifeminists, democrats and authoritarians, warmongers and peacemakers can ground themselves in the Bible, surely it is not the Bible itself that tells us which interpretation is final and true. The difficulty of articulating even formal criteria that would be acceptable to all parties in a dispute over the conflicting voices in Scripture suggests that, whether or not the fact is acknowledged, authority must lie outside the text and not within it.

The feminist example makes clear, however, that in failing to find certainty within traditional texts, we are not thrown back on personal subjectivity and desire. No feminist sits alone in her study and decides to seek a feminist Jesus or give priority to Genesis 1 because these approaches suit her own temperament or private view of the world. The quest for feminist role models and authorities *is a communal quest.* It emerges *out of a movement* of women and men struggling for social and religious transformation. Feminism *as a movement* teaches individual women to value their experiences as women, to criticize and reject texts that have subordinated and demeaned them, and to lift up sources that, even within a patriarchal tradition, seem to point to new ways of structuring social relations. A student recently asked me, very puzzled, why I had written no feminist papers in graduate school, and I answered, "Because I had no idea what a feminist paper was." I did not get my feminist perspective from God, but neither did I or any other individual woman invent it in a vacuum. We developed it together.

The feminist case suggests, then, that religious authority rests in a community of interpreters that—whether to enhance its own power or give voice to the experience of a larger community—seeks to understand texts and/or experience in ways that give meaning and structure to human life. I would claim that this is always where religious authority has rested. When the rabbis said that rabbinic enactments and modes of interpretation were given at Sinai, they were claiming authority for their own community. When Kabbalists proposed that *peshat* (literal meaning) and *drash* (midrashic meaning) are two important levels of a text, but that the mystical meaning is the most fundamental and profound, they were claiming authority for their community of interpreters. And so on for every group that has sought to shape the development of Judaism.

The knowledge that community has always functioned as an authority may provide cold comfort in our own situation. At least earlier interpreters, so we tell ourselves, *believed* that their interpretations gave the true meaning of Scripture and thus rooted the interpreters themselves in divine authority. Our self-consciousness about the authority of community, on the other hand, leaves us all too aware of the precariousness of our moorings.

I do not see a way beyond this self-consciousness, but I also think it need not be destructive. Awareness of communal authority can foster appreciation of diverse perspectives, help to challenge claims to absolute authority, and make us aware of our power to bring about religious and social change. Particular modes of interpretation emerge out of particular communities, but communities of interpreters seek to understand texts and experiences in ways that give meaning and structure to Jewish/human existence. Those who would speak on behalf of a community are accountable to others for their capacity to make sense and provide meaning, to offer the possibility of a whole life. Indeed, modes of interpretation become authoritative partly be-cause of their power to articulate the experience of ever-widening commu-nities. Authority is, or ought to be, responsive—to the meanings in Jewish sources, to the changing demands of Jewish and human community, to the Eternal You that sustains and enlivens all our efforts to give our lives purpose. There may be no way past communal authority into the mind of this Eternal You that would allow us to anchor ourselves in the absolute. But then even reaching for such foundation may entail an evasion of responsibility. "It is not in heaven," the rabbis remind us.

We are to be our own authorities—not against God, not without God, but also not in such a way that we dodge our responsibility to create the struc-tures of meaning we need to live our lives.

Beyond Egalitarianism

An interesting paradox is emerging in non-Orthodox Jewish communities. The very success of egalitarianism—the gains in equal access for women to educational opportunities, and fuller participation in Jewish religious life—has generated new questions and uncertainties about whether egalitarianism is enough. Over the last twenty years, barrier after barrier has fallen before women. We have found ourselves being counted in *minyanim* (quorums for prayer), going up to the Torah, leading services, becoming ordained as rabbis, and studying Talmud alongside boys and men. These new opportunities, however, have brought women up against the *content* of the tradition, and in doing so, have pointed to the need for changes far deeper and more frightening than the process of simply making available to women what all in the community acknowledge to be of value.

A rabbinical student finds herself studying a text that renders invisible her existence and experiences as a woman. A woman is called to the Torah and reads that daughters can be sold as slaves (Exod. 21:7–11) or that a woman's vow can be annulled by her father or husband (Num. 30). Women seeking to expand our Jewish lives discover that a tradition that seems to have a blessing for everything offers no Jewish forms for marking menarche or menopause. Ironically, it is only in gaining equal access that women discover we have gained equal access to a male religion. As women read from the Torah, lead services, function as rabbis and cantors, we become full participants in a tradition that women had only a secondary role in shaping and creating. And if we accept egalitarianism as our final stopping place, we leave intact the structures, texts, history, and images that testify against and exclude us.

Many non-Orthodox Jews are now stuck in a position of acknowledging the justice of women's claims to equality, but not knowing how to bring about deeper changes. Or feeling content that in some institutions the goal of equality has been achieved. Or feeling uncomfortable because even where the goal has been achieved, something is not quite working. If none of the steps toward equal access is easy, at least each is definable and measurable; one change opens to the next, and each is concrete and generally linked to a specific context of struggle (e.g., the Conservative movement, a particular synagogue). Beyond egalitarianism, the way is uncharted. The next step is not nearly so obvious as fighting for *aliyot* (the right to be called to the Torah) or ordination. Beyond egalitarianism, Judaism must be transformed so that it is truly the Judaism of women and men. It must become a feminist Judaism: not a women's Judaism or a Judaism focused on women's issues, but a Judaism that all Jews have participated in shaping. But how do we move from here to there? How does egalitarianism become the starting point for a fuller process of transformation?

I would suggest that there are at least five stages that any community has to move through on the path from egalitarianism to feminism or genuine equality:

1. The first stage is *hearing silence.* Indeed, the impetus to move beyond egalitarianism stems from hearing the silence of the Jewish tradition and of particular Jewish institutions and events concerning the history and experience of women. Silence is difficult to hear. When a silence is sufficiently vast, it fades into the order of things. We take it for granted as the nature of reality. When I went through three years of graduate school without reading a single word written by a woman, it took me a long time to notice. After all, men are theologians; who else should we study? Women have a long history of reading ourselves into silence. From child-hood bedtime stories to the biblical narratives, from male teachers to male books on male Judaism, women learn to people silences with our own shadowy forms.

Rebekah, Beruriah, and other individual women, a class on women in the Bible or a panel at the Y, are not disproofs of women's silence in Judaism. These are names and occasions we need to turn to *after* we have listened to silence, not in order to fill or deny it. Otherwise we miss the jolts against whose background particular women and events emerge:

"You shall not covet your neighbor's wife" (Exod. 20:14) (who is the community being addressed?); the absence of Miriam's prophecy or the record of Huldah's teaching (the hints in normative sources that there is so much more to women's leadership than the sources choose to tell us); a Talmudic discussion of whether a girl penetrated before age three should receive her full *ketubah* (marriage contract) (Ketubot 11a, b) (would women scholars ever have asked this question?); *a contemporary discussion of this Talmudic debate that assumes this is a reasonable question.* Women were agents throughout Jewish history, fashioning and responding to Jewish life and carrying its burdens. But women's perceptions and questions did not give form and content to Scripture, shape the direction of Jewish law, or find expression in liturgy.

2. The second stage is *making a space to name silence.* Both hearing and naming silence can refer to the large silences of Jewish history or the smaller silences within any particular movement or community. Hearing silence is often a private experience. Whether a community will move beyond egalitarianism is in part determined by whether or not it creates spaces for people to name the silences they hear. Often in particular egalitarian communities women's silence is interpreted either as accidental or as personal choice, or it simply leaves people resentful or befuddled. "We just don't happen to have many women who feel competent to lead Torah discussions." "I don't know why more men than women speak. A woman is leading the discussion; anyone can participate." The historical and structural impediments to women's speech thus get dismissed or overlooked, and the community is absolved from responsibility.

Communities need to set aside the time for members to speak the silences they hear. This might happen in an open meeting specifically called for the purpose. Participants might be asked to name the places where they feel silenced or hear women's silence. Discussion must take place initially without judgment and without challenge or cross talk, simply as an opportunity for people to speak their pain and their experiences. The list of silences provides a concrete agenda for a community to address.

3. The third stage is *creating the structures that allow women to speak*. What these structures are in particular contexts will emerge from the list of silences. In congregations where men dominate the Torah discussions, it might be decided that men and women will call on each other in alternation. In a Talmud class where women feel that the text ignores their questions and experiences, it might be agreed that women will lead the discussions for a certain period, with the understanding that the class is there precisely to hear women's questions about and responses to the text. In any context in which women are apparently free to speak but seldom take the opportunity, a program on gender differences in socialization, discourse, and learning styles may help both men and women to understand the personal and institutional barriers to women's participation, and to analyze the gender style of their own institution and events.

Crucial to allowing women to speak are women-only spaces—not women-only spaces that are auxiliaries to male ones, but spaces in which women meet to discuss and explore their experiences as women. Men can listen to women, but, by definition, they cannot be the ones to end women's silence, and there are many forces that prevent women from finding their voices in situations in which men are present. Women's discussion groups, Rosh Hodesh groups, retreats, and spirituality collectives are spaces in which, to use Nelle Morton's phrase, women "hear each other into speech." These spaces are sources of energy, empowerment, and creativity that potentially enrich the whole Jewish community.

4. The fourth phase is *taking the authority to fill in silence*. Once silence is named and space created, there is nothing to do but to take courage to speak. This is what is happening all over the country as women compose new blessings and liturgies, create rituals to celebrate important turning points in our lives, research our history and write new midrashim, reclaim our sexuality and explore our concepts of God. This is the phase where we create the content of feminist Judaism, and its time frame is open-ended, its agenda sufficiently broad to include every facet of Judaism.

Much of this exploration and creativity, however, is taking place outside the boundaries of particular Jewish movements or institutions. Whether feminist innovations will ultimately be integrated into the tradition depends to some extent on the earlier phases I have discussed. It is difficult for women to dare to take the authority to speak. But that authority will be acknowledged and welcomed only when members of the larger community open themselves to hearing silence and thus recognize the need for the inclusion of women's voices. Thus, to take one concrete example, through midrash, storytelling, and historiography, women are creating women's Torah. But women's Torah will be accepted and taught as Torah only as Jews acknowledge that at least half of Torah is missing. Will Hebrew Union College or the Jewish Theological Seminary confront the contradiction of educating women in institutions in which Torah is still defined entirely on male terms? That depends on whether they hear the silences built into their curricula.

5. The last phase is *checking back*. Speaking into silence entails enormous risk. It involves changes that are uncharted and whose direction is finally unpredictable. Not everything spoken into silence will be true or worth saying, and not everything said will finally feel Jewish. Any change that a community takes in the direction of transforming Judaism will necessarily involve feedback and evaluation. Did a particular liturgical or curricular change work? Whom did it empower? Did it create new areas of silence? Did it open new areas of Jewish experience and exploration? Did it feel Jewish? Why or why not? What is our operative understanding of "Jewish," and does it need to be expanded? Would we want to continue the change or experiment again? Would we want to teach the change to our children?

While such evaluation is crucial, it is equally crucial that it *follow* speaking into silence rather than precede it. Too often, questions concerning the appropriateness and boundaries of change are the first ones raised when feminists begin to alter tradition. Judgment is demanded in advance of any real experimentation. Will it be Jewish? is asked as a way of maintaining silence and continuing the status quo. But once we hear the silence of women, it becomes clear that repairing that silence will take all the creativity Jews can muster. Experiments in form, in content, in new relationships between women and men will all be necessary to make Judaism whole. There is time to decide the shape of the Jewish future—but that time is after those who have been silent have spoken.

Facing the Ambiguity of God

Much feminist work on God-language, including my own, has focused on particular aspects of God to the neglect of others. Feminist characterizations of the sacred have emerged largely out of two central experiences: coming to self-awareness in community with other women, and claiming the healing power of connection to the natural world. These experiences have generated a rich array of images for God focusing on female, natural, and nonhierarchical metaphors. Such images depict God as source, wellspring and fountain, mother and womb of life. God is Shekhinah, Goddess, all that seeks life; earth, moon, lover, friend—and so on.

It is entirely legitimate and even essential for a new community finding its voice to speak and write about God by drawing upon its own most fundamental experiences. In a profoundly misogynistic culture that has ruthlessly exploited the natural environment—and that has linked women with the natural world on many levels of practice and discourse—feminist metaphors for God elucidate long-buried dimensions of divinity. These metaphors are not just political correctives to dominant modes of seeing and being; they arise from and refer to real discoveries of the sacred in places we had long stopped looking to find it.

Insofar as feminist metaphors represent a deliberate attempt to capture particular aspects of experience, however, they are also necessarily partial. In a discussion in the *Journal of Feminist Studies in Religion* (Spring 1989), Catherine Madsen and a number of respondents criticized the "niceness" of God in feminist theology. Madsen argued that once God becomes Goddess or acquires female characteristics, she is connected too exclusively with the so-called female virtues of nurturing, healing, and caretaking, and is cordoned off from the savagery of the world. A "nice" female God does not take us sufficiently beyond traditional images, Madsen argued—any more than a

"Queen of the Universe" undoes the hierarchical nature of traditional male imagery.

A number of feminist writers and religious thinkers have begun to articulate a fuller and more complex account of the divine than the notion of a "nice" female God allows for. But I basically agree with Madsen that the ambiguity of God has not received enough attention in feminist discourse. Rereading the story of Nadab and Abihu in the annual cycle of Torah readings, I am struck by the extent to which the God who devoured Aaron's sons for offering "strange fire" (Lev. 10:1) is largely absent from feminist imagery. This God, the same who killed Uzzah for putting out his hand to steady the ark (2 Sam. 6:6–7), and who warned the assembled Israelites not to come too close to the base of Sinai lest they die (Exod. 19:12–13), seems to me to point to a profoundly important dimension of human existence. Unless the God who speaks to the feminist experiences of empowerment and connection can also speak to the frightening, destructive, and divisive aspects of our lives, a whole side of existence will be severed from the feminist account of the sacred.

The question of God's ambiguity is not the same as the classical problem of theodicy. Theodicy is a problem only if one accepts a series of propositions about the nature of God, most of which are irrelevant to my own understanding. Theodicy assumes not only that God is perfectly good and all powerful; it assumes that God's omnipotence is that of a person who acts and interacts as supreme ruler of history. According to this view, if God deliberately chooses not to intervene in a particular evil, then either there must be a higher theological explanation, or God must be blamed.

I do not believe in a God who stands outside of history and manipulates it and who therefore can be charged with our moral failures. The stories of Uzzah and Nadab and Abihu seem to me to present a somewhat different problem. Their deaths are not so much an expression of divine injustice as they are of divine unpredictability. These stories confront us not with a choice between God as good or evil but with the irrationality and ambiguity of the sacred. To use Madsen's term, the God of these stories is not "nice." S/he is not neat, sanitized, containable, or controllable. S/he does not easily fit our categories or conform to our expectations. But neither, of course, does the world that God created.

The God of these stories is an ambiguous God—the Goddess as energy of the universe, responsible for life and death and rebirth. S/he is a God who creates forms of startling fragility and beauty and also brings forth monstrosities that frighten and overwhelm us. S/he is the God who makes dry land rise up out of the waters and then washes it away with tidal waves and volcanoes. Creativity by its very nature seems profoundly ambiguous. The power of invention has yielded all the fruits of civilization, but the same power has also brought forth our civilization's horrors.

The ambiguity of life is a truth we all know on the small scale as well as the large. The experience of empowerment so central to feminism may allow women to make considered and important choices, but it does not guarantee that we will always choose rightly. Many movements for liberation generate new forms of tyranny or infighting; many women have been hurt in the name of feminism. In the same way, the Egyptians lost their lives when the Israelites walked safely through the Red Sea; the Palestinians lost their homeland when the Jews found one. On the other hand, it is not just projects begun with good intentions that often go awry. Choices made from selfish motives or dictated by circumstance sometimes lead to unanticipated good or open up new possibilities we could never have imagined. "Were it not for the evil impulse," said Rabbi Nahman B. Samuel, "man would not take a wife, or beget a child, or engage in business."

These truths do not absolve us from responsibility for the consequences of our choices, but they do point to ambiguity, contradiction, and paradox as fundamental aspects of our experience. One of the things I have always most valued about the Jewish tradition is its refusal to disconnect God from the contradictory whole of reality. "I form light and create darkness, I make weal and create woe—I, the Lord do all these things," Isaiah announces (1 Isa. 45:7). This has always seemed to me a far more religiously satisfying perspective than a theology that would close off huge areas of our experience and declare them devoid of sacred power. I do not know how a monotheist can choose to find God in the dry land and *not* in the tidal wave that destroys it—or only in our power to choose life and not also in our power to *choose* (see Deut. 30:15 and 19).

Yet I certainly understand why I and other feminists have not raced to deal with this aspect of God. It is not unique or central to feminist experience;

and in addition, it is difficult and painful. More than this, however, the ambiguous God threatens to bring us back to the images of domination we see as so problematic in the tradition. I and many other feminists have pointed to the destructiveness of hierarchical images of God such as Lord and King, images that draw upon and in turn justify oppression in society. But what if God as Lord points not simply to the manipulative ruler of history, the cosmic patriarch who authorizes numerous forms of oppression, but also the nonrational and unpredictable dimension of experience, the forces we cannot control or contain? How do we name the power in the world that makes us know our vulnerability, that terrifies and overwhelms us? Can we name this power without invoking images of Otherness? Can we jettison the Lord of history without also losing the Lord of contradictory life? Can we name the ambiguous God without resorting to the traditional metaphors that have rationalized oppression and denied the humanity of women?

I do not know the answers to these questions, but they bring me to a new place of wrestling with tradition. If I read the traditional liturgy from the perspective of God's ambiguity, then I suddenly see it in a new and ambiguous light. Kaddish, for example, is not simply a hymn to God's sovereignty; it is a hymn to God's sovereignty said precisely at the moment when I most deeply know my lack of power to preserve those I love. It is an acknowledgement of my own impotence exactly when I know myself as impotent. But should I pray to this contradictory God? Or should I pray *against* him or her? If I acknowledged God's ambiguity directly rather than burying it in images of praise would that make the ambiguity any easier to worship? Do I have to change "who creates weal and woe" to "who creates all things" in order to be able to say the words? And how do I continue to pray to the God who empowers me when I have confronted the equivocal nature of all power?

What's Wrong with Hierarchy?

No aspect of my feminist critique of Judaism provokes more demands to defend or explain myself than my critique of hierarchy. The assumption that a hierarchical understanding of relationships between people—and of the relationship between God and the world—is humanly destructive and antithetical to feminism raises serious questions. Is hierarchy all bad? Isn't it sometimes necessary? Doesn't leadership imply hierarchy, and how can any group exist without leadership? Isn't rabbinic leadership essential to the health of the Jewish community? Aren't there certain natural hierarchies—the hierarchy between parent and child, for example? Doesn't the assertion of norms—even the assertion that equality is better than hierarchy—itself create hierarchies?

These questions have not convinced me to abandon the critique of hierarchy, but they do make me want to clarify it. I see them as arising out of important concerns about the limits of nonhierarchical structures in feminist groups and in the Left more generally. But I think such questions also reflect an anxious equation of hierarchy and order that stems from a lack of experience with other models of leadership.

Feminist skepticism about the effectiveness of nonhierarchical models may have roots in the consciousness-raising groups of the 1960s and 1970s. These groups were usually committed to maintaining a leaderless structure that was simultaneously empowering and frustrating. On the one hand, specific techniques for sharing group time and space often enabled habitually silent women to find their voices and claim their experience. On the other hand, as Joreen pointed out in her now-classic essay, "The Tyranny of Structurelessness," the absence of recognized leadership often masked the formation of controlling cliques that remained unaccountable because they were unacknowledged. Moreover, as consciousness-raising groups wanted to move from discussion to action, they found that if they did not allocate responsibility and define structures of accountability, they became paralyzed.

If the critique of hierarchy is equated with early feminist repudiation of any kind of effective leadership, I can see why the critique would raise objections. But as Joreen pointed out even as she took critical note of the problems and contradictions of a "structureless" group, apportioning responsibility is not the same as endorsing hierarchy. The challenge is precisely to create group structures that maximize general participation while establishing clear norms of accountability.

In criticizing hierarchy, I am not opposing leadership, or even authority. Rather, my feminist suspicion centers on the essentialization of authority: the identification of authority with certain groups that are invested with power by virtue of their supposed nature. Thus the feminist critique of patriarchal social structures continually returns to Simone de Beauvoir's insight that men have been defined as the normative human beings, and women as Other. When this insight is refined further in light of other forms of dominance, it becomes clear that not all men are defined as normative either. White men, men who own land or have access to certain resources—or in the Jewish community, men with a particular kind of learning—are invested with the power to control and define community institutions and values. These are the hierarchical *dualisms* that feminists have criticized—the assignment of human beings to opposed and unequal categories on the basis of their presumed essential characteristics.

A different concept of authority would be the anarchist notion of "natural authority," the authority that resides in an individual by virtue of her or his competence and knowledge in a particular area. "In the matter of boots, I defer to the authority of the Bootmaker," says Bakunin—not out of any social constraint or any imperative stemming from the nature of the bootmaker, but because her or his ability elicits respect. All communities need to take advantage of those who have natural authority in different areas; not to make use of such people constitutes a waste of resources and ultimately flattens out individuality. But the fact that the bootmaker—or scientist, or rabbi, or CEO—is good at what s/he does will not endow him or her with intrinsic authority or authority outside specific areas of competence. Nor should the fact of competence in one area negate the authority of others in the community.

The test of nonhierarchical leadership or authority is the purpose and accountability of authority. Is authority aimed at securing and aggrandizing the power of the person who exercises it, or is it aimed at empowering others? If the latter, does the goal of empowerment gain concrete expression in the life of the community? The *havurah* (small, informal Jewish communities formed for prayer and study) movement, for example, was from its inception committed to the creation of nonhierarchical forms of Jewish religious community. Probably in any particular *havurah*, those with "natural authority" provided the initial leadership. In some *havurot*, that natural authority gradually was institutionalized, so that it became clear over time that certain familiar groups (e.g., women, or men without strong Jewish educations) were never taking leadership. But other *havurot*, through classes, skill sharing, and consistent rotation of leadership, found concrete ways to empower all members to share in responsibilities, so that the fund of natural authority was continually increased.

This test of the purpose of authority is helpful in considering the issue of so-called natural hierarchies—such as the hierarchy between parent and child and, in a different way, between teacher and student (or between rabbi and congregant). I would agree that inherently hierarchical elements exist in these relationships. Simply to wish or declare the two sides equal is self-deceptive and serves only to disguise the power dynamics that continue to operate despite lip service to equality. At the same time, I do not think that these examples legitimize hierarchy or negate the critique of it; rather they point to its profound dangers. As the intolerable prevalence of child abuse indicates, so-called natural hierarchies lend themselves to terrible abuses of power. To exercise power legitimately in such relationships means continually to undermine or work toward the demise of the hierarchy—to allow the child space for individuation and prepare him or her for independent adulthood. In the teacher-student relation, legitimate authority encourages learners to build on their strengths, define their own perspectives, and share the things they have to teach.

A hierarchy of values does indeed underlie this critique of hierarchy:

equality is better than hierarchy; legitimate power continually works to empower others so as to create greater equality. The feminist critique of hierarchy is not the same as an abdication of all norms. What a hierarchy of norms does not and must not do, however, is associate greater and lesser *values* with the nature of *persons:* so that, for example, men are depicted as always forming hierarchies and women as trying to relate more equally. This association of positive and negative values with groups of persons is precisely what establishes destructive patterns of communal domination.

And where does God fit in here? Isn't it all right, I am often asked, to have this one hierarchical relationship? Doesn't the notion that God is God, the only final authority, help to relativize and delegitimize the hierarchies between people? While it might seem that the notion of God as ultimate authority ought to function in this way, in reality it has been used far more often to support hierarchical dualisms than to subject them to criticism. Perhaps because the very idea of a male king ruling over the earth is already the product of human hierarchical thinking, it cannot, in any consistent way, free us from such thinking.

But let us suppose that the notion of God's authority does serve to delegitimize human domination. Why, still, would we want to imagine our relationship with God in terms of a model we reject in all our other relationships? If we ask of parents and teachers and rabbis that they nurture and speak to the peer in the child, student, or congregant, why would we want to be perpetually children in relation to God? If we understand the need to control others as disease and injustice in our social relationships, why should the experience of God as a dominant hierarch be liberating or holy?

Sometimes hierarchical imagery may express not just superiority and subordination in personal relationships, but also a sense of smallness and impotence before the mysterious and terrifying aspects of existence. But if we use such imagery to evoke the inherent inequality of the divine/human relationship, we also need to undermine that imagery in just the way we need to undermine all other hierarchies. The strand of protest against divine injustice that weaves its way through the Jewish tradition offers one means of destabilizing a hierarchical understanding of the divine/human relationship. Images of God as web, wellspring, or ground of life reflect a part-whole model of the divine/human relationship rather than a dualistic one, and thus avoid the hierarchical separations that divide the dominator from the dominated. Or perhaps the notion of natural authority is also a fitting image for the divine. Is not God the ultimate natural authority, never actually wielding the bolts of lightning that punish or coerce us, but addressing and persuading us through something deep in ourselves and through the web of our interrelations with a complex and changing world?

About Men

"What is the place of men in a feminist Judaism?" "What can I do?" "Where do I fit in?" Men ask these questions, sometimes plaintively, sometimes angrily, whenever I speak on Jewish feminism. I find it difficult to answer the questions directly. For one thing, if I do not want men to define the role of women in the Jewish tradition, what right have I to define men's place in a new Jewish order? For another, these questions at times sound suspiciously like appeals for women to remain in our caretaker role. They are requests not simply for guidance but for reassurance, for continuing affection and regard. One sure implication of a feminist Judaism, however, is that just as women are learning to support and empower each other, so men will need to learn to do the same. Women have enough work creating a Judaism that acknowledges our presence without also being expected to take care of men. We need the help of men who can be responsible for their own Jewish lives and who can recognize the ways in which sexism has deformed those lives.

Once the problem with such questions is acknowledged, however, it is also true that men have a vital role to play in shaping a feminist Judaism. They can take many concrete steps to function as agents of change and allies in the struggle for a feminist Judaism. These steps fall into two broad categories: letting go of traditional forms of male power and exploring their Jewishness within a feminist (i.e., genuinely egalitarian) framework.

Letting Go

1. An excellent first step in divesting oneself of the prerogatives of male power is to read Esther Ticktin's "A Modest Beginning" and make a commitment to the new halakhot she proposes there. This article, first

printed in the *Response* anthology on women in 1974 (and reprinted in 1976 in Elizabeth Koltun's anthology *The Jewish Woman*), has never received the attention it deserves. Ticktin suggests concrete ways in which men can begin to let go of male privilege while at the same time raising the consciousness of others. She suggests, for example, that men refuse to accept an *aliyah* (call to the Torah) in any congregation where women cannot have an *aliyah,* and give the reason for their refusal. And she asks that traditional men, for whom certain forms of nonparticipation are not yet possible, at least refrain from speaking to women about events and privileges that exclude women (e.g., in Orthodox synagogues, dancing with a Torah on Simchat Torah).

My favorite example of the practice of Ticktin's principles involves a prominent member of the Jewish renewal movement who was asked by Hasidim on an airplane to help make the morning minyan. "Does your minyan count women?" he asked them. "I'm sorry, but it is the halakhah of my community to count women in a minyan." The multiplication of such simple acts helps sow the seeds of a feminist Judaism.

2. Interrupt and argue with the conscious and unconscious sexism of male friends and colleagues. Whites have learned from black people that if we really care about ending racism, then it is our responsibility to name and stop it wherever we see it. Just as we should not have to wait for a black person to be in the room to intervene in racist situations, men should not have to wait for women to put a stop to sexist conversation or conduct. Indeed, because of the pervasiveness of racism and sexism, it is often more effective when members of the dominant group interrupt or halt oppressive behavior.

Allies of Jewish feminists can refuse to participate in sexist banter or to tolerate JAP jokes. They can persistently question the conscious or unconscious exclusion of women from a thousand synagogue and Jewish community undertakings. They can examine their own work and teaching, writing, and communal projects to see if they make room for women and women's experience.

3. Never say, "We are not talking about that now" when women raise issues concerning the oppressiveness of a particular text, context, or situation. This line, which I heard all through graduate school, is continually used to avoid examining the problems and erasures of tradition. "We're not talking about Karl Barth's view of women as ontologically subordinate right now, we're talking about his doctrine of revelation." "We're not talking about the abusiveness of this Talmudic passage, we're talking about Rashi, or how to follow the argument." Think about the political consequences of this silencing. When an individual or text is clearly anti-Semitic, can Jews put the anti-Semitism neatly aside while we deal with the "real issues," or is anti-Semitism the first thing we need to have acknowledged and addressed?

Dealing with feminist issues can indeed derail discussion, cause carefully planned projects or talks to be laid aside, and take events in unexpected and sometimes frightening directions. If we temporarily turn from Rashi or modes of rabbinic argument, for example, to look at the *content* of Talmudic assumptions about women's sexuality, there is no question that the lesson will be exploded open. But the train of Jewish tradition has been barreling along on its patriarchal track for three thousand years. Laying some new line is a priority that rightfully interferes with business as usual. *Im lo akhshav eima'tai?* (If not now, when?) When else shall we talk about women's issues—in specifically planned sessions that only a small number of already committed people will attend? How then will we ever learn to conduct our communal business in new and different ways?

Discovering and Exploring

Jewish feminism not only offers a wide-ranging critique of the subordination of women in Jewish religious and institutional life, it also offers a vision of a new Jewish order. It calls us to imagine a Jewish community organized to enable the participation of all its members, a Jewish history made whole, a revitalization of Jewish God-language, a broader definition of the Jewish family, and a new sexual ethic. It invites Jewish men to a reconsideration of their own Jewish humanity, its contours and its meaning.

1. Meet with other men. Write midrash. Talk about your relationship with God. Talk about Jewish spirituality not as universally Jewish, but as male spirituality, a direct outgrowth of your experience as men. Discuss what it feels like to let go of power, and welcome the range of emotions—from fear to laughter—that this prospect raises. Organize groups and develop rituals to guide each other through the process of relinquishing power. Talk about what might be on the other side of a patriarchal Judaism. Experience the power of particularity and the power of taking up a shared burden.

2. Talk with women. Listen—hard. Argue with women—not as one who owns the agenda but as one who has an equal stake in creating the Jewish future. Share your midrashim, your new liturgy. Participate in and organize joint projects, listening closely to women about how new endeavors have worked from their perspective. Go back and talk more with men.

I realize these suggestions are more amorphous than my first three, but it is precisely the daunting and open-ended task of shaping a new Judaism that finds Jewish feminists least able to tell men where they fit or what their role is. We do not have the answers, and it is not our job to find them. We know we are raising issues that are fundamental to Jewish life and the human community. In responding to these issues out of the particularities of their own experience—and in finding and defining new sorts of questions—Jewish men enter into a necessary dialogue out of which a new Jewish future can emerge.

The Year of the Agunah

On March 9, 1992, on the Fast of Esther, the International Committee for Agunah Rights (ICAR) declared 5753–54 (1993–94) the "year of the *agunah.*" (The Hebrew *agunah* literally means "woman in chains." Within the system of Jewish law, *agunot* are women whose marriages have ended, either through separation, or the disappearance or unattested death of the husband, but who are unable to remarry because they do not have a *get,* the religious bill of divorce.) The ICAR declaration was preceded and followed by a flurry of articles on Jewish divorce in both the secular and Jewish press. But because the intensified media attention has not led to any resolution of the terrible predicament of *agunot,* I want to take up the issue here, locating it in the context of women's situation in Judaism.[1]

The existence of *agunot* is a crime against women, a disgrace to the Jewish community, and a violation of human rights that demands immediate remedy. It is also a symptom of the systemic exclusion of women from power and authority in traditional Judaism. It points to the far-reaching work that will have to be done before women can define Jewish practice and values on an equal footing with men.

While in the past, *agunot* were generally women whose husbands had disappeared—during war, or in the course of travel, for example—today the majority are victims of husbands who deliberately withhold a *get,* either for purposes of extortion, or to keep their wives in limbo. The very existence of *agunot* as a category of person within Judaism is an outcome of the fundamental power imbalance in Jewish marriage. According to Jewish law, when a man marries, he formally acquires rights to a woman's sexual function, and when he divorces, he relinquishes those rights so that the woman can marry another. Both these actions are nonreciprocal: a husband can acquire and divorce a wife, but a woman cannot acquire or divorce a husband.

While this basic inequality is the precondition for the existence of *agunot,* women's powerlessness is further magnified by a larger religious system that is also entirely under male control. The typical *agunah* is a right-wing Orthodox woman with a large family and no secular education, whose marriage has simply become too abusive to endure. In cases where a woman's husband refuses her a *get,* she can find herself in a nightmare realm, bargaining away her means of survival and occasionally even custody of her children.

To write and receive a *get,* spouses must appear before a *beit din* (rabbinical court), but the system of *batei din* (plural) is completely unregulated, with no procedures for appeal. It is not regarded as a conflict of interest for a rabbi on the *beit din* to have a personal relationship with one of the divorcing parties. Since men are far more likely than women to know the *beit din* system and have a strong personal relationship with a rabbi, women enter the proceedings at a distinct disadvantage. Some courts force a woman appearing for a *get* to sign a document agreeing to litigate all aspects of the divorce, even in cases that have already been decided in civil court.

When one compares civil court decisions with those of rabbinical courts, the latter are almost always less favorable to women. Civil courts, for example, will generally allow a divorcing woman with children to remain in the family home for some period, but it is the standard practice of rabbinical courts to force a woman to sell her home immediately. In this and other ways, women are forced to give up important rights in order to gain their freedom. The result is that fear of becoming *agunot* keeps many Orthodox women in abusive relationships, enabling men to hold them hostage even before the issue of divorce arises.

In part, the existence of large numbers of *agunot* is the product of a failure of courage on the part of rabbinic authorities to implement the halakhic solutions to the problem that a number of prominent Orthodox rabbis have proposed. But the persistent exploitation of the inequities of Jewish divorce law is also a more deliberate attempt to curtail women's power in a time of social change. In a period when even very sheltered women are beginning to see the possibility of taking control of their lives, elements within the Orthodox community are using the fundamental inequity of Jewish law to ensure women's powerlessness and to reinforce the status quo.

Why should non-Orthodox Jews care about the issue of *agunah,* which, at least superficially, seems a purely Orthodox problem? I suggest that this is-sue affects all Jews in three ways.

First, questions of family status can touch the life of any Jew. Given the movement of American Jews across denominational boundaries, and given that in Israel, all matters of marriage and divorce are decided by halakhah (Jewish law), any Jewish woman can find herself unable to remarry because she has not received a *get*, or find that her children are declared *mamzerim* (bastards) because she remarried and had children without a valid *get*. Sec-ond, as an ethical issue, the existence of *agunot* should receive the attention of the whole Jewish community. Many individual Jews have devoted their thought and energy to aspects of the oppression of women in the larger soci-ety and in other cultures. The existence of *agunot* is Judaism's most profound crime against women and as such deserves to be a Jewish priority. Third, while the non-Orthodox movements have eliminated the problem of *agunot*, they have not systematically addressed the fundamental inequality of Jewish marriage which generates the problem in the first place. Thus the Conserva-tive movement has added a clause to the marriage contract that provides a way to bring a recalcitrant husband before a *beit din*, but it has not sought a way to allow a woman to *give* a *get*. The Reform movement has done away with the need for a *get*, and the Reconstructionists are working on a recipro-cal bill of divorce, but neither movement has created the new *ketubah* (mar-riage contract) and wedding ceremony that would establish Jewish marriage on an equal basis.

What can Jews do to ameliorate the dilemma of *agunot*? Individual women who are not yet married can protect themselves in advance to some extent by insisting on a prenuptial agreement specifying that, in the event of a civil divorce, the couple will submit to the arbitration of a *beit din*. For New York women who are already *agunot*, the state's amendment to the Domestic Relations Law, passed in August 1992, allows a judge who is determining eq-uitable distribution of property to take into account any barrier to remar-riage, including the failure of the husband to give a *get*. This law has helped a number of women, but some rabbis in Agudath Israel, a right-wing Ortho-dox organization, are seeking its repeal on the grounds that it results in a coerced *get*, which is halakhically invalid. (Compare the opinion of Maimonides, who says that a husband may be beaten until he says "I am willing" to give a *get,* and the *get* is not considered coerced and is valid.) New Yorkers can monitor challenges to the law and support those fighting to maintain it.

The need to turn to the civil authorities to find a remedy for *agunah* is an embarrassment to the Orthodox community, constituting an acknowledgement on the part of halakhic authorities that have failed to deal with a burning social and ethical problem. In the absence of an effective solution, some Orthodox synagogues are putting pressure on recalcitrant husbands by ostracizing them from the community. Unfortunately, given the fragmentation of American Orthodoxy, it is easy for such men to switch to other congregations, where they can be called to the Torah, teach, and even serve as rabbis.

Rivkeh Haut and Susan Aranoff, two of the cofounders of Agunah, Inc., an organization seeking reform of the *beit din* system and a halakhic solution to the problem of *agunah,* argue that the persistence of *agunot* undermines the moral legitimacy of Orthodoxy. On the one hand, Orthodox rabbis argue that, for the sake of Jewish unity, all marriage and divorce procedures should adhere strictly to halakhah. On the other hand, they are unwilling to address the vulnerability of women who enter into halakhically valid marriages. Moreover, while Orthodox rabbis are always bemoaning intermarriage and low birthrates, their failure to free *agunot* is keeping large numbers of traditional women who would love to have children, or additional children, from remarrying. Haut suggests that non-Orthodox Jews seize opportunities posed by weddings, bar mitzvahs, lectures, and other public events to challenge Orthodox rabbis with these questions: "What are you doing to help *agunot?* How can you ask us to become Orthodox or to be converted or married by Orthodox standards when you are permitting this terrible situation to exist?" Moreover, no interdenominational discussion of intermarriage or Jewish birthrates should take place that fails to raise this issue.

Meanwhile, desperate *agunot* and their supporters are becoming more militant. Agunah, Inc., which is an Orthodox feminist group, has organized demonstrations at Agudath Israel conferences. It and G.E.T. (Getting Equitable Treatment), another organization for *agunah* relief, have picketed the homes, businesses, and synagogues of men who are withholding *gittin* from their wives. The founding of ICAR represents an attempt to marshal the energy of organizations throughout the Jewish world, from those focused specifically on questions of divorce to broad-based groups such as Hadassah. The goal is to get the Israeli rabbinate to formulate a halakhic solution to the problem of *agunah* that halakhic Jews worldwide will find acceptable.

As Susan Alter, the third cofounder of Agunah, Inc., points out, this goal has a certain irony. Orthodox women pressing the rabbinate for halakhic change are asking those who have oppressed them to find a way to alleviate that oppression. But since oppressors are not known for spontaneously surrendering their power out of sympathetic identification with their victims, Israeli or American rabbis are unlikely to act until the shame and cost of wielding power in this way are made to outweigh its rewards. While all Jews can increase the pressure for a creative halakhic response to the issue, those of us in communities where women have a voice can reexamine the deeper problems with marriage, divorce, and rabbinic authority that generate *agunot* in the first place. Getting Orthodox rabbis to solve the problem of divorce within a framework that denies the agency of women is a necessary short-term remedy. Changing the foundations of Jewish marriage and empowering women to participate in the formulation of Jewish law are the only solutions that will prevent abuse in the long haul.

Preaching Against the Text

This previously unpublished piece was first delivered in a slightly different form as the ordination sermon at Hebrew Union College, Cincinnati, in 1997.

A rabbi friend once told me that when he was a student at Hebrew Union College, he was taught never to preach against the weekly Torah portion. Instead, he should always seek out something positive in the text that he could lift up as a moral or spiritual lesson that would instruct and inspire. This advice captures a central strategy of many liberal Jews who grapple with issues of continuity and change in relation to Jewish tradition. One way of maintaining a connection with tradition is to affirm its values when they accord with contemporary sensibilities—and ignore them when they do not.

The prophetic reading that accompanies the first Torah portion in the book of Numbers seems a perfect example of the kind of text that calls out for this strategy. The first chapters of Hosea are one of the more horrendously misogynist passages in the Tanakh, and yet they end with a magnificent statement of covenant love and faithfulness that seems to express the highest ideals both of marriage and of the relationship between God and Israel: "And I will espouse you forever: I will espouse you with righteousness and justice, and with goodness and mercy." Why *not* focus on this verse and forget about its context? Since contemporary Jews are forced to pick and choose from among the riches and contradictions of tradition, why *not* pick what we like and discard what we don't, building our spiritual lives around the parts of our history that continue to speak to us?

To answer this question, it is necessary to explore the framework of God's declaration, "And I will espouse you forever." In the first chapter of Hosea, God instructs the prophet to get "a wife of whoredom" and beget "children of whoredom," in order to symbolize Israel's apostasy in worshipping other gods. In speaking in powerful and shocking terms about marrying a prostitute, Hosea dramatizes a trope found in a number of the prophets: he compares Israel's faithlessness to God to a wife's faithlessness in a marriage.

Renita Weems, in her excellent book *Battered Love: Marriage, Sex, and Violence in the Hebrew Prophets,* examines the many variations on this trope found in Hosea, Jeremiah, and Ezekiel. All these prophets use explicit and provocative female sexual imagery in order to direct the attention of their male audiences to the inevitability of divine judgment. Exploiting what were probably widely held attitudes toward marriage, they choose the metaphors of promiscuity, lewdness, and shamelessness to cast Israel's religious misbehavior in the strongest possible moral terms. While other central prophetic metaphors—judge and litigant, parent and child, master and slave, king and vassal—represent the divine/human relationship as hierarchical and bound by mutual obligations, the marriage metaphor conveys with unique clarity and power the ways in which Israel's idolatry not only disappoints God but dishonors and humiliates him.[1]

From a feminist perspective, this metaphor presents a number of difficulties. First, it legitimates the understanding of marriage that provides the basis of the analogy to God's behavior. Metaphors work when they get us to reorganize our thinking about a subject by bringing it into relation with something well known to us, but previously perceived as unconnected. In the case of the marriage metaphor, the prophets try to convince their listeners that there is a similarity between the rights, expectations, and feelings of a husband married to an adulterous wife and God's responses to Israel's disgraceful behavior. But to be effective, the marriage side of the analogy must be taken for granted. *Of course* women's sexuality is deviant and dangerous, posing a constant threat to male honor and prestige; *of course* husbands might appropriately respond to a wife's promiscuity with outrage and abuse. What's new and startling about the metaphor is not its view of marriage as hierarchical and abusive, but that it draws a parallel between the religious apostasy of elite men and the disgusting wantonness of women.[2]

Second, the effect of the metaphor is to vindicate the husband or God from blame for his abusiveness, and to place on the subordinate party the responsibility for any punishment. When God says of Israel, "Else will I strip her naked and leave her as on the day she was born: And I will make her like a wilderness, Render her like a desert land," we are not to see him as a raging husband completely out of control "who threatens and beats his wife simply because he has the power to do so." On the contrary, the text constructs *him* as the victim who is just responding to Israel's infidelity. In Weems's words, "[God] has been driven to extreme measures by a wife who has again and again dishonored him and disregarded the norms governing marriage relations."[3] It is not very difficult to hear in the Haftorah the voice of the batterer who disclaims responsibility for his actions, explaining that if only his wife had behaved properly, he would not have been forced to beat her.

Third, as Drorah Setel has argued, this imagery fits startlingly well into a number of contemporary feminist definitions of pornography. Andrea Dworkin, for example, defines pornography as "the graphic depiction of women as vile whores," which is exactly the burden of prophetic rhetoric. Helen Longino suggests that pornography "describes degrading and abusive sexual behavior so as to endorse and/or recommend the behavior represented." Other characteristics of pornography are also found in prophetic language: "Female sexuality is depicted as negative in relation to a positive [or] neutral male standard; women are degraded and publicly humiliated; and female sexuality is portrayed as an object of male possession and control ..."[4] In seeking to shape the Israelite elite's understanding of its relationship to God and the nature of divine activity, Hosea assumes and reinforces an objectified and degraded view of women's sexuality, a view the contemporary reader is easily seduced into taking for granted in much the same way as the prophet's original audience.

In the last part of the Haftorah reading, there is a sudden shift in tone and substance. The rhetoric of abuse gives way to the rhetoric of romance as God reminds Israel of the halcyon period of their courtship and promises restoration of their days of devotion and mutual trust. But if we place the proffered vision of intimacy and reconciliation in the context of this analysis, we can see that it serves only to reinforce the notion that God or the husband is ultimately decent and reasonable, and thus leaves male power over and aggression against women unchallenged. Weems points out that there are at least two aspects of the marriage metaphor that were likely to be shocking to the prophet's listeners. One was the suggestion that Israelite men are in certain respects like unfaithful women; the other was the notion that the betrayed husband might exercise forbearance and forgive his wife. His willingness to overlook her depravity marks him again as the finer one in their relation-ship. Not only does the husband have social and economic power, he is also morally superior to his wife in that he forgives her rather than having her stoned to death. One can hear behind the sudden emotional shift of the chap-ter the emotional manipulation that makes it so difficult for women to leave battering relationships: I promise you, all will be fine now, it won't happen again, I forgive you; and besides, it was all your fault anyway.[5]

Why say all this? Why try to take the pleasure out of a beautiful passage —and one so many couples choose to inscribe on their wedding bands? My first answer to this question is that it is intellectually dishonest to focus sim-ply on the positive aspects of tradition. Individual religious ideas and values have contexts; they are connected to other ideas. They are parts of systems that seek to express and establish particular worldviews. Why engage with tradition if we're not prepared to look at the ways it shapes us for good *and* for evil? A lot of poetry besides Hosea speaks of the value of faithfulness; we do not need the whole ambiguous witness of Jewish tradition to affirm the im-portance of family. To wrench what we like out of context and ignore the rest is to engage in a kind of pretense, to act as if we were deriving our values from tradition when what we are actually doing is seeking support for our own convictions.

Such intellectual dishonesty might be excused were it to serve a spiritual purpose. But I would argue that failure to grapple with the hard parts of tra-dition is spiritually and socially corrosive because it leaves destructive ideas intact to shape our consciousness and affect our hearts and minds. Hosea's vi-olent threats do not cease to reverberate with the dynamics of battering in contemporary relationships when we choose to focus on "And I will espouse you forever." While the prophets are not responsible for abuse in modern marriage, their rhetoric presupposes and can legitimate present-day abuse, just as it did in their own time.

Remaining silent about the negative aspects of tradition not only leaves them to do their work in the world, it also deprives us of an important spiri-tual resource. In congregations, in Hillels, and in other places rabbis serve, many Jews are in pain. Sometimes they are in pain and feel they have been wounded directly by some aspect of Jewish tradition. More often, they have been hurt by injustices or abuse described and sometimes reinscribed by tradition, but not immediately attributable to its influence. In either case, what they frequently need and seek are not simply spiritual ideals they can counterpose to the bitterness of their experiences, but places to name and explore the contours and causes of their pain. Passages like the Haftorah provide wonderful starting points to talk about the reality of abuse, its origins and emotional dynamics—*and* how one can learn to refuse it. In this sense, learning to read and preach against the text is not just an intellectual exercise in criticizing tradition, but a way of claiming one's experience—in relation to the Haftorah, as women, as sexual persons, as survivors of battering. Viewed in this light, acknowledging those aspects of tradition that need to be repudiated and exorcised is a necessary moment in the process of creating something new. It is part of the quest for metaphors for intimacy and faithfulness that are not rooted in the conventions of patriarchal marriage and that do not accept these conventions as givens.

I do not believe that we have any choice other than to make choices about what we accept and repudiate in tradition. But we do have a choice as to whether we leave the negative to do its silent, poisonous work like an old family secret, or whether we turn and grapple with ambiguity and ugliness, and force them to yield up meaning. Confronting the hard places in tradition and in our lives is neither comfortable nor easy. But it is a necessary step in shaping a Judaism that is inclusive and life-giving, in continuity with tradition and yet responsive to the contemporary world.

Expanding the Jewish Feminist Agenda

Jewish feminists have succeeded in changing the face of Jewish religious life in the United States beyond the wildest dreams of those of us who, in the late 1960s, began to protest the exclusion of women from Jewish religious practice. Thirty years ago, who could have anticipated that, at the turn of the century, there would be hundreds of female rabbis representing three Jewish denominations, untold numbers of female Torah and Haftorah readers, and female cantors and service leaders in synagogues throughout the country?

Who could have imagined that so many girls would expect a full bat mitzvah as a matter of course, or that Orthodox women would be learning Talmud, mastering synagogue skills, and functioning as full participants in services of their own?

Equal access to all the roles and responsibilities of Jewish religious life has been—and remains—a hard fight for women in many individual congregations, and it has been far easier to achieve than transformation of the *content* of Jewish liturgy and teaching. Yet even in this more difficult area, there have been steps toward change. Birth ceremonies for baby girls, experimental liturgies, new denominational and alternative prayer books reflecting women's presence and/or offering new God-language, feminist midrash and commentaries on biblical texts, are all part of the American Jewish scene. It is true that institutionalizing these gains remains an enormous challenge. But enough has been accomplished that it seems appropriate for Jewish feminists to ask, what next?

What is next, I would argue, is moving beyond a single-minded focus on internal religious issues and synthesizing the concerns of religious and secular Jewish feminists. Up until now, there has been a remarkable lack of conversation among feminists addressing religious questions, those criticizing the absence of women's leadership from major Jewish communal organizations, and those working on a host of social and political issues, from racism to poverty to the rights of Palestinians. Even where some of the same people have been active around these different questions, there has been strangely little cross-fertilization in terms of analysis and strategies.

I cannot speak for the secular side, but I think the task of religious feminists in the new millennium is to end this counterproductive division of labor. How can we hope to solidify the gains of the last decades without sophisticated analyses of power in the Jewish community and in the larger society? How do we begin to theorize and act on the ways in which creating a more just Judaism is but a small piece of the larger task of creating a more just world?

Jewish feminists have difficulty transforming Jewish liturgy and integrating the insights of feminist scholarship into Jewish education not simply because of religious barriers but also because of lack of access to power and money. A 1998 study commissioned by Ma'yan, The Jewish Women's Project in New York, documented the deplorable absence of women from the boards of major Jewish organizations. Of 2,315 members representing boards of 45 important national Jewish organizations, only 25 percent were women. Although this study has yet to be integrated with an analysis of feminist progress on religious issues, surely the difficulty of institutionalizing feminist curriculum projects or of finding funding for major feminist commentaries is related to the absence of women from the halls of power. Moreover, boards of Jewish organizations are themselves being rendered increasingly irrelevant by the wealth of a small number of individuals whose private foundations have the power to set the agenda for their communities. This concentration of power and money in the Jewish community points to the necessity of connecting Jewish issues with larger social problems because it is part of the growing economic inequality in the United States and around the globe.

Jewish feminists have been extraordinarily successful in reshaping the internal landscape of American Jewish religious life. Now it's time to connect issues of religious justice with issues of power and to start working for the redistribution of power and resources within the Jewish community and in the larger society.

The Continuing Value
of Separatism

For the increasing number of American Jewish women who live and/or grew up in egalitarian Jewish communities, the need for separate women's spaces is less self-evident than it was in the early days of Jewish feminism. Thirty years ago, when even liberal synagogues offered few opportunities for women to take leadership roles or participate as equals in public worship, women-only groups provided rare opportunities for women to begin to examine barriers to equality, articulate critiques of Jewish ritual and God-language, ask daring new questions about women's history, and acquire skills long denied them. At the beginning of the twenty-first century, as women's full access to public roles is the norm in more and more congregations, separatism often feels like reneging on a bargain that, while rarely made explicit, is still morally and psychologically compelling. If the synagogue, and particularly the *bimah* (platform for prayer), are no longer clubs marked "for men only," then why should women create women-only spaces that seem as exclusive as the men's spaces of previous generations? Doesn't a commitment to egalitarianism involve a commitment on the part of both women and men to make integrated spaces work for everyone?

This general skepticism about the continuing value of separatism might apply with special force to women's seders, currently proliferating in communities and on college campuses around the country. Because the Passover seder celebrates a founding moment in the history of the Jewish people, it is a ritual that seems to cry out for inclusive community. As part of the throng brought forth from Egypt "with a mighty hand and an outstretched arm"— and, indeed, as crucial actors in the events leading up to and surrounding the Exodus—women have a rightful and important place at the communal Passover table. The fact that most seders are celebrated in the home, moreover, rather than in public institutions, means that any particular seder is likely to include a substantial proportion of women. Some of these women may find that small communities of families and friends provide more comfortable contexts for experimenting with leadership, participation, and the content of the seder than do synagogue-based rituals.

Yet, at the same time that Passover seems like an especially inopportune moment for separatism, the Festival of Freedom also crystallizes the contradictions surrounding women's inclusion and exclusion that continue to characterize even liberal Judaism, and that point to the great unfinished agenda of Jewish feminism. I leave aside the massive preparation that the holiday requires and that continues to fall in women's domain, so that all too many women are unable to join fully either in the seder itself or in the leisurely enjoyment of the festive meal that they have prepared. Beyond the important point that Jewish feminists need to challenge the gendered division of labor and not simply women's exclusion from public religious roles, there is another dimension of women's marginalization at the Passover table that women's seders address. Just as women's often invisible work and energy are the essential "background" of the seder celebration, so women's work and contributions are relegated to the background of the haggadah. Although the biblical account of the Exodus makes clear that women participated in the liberation of the Jewish people as midwives, rescuers, and cultic leaders, not a single woman is mentioned by name in the haggadah itself. And while, to be sure, the haggadah focuses on *God's* role in the Exodus, so that even Moses is referred to only briefly, a parade of rabbis and patriarchs flows in and out of the text—a text that repeatedly adjures *men* to teach their *sons* the story of the going out from Egypt. Inclusive translations that change "son" to "child" do not thereby make women visible or give substance to the shadowy forms of Mrs. Rabbi Eliezer, Joshua, and Akiba. These women hover outside the boundaries of the text, just as they obviously were excluded from their husbands' paradigmatic seder.

It is this crucial contradiction between the increased participation of women in all aspects of Jewish life and the *content* of the tradition that, in my view, provides the warrant and necessity for women-only spaces, including women's seders. Such seders function on several levels. First, they furnish occasions for women to *sit* and/or to serve themselves, rather than always caring for others. Second, they are contexts in which women have special opportunities to teach and preside—a dimension of women's seders that may be especially important to those from traditional backgrounds. Third, in a knowledge-based tradition in which those without extensive Jewish educations—educations traditionally unavailable to women—often feel inadequate and silenced, women's seders allow those present to claim ownership of their Judaism and begin to take power to shape and transmit it. Fourth, and most important, women's seders allow participants to redefine their relationship to tradition by raising questions and exploring perspectives that would most likely be regarded as distractions in the framework of an ordinary seder. Whether a particular women's seder uses the haggadah as a starting point for talking about the incomplete liberation of women or attempts to highlight women's roles in the story of Jewish liberation from Egypt, it is still almost entirely in separate spaces that women have the opportunity to critique normative texts and to create alternative rituals and liturgies that place women at the center.

Women's space is important, as I see it, precisely insofar as it becomes *feminist* space: space for questioning the received tradition and for pioneering new forms of Jewish expression that have the potential to transform the self-understanding of the whole Jewish community. Not all women's spaces are feminist spaces in this sense. Feminism entails a personal and political commitment to religious and social change, a commitment that is neither a natural outgrowth of being a woman nor necessarily limited to women alone. Feminism involves adopting a set of critical lenses for viewing Judaism and the world—lenses that must be turned on women's seders themselves whenever they fall into speaking about "the feminine" instead of women, or whenever they define women or feminism in monolithic terms. Separatism is important not because women as women have some unique and shared vision that the Jewish community needs, but because women have been excluded from the formulation of Jewish texts and traditions, and because men's comments, questions, and agendas tend to be taken more seriously in integrated contexts, while feminist questions and perspectives are often trivialized and treated with impatience.

If it is the critical and transformative perspective of women's seders that constitutes their rationale and main contribution, then the presence of men at such seders is by no means an oxymoron. I have learned over many years of teaching Jewish feminism and participating in feminist liturgies in a variety of contexts that men who are willing to take part in such events on women's terms can enter fully into their spirit and make powerful and important contributions to the proceedings. On the other hand, given the ways in which gender-role socialization can lead even assertive and feisty women to defer or fall silent in the face of certain kinds of male posturing, given the many forces still aligned against women claiming the right to shape and transform Jewish tradition, and given the ways in which women's leadership continues to be feared and undermined, it must be up to the women planning any particular seder to decide whether it makes sense to invite men to the event.

Whether women's seders will be a temporary means to a more inclusive tradition or a permanent feature of Jewish life, it is much too soon to judge. For now, there is no conflict between the continuation of women-only spaces and their contribution to a richer Judaism for all. The wonderful new ritual innovations, poems, songs, and pieces of liturgy that have been created for women's seders provide invaluable resources for incorporation into family and community seders. At our family seder, we always put the cup of Miriam next to the cup of Elijah, read some poems about the importance of women's history, and celebrate the midwives' civil disobedience. There is no reason why, as families mention the Holocaust, contemporary poverty and homelessness, or peace in the Middle East at their seder tables, they should not also make the role of women in the Exodus and in Judaism a theme for the seder. But the experimentation that is generating this new material and making it available for wider use takes place at women's seders, where the restoration of women's rightful place in the reenactment of the central event of Jewish history is not *a* theme but *the* theme.

It may be that some day, all haggadahs and all seders will reflect the idea that the whole Jewish people went forth from Egypt. Until that day arrives, women's seders remain necessary—both for individuals trying to claim a history from which they and their foremothers have been erased, and for the future of a Jewish community that has yet to fully realize the liberating vision of Passover.

IV

Sexuality, Authority, and Tradition

Sexuality and Teshuvah

Leviticus 18

Of all the readings for the High Holy Days, the Torah portion for the afternoon of Yom Kippur seems the most puzzling and even bizarre.[1] Coming after the awe-filled description of the service of the high priest and before the reading of Jonah, with its clear focus on repentance and forgiveness, Leviticus 18—a list of forbidden sexual relations—seems to bear little relation to the themes of the day. Yom Kippur is a time for self-examination, for reflection on one's sins and one's relationship with God. Of the many ways in which it is possible to transgress the divine commandments, why should sexual violations be singled out to be described in all their concreteness? How does reading Leviticus 18 forward the movement of the liturgy?

A possible historical explanation for the Torah reading is provided by a statement in the Talmud. Mishnah Ta'anit 4.8 says that *Tu B'Av* (the fifteenth day of the month of *Av*) and Yom Kippur were the happiest days of the year. On the afternoons of these days, the daughters of Jerusalem would go out in white clothing and dance in the vineyards, while young men would come and choose their brides. Lamentations Rabbah 33 comments on the appropriateness of Yom Kippur as a day for dancing, pointing out that it is a day of forgiveness and expiation. In light of these indications that the solemnity of the day once gave way to rejoicing by the afternoon, the reading of Leviticus 18 might be understood in one of two ways. It could be a strict warning not to get carried away by an excess of exuberance, or it could be a reminder to prospective spouses of what relationships are permitted and prohibited.

The existence of historical reasons for reading Leviticus 18 does not necessarily make the portion meaningful in the contemporary context, however. Not only is the notion of Yom Kippur as a day for choosing brides at best a distant memory, but the specific content of the chapter is in many ways disturbing. Its profound male-centeredness, its silences, its focus on purity, its condemnation of certain sexual practices that many Jews today find entirely acceptable, are more likely to provoke a sense of alienation from the service than to promote self-reflection. It is probably partly to avoid evoking this alienation that many non-Orthodox congregations substitute Leviticus 19 for Leviticus 18 on Yom Kippur afternoon. As a list of fundamental ethical (and cultic) precepts that define holy community, Leviticus 19 seems more in keeping with the themes of wide-ranging self-scrutiny and commitment to *teshuvah* (repentance).

As someone who has long been disturbed by the content of Leviticus 18, I had always applauded the substitution of an alternative Torah reading—until a particular incident made me reconsider the link between sex and Yom Kippur. After a lecture I delivered in the spring of 1995 on rethinking Jewish attitudes toward sexuality, a woman approached me very distressed. She belonged to a Conservative synagogue that had abandoned the practice of reading Leviticus 18 on Yom Kippur, and as a victim of childhood sexual abuse by her grandfather, she felt betrayed by that decision. While she was not necessarily committed to the understanding of sexual holiness contained in Leviticus, she felt that in quietly changing the reading without communal discussion, her congregation had avoided issues of sexual responsibility altogether. She wanted to hear her community connect the theme of atonement with issues of behavior in intimate relationships, to have it publicly proclaim the parameters of legitimate sexual relations on a day when large numbers of Jews gather.

As a result of this conversation, I began to rethink the connection between *teshuvah* and reading about sex on Yom Kippur. It struck me that the appeal of Leviticus 19 as an alternative Torah reading is not without its problems. Leviticus 19 makes a more comfortable reading because its injunctions are broader and more foundational. It reiterates a number of the Ten Commandments, links kindness to strangers with the experience of Egyptian slavery (verses 33–34), and enjoins the community to "love your neighbor as yourself" (verse 18). Yet injunctions that are broader are also more easily evaded, while the disturbing concreteness of Leviticus 18 reminds us that love of the neighbor begins at home. The family is the first sphere in which we learn about both love and domination, and it is also the closest and most frightening context in which we can begin to make changes in our relationships with others. As many voices in our society draw attention to the high incidence of incest and other forms of sexual abuse within the family and the ways in which patterns of family interaction are passed on through the generations, it becomes clear how important it is to connect the notion of atonement to the quest for holiness in intimate relations. Focusing on the issue of sexual boundaries may be a very important exercise for Yom Kippur because it makes *teshuvah* concrete in ways that touch on a central area of both personal and communal life.

Problems with Leviticus

Yet if, in theory, it is entirely fitting to read about sexuality on Yom Kippur, the actual *content* of Leviticus 18 is deeply disturbing. Indeed, from a feminist perspective it seems that, far from fostering holiness in interpersonal relations, the chapter reflects and supports those structures of domination that undergird sexual and family violence. Thus, reading or not reading Leviticus 18 can be equally problematic. On the one hand, as my interlocutor made me realize, gliding silently away from the difficulties Leviticus 18 poses evades the responsibility of communal self-examination and *teshuvah*. On the other hand, chanting it as sacred text colludes in promoting its values. In this situation, the question becomes not so much *whether* to read or not, but *how* to read, interpret, and appropriate the text in ways that are transformative.

The task of transforming Leviticus 18 begins with examining its problems, problems that start with its foreign context. Leviticus 18 is part of a larger Levitical "Holiness Code" (chapters 17–26) that lays out laws and ordinances incumbent on the entire people of Israel in order that they can attain holiness.[2] While, for the priestly authors of the code, holiness is not unconnected to morality, it is understood primarily through the categories of purity and pollution. Thus, while I just argued on moral grounds for reading Leviticus 18 on Yom Kippur, it is striking that the language of the chapter is not the language of right and wrong, but of abhorrence and defilement. "Do not defile yourselves in any of those ways, for it is by such that the nations that I am casting out before you defiled themselves. Thus the land became defiled; and I called it to account for its iniquity, and the land spewed out its inhabitants" (verses 24–25).[3] The fact that the land itself can be contaminated suggests that holiness is at least partly identified with the avoidance of a quasi-physical contagion or pollution, a pollution that is dangerous to both individuals and the community.[4] Mary Douglas argues in her classic work *Purity and Danger* that the purpose of pollution beliefs is to impose order on the chaos of experience. Pollution arises from the violation of social boundaries and classifications, and from the failure to conform to one's class. Pollution rules can reinforce moral principles and moral indignation—as they do in Leviticus 18, where defilement is caused by individual behavior—but pollution is not identical with morality and involves a mystical surplus that cannot be reduced to it.[5]

Although these ideas are strange to the contemporary consciousness, it is not most centrally its remoteness that makes Leviticus 18 problematic, but the character of the social order that pollution laws protect. My interlocutor wanted to hear Leviticus read on Yom Kippur because, as a victim of sexual abuse by her grandfather, she wanted it proclaimed in the presence of the assembled community that the violation of granddaughters by men in power over them is morally unacceptable. But as I pointed out to her, it is not the purpose of the incest prohibitions of Leviticus 18 to protect the young and vulnerable. The laws address the situation of extended patriarchal families in which the honor and authority of male heads of household is the primary social value. Thus the first two incest rules in chapter 18 (verses 7 and 8) do not forbid the father/parent to sexually violate a child, but rather forbid *the son to violate the sexuality of his father* by committing incestuous adultery with the father's wife. The less powerful party is instructed not to dishonor the powerful, while the wife's sexuality is treated simply as her husband's possession. The other incest laws in verses 9–18, all of which are addressed to a male audience, serve several different functions: they protect the purity of the line of descent, they encourage exogamy, and they maintain order and reduce the likelihood of jealousy and conflict within the (polygynous) family group.[6] While this last purpose may work to the benefit of women, by outlawing marriage with two sisters, for example (verse 18), it is not women's concerns and interests that animate the text. Moreover, that it is not the intent of these rules to defend the weak is indicated by the striking absence of any mention of the most prevalent sexual violation, namely father/daughter incest. While both the rabbis and many contemporary commentators take it for granted that such incest is subsumed under other categories, it is not clear that such an assumption is supported by the Biblical text.[7]

The marginalization of women within the social world presupposed by Leviticus 18 is underscored in a different way by the prohibition of sex with a menstruant in verse 19. On one level this prohibition fits quite seamlessly into the purity-related concerns of Leviticus and the associated concepts of pollution and defilement. Leviticus 15 defines a number of bodily emissions as defiling—semen and any other discharge from the penis, menstrual blood, and nonmenstrual bloody discharge from the vagina—and sets out the proper procedures for purification. Since semen and menstrual blood are separately polluting, mixed together they represent a double danger to the community.[8] On another level, however, as Howard Eilberg-Schwartz points out in *The Savage in Judaism,* when menstrual blood is viewed not simply as a body fluid, but specifically as *blood*, it is negatively marked in a particular way. Unlike the blood of circumcision, which represents entry into the covenant and the end of the male infant's impurity caused by the mother's blood at birth, menstrual blood is contaminating. The prohibition of sex with a menstruant, repeated more forcefully in Leviticus 20:18, is part of a symbolic complex in which menstrual blood has many ugly associations.[9] The prophets link menstrual impurity with adultery, idolatry, and murder. Ezekiel, for example, compares God's revulsion at Israel's violence and idolatry with disgust at the "uncleanness of a menstruous woman" (36:17). The book of Lamentations likens Jerusalem's degradation after the exile to a menstruating woman whose "uncleanness clings to her skirts" (1:9).[10] Thus, as Eilberg-Schwartz puts it, "menstrual prohibitions may be the sign par excellence of 'the difference of woman from man . . . her eternally inexplicable, mysterious and strange nature. . . .' "[11] Reading Leviticus 18, then, activates and reinforces a host of negative religious and cultural attitudes surrounding women's bodies.

The proscription of male/male intercourse in Leviticus 18:22 raises analogous purity-related and ethical issues. The original significance of this law is difficult to recover. Although the verse is most often read as a general condemnation of male "homosexuality," in fact, the prohibition against a man's lying down "the lying down of a woman" probably refers specifically to the insertive role in anal intercourse.[12] Because this law appears only in Leviticus

(18:22 and 20:13) and not in other legal collections in the Bible that deal with sexual relations, it should probably be understood in connection with the distinctive concerns of the Holiness Code. Saul Olyan suggests that it be interpreted in the context of Leviticus 18's anxiety about mixing defiling fluids. Just as it is dangerous to mix semen with the blood of a menstruant, so, in this case, it is dangerous to mix semen with excrement, a substance that is also seen as defiling in other holiness contexts.[13]

Even if the original issue behind Leviticus 18 is quite limited, however, the history of its use and interpretation cannot be ignored. While in the Bible itself, male/male anal intercourse does not become a metaphor for other sorts of sin and defilement in the way that menstrual impurity does, the verse has long been understood as a judgment on all male homosexual relations and has provided a sanction for both Jewish and Christian homophobia. In contemporary debates about the status of gays and lesbians within Judaism, Leviticus 18:22 is often treated as divinely ordained and eternally binding by people who otherwise have little use for the directives of Leviticus. Thus to read this passage on Yom Kippur without discussion or comment is to lend support to a larger environment of social prejudice and discrimination against gays and lesbians.

A more general problem with Leviticus 18 that makes it alien to a contemporary perspective is the extent to which its rules are act-centered. The chapter forbids a series of discrete behaviors that are linked by particular themes and purity-related concerns. Not only must the underlying principles at stake be deduced from the specific regulations, but also these principles have little to do with the emotional and psychological dimensions of sexual experience that today are considered so central to evaluations of sexual morality. Related to this, Leviticus 18 offers no *positive* vision of holy sexuality. Instead, holiness is defined as avoiding defilement—by *not* copying the practices of Egypt and Canaan and by *not* violating the categories and boundaries that order and preserve the social/religious world.

In terms of thinking about the Torah reading for Yom Kippur afternoon, then, Leviticus 18 poses a dilemma. On the one hand, the link made by the reading between *teshuvah* and sexuality is very important. Ideally, reading Leviticus 18 should encourage us to focus on the quality of our family relationships as they affect the nature of communal life. In positing a connection between individual behavior and the viability of the whole land, the chapter draws attention to the ways in which the character of intimate relationships has ramifications way beyond the interpersonal sphere. On the other hand, the moral, emotional, and psychological components of that link that are so central to us are not the concern of Leviticus, so that we can find meaning in the text only by using it as a starting point that is fairly quickly left behind. Thus it is not surprising that many synagogues have chosen to substitute a different Torah reading for Leviticus 18—or that many individuals have solved the problems it poses by coming to *minchah* (the afternoon service) a little late!

Transforming Leviticus

How, then, does one hold on to the value of connecting *teshuvah* and sexuality without denying the very real difficulties of Leviticus 18? Or, put another way, how does one affirm the insights of Leviticus into the necessity for sexual boundaries and into the link between communal well-being and interpersonal behavior without abandoning the victims of its hierarchical and purity-centered worldview? It is easy enough to set out the contradictions of reading Leviticus in an essay for a book, but bringing a critical consciousness to the Torah reading on Yom Kippur makes it difficult to focus on the tasks of self-examination and repentance. The synagogue on Yom Kippur is not a classroom in which to analyze the sociology of the liturgy. It is supposed to be a place to meditate on our relationship with God and to seek atonement. From this point of view, it may make sense to substitute Leviticus 19 for 18, because, while the readings raise similar purity-related issues, Leviticus 19 also contains injunctions that fit with less distraction into the themes of the day.

To my mind, however, there is no easy way around the tension between a critical consciousness and the ability to focus on worship and self-reflection. The fact that Leviticus 19 contains, alongside its profound moral injunctions, ritual commandments that seem utterly devoid of ethical content may serve only to highlight the gulf in worldviews between Leviticus and ourselves. To a large extent, this tension is inherent in the erosion of religious authority that was part of the emergence of modern science and historical criticism. There are many places in the Yom Kippur liturgy where an abyss may suddenly open between the text and ourselves. Rather than seeking a way around this dilemma by changing the Torah reading, we might better address it by placing the reading in a larger context of communal wrestling with and transformation of Torah.

In the aftermath of my conversation about these readings, I tried to envision a different way of dealing with Leviticus 18 other than simply substituting another portion without communal discussion. It occurred to me that small groups of Jews in many different contexts might grapple with issues of sexual responsibility and try to create statements of sexual values that engage both Leviticus and contemporary experience. Leviticus 18 enjoins Jews to holiness in the arena of sexual behavior. What constitutes holiness today? What would it mean to begin to do *teshuvah* in this area of our lives—both as a personal process, internal and behavioral, and as a Jewish community contending with the legacy of a hierarchical, patriarchal sexual ethic?

To ask such questions is to approach the Torah not as a static document that brings us a set of eternal truths, but—to use Rachel Adler's image—as one end of a bridge that might possibly carry us toward where we want to be. Borrowing Robert Cover's metaphor of law as a bridge between our present moral universe and those alternative universes a people might create through its concerted communal action, Adler suggests that Leviticus 18 is still usable if we think of it as part of the Jewish historical teaching about sexuality that is holding down one end of the bridge.[14] As every lesbian and gay man listening to the *minchah* Torah reading on Yom Kippur knows, Leviticus 18 has shaped Jewish life and consciousness for good and for evil. Erasing it from the *makhzor* (High Holy Day prayer book) will not in itself eradicate the homophobia it helps generate and justify, any more than ceasing to read about menstrual taboos will generate a new set of positive attitudes toward women's bodies.[15] Leviticus 18 is read, however, in the context of congregations whose members, whether or not they are consciously critical, are generally living out very different sexual norms. Thus if Torah, like law, is a bridge between past and future, it is being reshaped on the ground by Jews whose attitudes and behaviors are necessarily affected by contemporary social movements and sexual values. This process of reshaping can become a more fully Jewish process—and a process of *teshuvah*—if it involves conscious engagement with Leviticus 18 and other traditional sources with the intention of moving toward a new sexual ethic.

Grappling with Leviticus from a contemporary feminist perspective involves importing a set of assumptions radically different from those of the text. Any feminist reworking of Leviticus would have to address the ways in which many of its premises—for example, that the nakedness of the *fathers* is more in need of protection than the nakedness of daughters, or that menstrual blood is defiling—produce and support the sexual injustice that a sexual ethic should address and correct. While such a reworking would certainly attend to the social structures that undergird and make possible holy relationships, it would also be more person-centered, focusing on the qualities of human connection rather than on the supposedly intrinsic nature of particular sexual behaviors. It might be aware of the dangers of too easily equating certain feelings with holiness, yet it would at least attend to the place of feelings as a dimension of holy sexuality. Rather than understanding defilement as a quasi-mystical reality, the avoidance of which protects the privilege of the powerful, it would see it as the outcome of abuse of power and the violation of the vulnerable. Attempting to articulate both basic standards of sexual decency and a vision of possible holiness, it would attempt to connect sexual values with those ethical values that ought to guide all relationships. Rachel Adler points out that the exhortation in Leviticus 19:2, "You shall be holy, for I, the Lord your God, am holy," comes at the juncture of two sets of commandments. Leviticus 18 deals with sexual boundaries, while Leviticus 19 offers some basic principles for creating a just and loving community. Insofar as "you shall be holy" refers to both sets of laws, it is possible and necessary to rethink the laws of sexual relations, not as a discrete set of rules bearing on a unique capacity to sanctify or defile, but as a subset of the laws about justice toward the neighbor.[16]

Over the past few years I have participated in, or helped to facilitate, a couple of groups that have begun the process of rethinking Leviticus. In particular, Su Kasha, a lesbian and gay *havurah* (small, informal Jewish communities formed for prayer and study) in New York to which I belong, has been engaged in this project for over a year.[17] Each spring, as we have struggled with *Acharei Mot* and *Kedoshim* (the Torah portions that contain Leviticus 18 and 20), we have found ourselves questioning our relation to a tradition that sees male/male sex as an abomination. Writing our own Leviticus 18 has provided the opportunity to move beyond anger and a sense of victimization and to explore our own assumptions, values, and differences. We began the process of rethinking Leviticus with a lengthy and serious discussion of the chapter, in which we laid out the text's interests and assumptions and examined what in it we rejected or affirmed. We also studied portions of the Song of Songs in order to place Leviticus in the context of a complex and multivocal tradition. We then entered into an open-ended and wide-ranging conversation about our own concerns, trying to delineate important lines of sexual responsibility and to explore our own values and "bottom lines" within them. We agreed that we would try to express our sexual ethic in positive terms, affirming our responsibilities to ourselves, to individual others, and to a larger community. We also agreed that, for the sake of coming up with an actual document, we would work toward consensus, although we were at the same time aware of many differences among us.

The process of trying to articulate our own sexual ethics has been challenging and exciting, eliciting insight along with playfulness. Engaging in the project has made us aware of the extent to which we normally dwell in the same zone of silence around sexuality that leads to the quiet substitution of Leviticus 19 for 18 on Yom Kippur. Although our culture is saturated with sexual images, there is an enormous gap between media fixation on sexuality and pressures toward sexual activity, and the capacity of individuals to speak comfortably about and claim responsibility for their own sexuality. Rethinking Leviticus provides an opportunity to grapple with the painful contradictions between traditional sexual values and the realities of people's lives, and to think through the meaning of holiness in light of these conflicts. As Su Kasha has explored our agreements and talked through our differences, it has become clear to us that the point of the exercise is the process itself. Even though we have focused on creating a new text, we are aware that that task has provided a context for conversations that have been more important than the finished product—especially since any new document would function only as a basis for further discussion, either among ourselves or for others. In the spirit of providing a model for a process that any group can engage in, I have appended to this essay sections of a draft of the Su Kasha ethic, an ethic that is very much in process.

Conclusions

The task of rethinking Leviticus 18 seemingly takes us far away from the specific context of the Torah reading on Yom Kippur afternoon. Like criticizing Leviticus altogether, it is not so much a job for the holiday as for individual and group reflection during the rest of the year. Moreover, it is a rare congregation or *havurah* that would actually read a new statement of sexual ethics in lieu of the Torah reading, and, probably, the act of doing so would deflect attention from the task of self-reflection to arguments about specific content, or the status of Torah. On another level, however, rethinking Leviticus connects the theme of repentance to the ongoing life of the Jewish community. It is an act of communal *teshuvah*, both in relation to those who are marginalized and anathematized by Leviticus 18 and those who are abandoned when it is abandoned without considered discussion. In this sense, continuing engagement with Leviticus provides a context that can enrich the experience of Yom Kippur. It allows us to move out from the Torah reading to thinking about *teshuvah* in our personal relationships in a way that is both rooted in tradition and attentive to the realities of contemporary life. And it affirms a central insight of Leviticus 18: the relationship between holiness on the interpersonal and communal levels.

Appendix: The Su Kasha Ethic (Selections)

I have selected those sections that, after laying out some basic assumptions, speak most directly to issues of interpersonal and communal sexual values and responsibility.[18]

You Shall Be Holy as I Am Holy

We believe that we honor the image of God by honoring the body. Through our bodies we can connect with each other, the world, and the sacred.

We affirm that each human being has sensual feelings from the beginning of life and that sensuality is the foundation of sexuality. Children have the right to grow up enjoying their bodies, to be nurtured by appropriate touch, and to have a positive physical self-image. These positive experiences are a foundation for a healthy adult sexuality.

We affirm that each human being must be taught that the awakening of sexual feeling and the desire for sexual activity are natural and good, and that an understanding of how to express sexuality must also be taught. It is good to talk about sexuality.

We affirm human sexuality in all its fluidity, complexity, and diversity. Many of the proscriptions on human sexuality that were established for the survival and differentiation of small tribes in earlier cultures have become tools of oppression and destruction in today's world and therefore unacceptable.

We affirm that human sexual diversity is part of the richness and diversity of life. We envision a society in which sexual behavior, whether heterosexual, bisexual, homosexual, or celibate, is all considered healthy; and in which sexual ambiguity, including hermaphroditism, androgyny, and transgenderedness, is affirmed and neither feared nor despised.

We affirm that we all have the right to make decisions about our own bodies.

We affirm the goodness of sexual pleasure independent of the goal of procreation.

Sexual Responsibilities to Others No person twenty-one or older shall have intercourse with any child sixteen or younger.

All sexual activity between people must be consensual. No person shall touch another person without that person's permission.

No person shall abuse, exploit, control, humiliate, do violence to, or harm another human being physically, emotionally, or in any other way in the course of sexual expression.

If or whenever one person withdraws permission, the other must stop.

As our bodies are holy, we shall not do violence to others or put others in danger or at risk of disease through sexual behaviors.

No person shall have unprotected sex with any partner if s/he knowingly has any sexually transmitted disease.

Each person must take responsibility for the consequences of sexual activity, including pregnancy and children.

Sexuality shall not be used as an expression of status or power, and no person shall use status or power to gain consent for sexual activity.

Partners shall be forthright about sexual activities outside their primary relationship.

The Communal Context of Sexuality No person shall project sexual stereotypes on any person based on that person's perceived age, gender, sexual orientation, or membership in a racial or ethnic group.

It is the responsibility of the Jewish community to raise and discuss issues of sexuality and to help give parents the tools to discuss sexual issues with their children.

Communities have the responsibility to create spaces and contexts that allow for the discussion of and for the varieties of sexual expression and that acknowledge the variability and fluidity of sexual identities.

Sexual Orientation
and Human Rights
A Progressive Jewish Perspective

Progressive discussion of the question of homosexuality and public policy must start from a curious and important contradiction between theory and politics around gay, lesbian, and bisexual rights.[1] At the same time that various social constructionist understandings of sexuality have become widely accepted in academic circles, providing the foundations for historical research and discussions of sexual identity, the gay, lesbian, and bisexual movement has tended to depict sexual identity as inherent and unalterable.[2] Particularly as the New Right has made homosexuality an important battleground in its struggle to enshrine in law traditional sexual and "family" values, lesbians, gays, bisexuals, and our allies have argued strongly that some people are just born with an attraction to their own sex that is at once ineradicable and a fundamental part of identity. It is my contention in this essay that, while biological arguments may be strategically useful, it is ultimately a mistake to ground support for gay and lesbian rights on biologically based understandings of sexual orientation. A progressive position, I will argue, must use the insights of social constructionism to place the issue of homosexuality in the larger context of the feminist critique of gender roles, compulsory heterosexuality, and traditional sexual ethics.[3]

The Liberal Jewish Discussion

The emergence of the gay rights movement has precipitated an ethical crisis within many U.S. religious denominations. The existence of increasingly visible and vocal lesbians, gay men, and bisexuals within every religious group has forced denominational bodies to take stands on a host of issues related to homosexuality. Task forces and the debates attending them have often generated anger, bitterness, and deep division between those who would protect what they see as the integrity of tradition and those who would defend the rights and integrity of gay and lesbian members.[4] One of the more striking aspects of the current debates about homosexuality and religious tradition is the similarity of arguments across religious lines. Within Jewish, Catholic, and Protestant contexts, conservatives point to the supposedly unrelieved condemnation of homosexuality in both the Bible and religious tradition, while many liberals appeal to the supposed innateness of homosexuality to reinterpret or question the contemporary validity of the same limited number of texts.

In the Jewish discussion, Leviticus 18:22 and 20:13 are taken as the key biblical passages condemning homosexuality and defining it as an abomination. Exegeses of other texts—the Sodom story, for example, or the rape of the Levite's concubine in Judges—simply confirm the Levitical prohibitions.[5] While lesbianism is not mentioned explicitly in the Tanakh, the rabbis find a reference to it in Leviticus 18:3: "You shall not copy the practices of the land of Egypt...or the land of Canaan." The Sifra (a legal commentary on the book of Leviticus) interprets the practices in question as a man marrying a man and a woman marrying a woman, a position that is codified by Maimonides.[6] The rabbis also explore the meanings of the term *to'evah* (abomination) and elaborate on the Levitical injunction against male homosexuality, arguing that it applies to both the active and passive partners.[7] All in all, traditional references to homosexuality are very sparse, a fact that many conservatives interpret as signaling the rarity of homosexuality among Jews.[8]

I agree with conservatives that the weight of Jewish tradition is against homosexual relations. Indeed, what strikes me as far more compelling than the small number of sources actually addressing the issue is the pervasive assumption that heterosexual marriage is the norm for adult life. To my mind, the central issue for the contemporary debate is not the meaning of this or that particular passage—though I certainly recognize the strategic importance of new interpretations in enabling halakhic (Jewish legal) change—but the meta-halakhic question of the authority of traditional teachings on sexuality. This question can be further broken down into at least two others. First, since halakhah (Jewish law) is an evolving system, always responding to new social, economic, and political conditions, are there grounds for halakhic change on the issue of homosexuality? And second, how should gay rights advocates within Judaism understand their relationship to halakhah?

In response to the first question about the grounds for halakhic change, halakhic liberals have adopted the same argument used by much of the gay rights movement in the public arena. They have highlighted new data on the fundamental and ineradicable nature of sexual identity, claiming that it undermines the Torah's prohibitions. Hershel Matt, for example, who was the first rabbi to call for change in Jewish attitudes toward homosexuality, argued that "the clear and consistent assumption behind all of the Torah's commands and prohibitions is . . . that human beings have freedom to obey or disobey them."[9] Where such freedom does not exist, violations of Jewish norms are judged more leniently. Matt pointed out that, while the Torah and tradition clearly presuppose that homosexual acts are freely chosen, contemporary evidence suggests that homosexuality is a "basic psychic orientation, involving the deepest levels of personality," and that, most important, it is almost impossible to change.[10] On the basis of this evidence, he argued for full acceptance and respect for constitutional homosexuals who otherwise live faithfully by Jewish law.[11]

When the law committee of the Conservative movement debated the legal status of homosexuality in 1991–92, the whole issue of choice was very much to the fore. Elliot Dorff, for example, in calling for a broad reconsideration of Jewish sexual values, emphasized the centrality of choice in his evaluation of homosexuality. He argued that it is *the* critical factor pressing the movement to rethink its halakhic position. All Jewish traditional sources, he said, assume that homosexuality is a violation of the law because it is a matter of choice. We now know, however, on the basis of both scientific research and the testimony of gay and lesbian Jews, that this is not true. Yet while the new data convinces Dorff that it is inappropriate to see homosexuality as a moral abomination, he does not yet find it sufficiently conclusive to justify fully overturning traditional Jewish norms.[12]

Matt and Dorff put forward a widely promulgated argument that can be very powerful in both the religious and the civil spheres. Since there is no point in legislating against or punishing people for what cannot be changed, it seems that, could researchers only pinpoint the mechanisms through which homosexual identity is acquired or transmitted, not only would halakhah have to accommodate this new knowledge but also sodomy statutes and discrimination against gays and lesbians would have to disappear. Such arguments do not simply take the teeth out of traditional prohibitions, moreover. They do so in a way that performs three important functions: (1) they allow for formal acknowledgment of traditional sources of authority; (2) they cause minimal disarray to traditional sexual values; and (3) they provide reassurance that accepting homosexuals will not increase their numbers.

Perhaps the central appeal of empirical studies pointing to the inborn nature of homosexual identity is that they allow proponents to support social change from within the framework of halakhah or commitment to the authority of Scripture. Thus, a number of the religious thinkers who draw on biological arguments distinguish between "true" or "obligatory" homosexuals and those who *could* lead heterosexual lives.[13] Hershel Matt, for example, argued that while a truly Jewish approach would counsel compassion for the constitutional homosexual, homosexuals or bisexuals who deliberately violate the Torah for their own pleasure or who could change with some effort still remain bound by the Torah's standards.[14] Since Matt never actually placed anyone in the category of gays who deliberately reject tradition, it appears that the concept of "situational" homosexuality functioned in his thought as a formal marker that allowed him to affirm tradition even while changing it. If constraint is the criterion for gay legitimacy, in other words, then halakhah or traditional social norms can still be affirmed as applying to those who have choice—should any such people exist. In this way, biological arguments provide a ready means of responding to social change without having to question tradition at a fundamental level.

Second, precisely because such arguments remain within the framework of tradition, they allow for acceptance of gays and lesbians with minimal disruption of sexual norms. As Hershel Matt expressed it, Torah norms apply to all who are capable of living by them. Obligatory homosexuals are "God's exceptions," who can live fully and faithfully by Torah's standards "except for the sexual identity of their mate[s]."[15] This formulation, like much of the recent rhetoric of the gay rights movement, assumes an assimilationist model of homosexual identity in which gays and lesbians are normalized through acceptance of dominant values. The fact that many gays and lesbians have adopted dominant family patterns, forming committed monogamous relationships and rearing children together, provides further grounds for this argument.

Third, constitutional constraint as the measure of homosexual acceptability also serves to define a certain discrete minority of the population as gay or lesbian while assuming that everyone else is naturally heterosexual. This construction does two things. It allows gay and lesbian activists and their allies to organize on the basis of a readily available and widely understood vocabulary of minority rights that fits with U.S. political rhetoric and sensitivities.[16] And it also helps to allay anxieties about the potentially deleterious effects of accepting gays and lesbians, particularly on the formation of young people's sexual identities. Again Hershel Matt illustrates a line of argument that has been used repeatedly in both the religious and civil arenas. After considering whether gays and lesbians ought to be ordained, and thus allowed to function as guides and role models, he concludes that since "one does not choose to *be* homosexual, a homosexual rabbi could not influence a person to *become* homosexual."[17]

Problems with the Liberal Position

Since, in the inflamed and often anxious context of religious and public debate, the limits of the liberal position are also its strengths in terms of gaining allies, criticizing these arguments feels a bit like the proverbial "biting the hand that feeds." Religious liberals like Hershel Matt have been courageous and important allies of gays and lesbians. Moreover, the notion of a fixed homosexual identity has provided a firm foundation for gay and lesbian organizing. It has furnished the basis for a civil rights argument in the religious and larger communities. And it has convinced some skeptics and turned them into friends. Despite these achievements, however, I would argue that the liberal position is riddled with contradictions that ultimately undermine its effectiveness and point in the direction of a more far-reaching analysis. Rather than seeking to establish gay, lesbian, and bisexual rights on the narrowest possible grounds, bisexuals, lesbians, gays, and our allies need to confront the evidence pointing to the complexity of sexual orientation, and then situate the issue in the larger context of a reexamination of sexual identity and sexual ethics.

As I can indicate only briefly, claims about the "givenness" of gay identity are often based on faulty research and misrepresent or ignore evidence that undermines their premises. First, the great majority of studies—biological, psychological, and sociological—on which arguments for a fundamental and irrevocable sexual orientation are based ignore the experience of lesbians. The same androcentrism that has affected every other area of human knowledge, entering into the creation of fundamental paradigms and shaping the formulation of basic questions, also has informed sexological research.[18] This fact has skewed the data in several significant ways: (1) Although researchers often speak of "homosexuality" as if it were a unified phenomenon both within and across sex lines, in fact a number of the biological mechanisms that have been proposed to explain homosexuality in men cannot be generalized to lesbians.[19] (2) Studies of lesbian communities have yielded understandings of sexual identity that are far more complicated than the better-known gay male accounts of an early and irresistible same-sex attraction. There seem to be several distinct trajectories of lesbian identity development, only one of which supports the idea of sexual orientation as a fundamental constitutional element outside of conscious control.[20] (3) These same studies suggest that the relationship between identity and behavior is also complex and contradictory. Not only are identity labels not terribly reliable predictors of actual sexual practices, but they are also fluid over time.[21] (4) Perhaps most significant, the experience of many lesbians challenges the opposition between nature and choice that grounds so many arguments about homosexuality. Many lesbians see their sexuality both as consciously chosen *and* as reflecting who they truly are.[22] Their lesbianism is a choice, but an erotic choice, not a purely political one, and certainly not arbitrary.

Second, if studies of lesbian lives challenge the notion of clear sexual categories, the existence of bisexuality is even more disruptive. Indeed, bisexuality is so problematic for both heterosexual and gay and lesbian self-understandings that in virtually all arguments about sexual orientation, it is formally acknowledged and then substantively ignored. All the religious liberals, Jewish and non-Jewish, pay their respects to the Kinsey scale and the supposed bisexual potentialities of all human beings—and then proceed to argue on the basis of a binary understanding of sexual orientation as if these did not exist. Moreover, large numbers of bisexuals—including married men who engage in homosexual activity—are labeled as gay in studies of homosexuality, a fact that thoroughly confuses neat categories of any kind.[23] Indeed, the presence of bisexuals in homosexual research samples points to the fundamental methodological absurdity of biological research on homosexuality. By superimposing binary categories on complex data and then taking for granted the question of whose brains or glands will be dissected, such research presupposes what it seeks to explain.

The reason that Matt, Dorff, and others ignore this large body of evidence pointing to the complexity and malleability of human sexual identity is connected to the strengths of their arguments that I outlined before. It is precisely the point of this perspective to leave untapped the potential of gays and lesbians to raise far-reaching questions about the sex-gender system. It is the restrictedness of the arguments that makes them acceptable. Assuming that gays and lesbians are "just like everyone else" except for the quirk of their sexual orientation, the liberal position attempts to normalize them within the framework of a heterosexist system that will now be adjusted at its margins.

This argument ignores the fact, however, that from the perspective of the same heterosexist system, gays and lesbians are *not* like everyone else. Within both the Jewish and U.S. contexts, primary emotional and sexual bonds between women are invisible and unthinkable.[24] Judaism does not condemn sex between women to the same degree as it condemns sex between men because "nothing happens" between women; it is the presence of a man/ penis that defines the possibility of sexual relations.[25] Gay men, while acknowledged to exist, are profoundly threatening, for they expose the erotic underpinnings of the homosocial social order. They challenge the dominant understandings of masculinity and male sexuality, standing in an ambiguous relationship to male privilege.[26] To take gay and lesbian experience seriously, then, rather than incorporating it at the margins of the dominant system, would necessitate raising fundamental questions about a heterosexist, patriarchal social order, about gender roles, and about the fluidity and nature of human sexuality. This larger project, which was initially what the gay liberation movement saw itself as about, is far more threatening to traditional religious values. Yet it also has the potential to begin a conversation that addresses the complexity of people's lives, and that might lead to a new understanding of the nature of eroticism and its relationship to the holy.

Toward a New Perspective

Let me be clear, before I move on, about the limits and intent of my critique of the liberal position. I am quite aware that the danger of the evidence I have cited is that it can be interpreted to mean that all sexuality is fluid on an individual level, and that anyone can at any time choose or be taught to conform to religious norms. This would increase the pressure on gays and lesbians to undergo psychotherapy or other programs for change to bring them into conformity with religious injunctions. But historical and sociological studies that may be quite important and useful on the social level do not explain how individuals come to define themselves in relation to particular sexual categories; nor do they indicate that such categories can be changed according to whim.[27] Thus, I do not want to dispute or diminish the claims of those gays and lesbians who "always knew" that they were gay or lesbian and/or who feel themselves such from birth. My point is to make room for the variety of human sexual experience, to shift the burden of proof from the individual, who must now fit her or his life into a restricted set of sexual narratives, to the categories of sexual self-understanding themselves. *The question then is not, Is this person truly gay or lesbian and thus deserving of acceptance by his/her religious community? but, Where do we get our sexual categories, and what religious, social, political, and economic functions do they serve?*

This is the crucial shift in starting point: from seeking to justify the existence of gays and lesbians within a particular religious framework to seeking to understand—and dismantle—the categories that create the need for such a justification;[28] from seeking to enlarge the umbrella of our sexual categories so that they cover minorities at the margins, to assuming the diversity of human sexuality along many axes and proceeding from there. Lesbians and gay men are not a "them" whose presence needs to be justified; *we* are part of every religious community. We are members and leaders of congregations, parents, children, clergy, laity, active and engaged, bored, angry, and alienated.

Just as Pogo declared, "We have met the enemy and he is us," so gays and lesbians are already part of that "we" that imagines itself as extending (or denying) rights to those "others."[29]

Having said early on that I agree with conservatives that the weight of tradition is against homosexual expression, I am now suggesting that it is the tradition's boundaries and categories that require justification. This shift in perspective is in many respects an extension of feminist arguments I have made throughout my work. First, I would contend that Jewish sexual norms are rooted in concerns about purity, status, and control of women's sexuality that serve the interests of male elites and that have long ceased to reflect the ethical insights or values of contemporary Jews. In this context, the current crisis in traditional sexual standards, of which debates about sexual orientation are only a part, provides an excellent opportunity to expand the range of voices participating in the development of Jewish sexual values, and thus the range of experiential and ethical insight on which the tradition can draw.[30] Second, and I will develop this point further, what we take to be full and authentic tradition is itself shaped from the perspective of the same elites. If we place at the center those the dominant tradition has marginalized or condemned, we broaden our sense of Jewish historical possibilities in which current arguments and judgments are grounded. Third, drawing on a wider range of texts and appealing to Jewish values other than those used to condemn homosexuality, I would argue that starting with the experience of the marginalized is itself thoroughly authorized by Jewish tradition.

Criticizing Compulsory Heterosexuality

This shift from a "gay as other" to a gay-centered perspective does not mark the end of encounter with tradition but rather the beginning. Such an encounter has at least three dimensions, each of which is just in its earliest stages of development. The first is a critical examination and analysis of the ways in which Judaism helps to create and enforce a system of "compulsory heterosexuality."[31] This phrase refers to the complex political and social processes through which a polymorphous human sexuality comes to be channeled and expressed in certain narrow and definite ways. It names the complex web of ideologies and institutions through which people learn how and are made to be heterosexual. Over the course of the last twenty-five years, feminists have shown how gender roles are communicated from birth and enforced by social and ideological structures as diverse as family, peer group, school, medicine, religion, and workplace. Still much less visible are the ways in which expectations of heterosexuality are imparted and maintained through all the same mechanisms. The romantic fairy tales told to children; the grade school readers, even in their multicultural versions; the obsessions of the media; the constant questions, "Do you have a boyfriend/girlfriend yet?" all convey the assumption of heterosexuality, at the same time that social ostracism, beatings, military discharges, psychiatric incarceration, job firing, and the like enforce the boundaries of acceptable behavior, punishing those who fail to get the message and trying to force them back into line. So pervasive is this network of stories, expectations, rewards, and punishments that it is as invisible and taken for granted as the air we breathe.

The analogy between compulsory heterosexuality and gender roles as political and social institutions is not accidental. Gender roles are a mainstay of compulsory heterosexuality and are, in turn, sustained by it. Part of the task of a gay critique of Jewish tradition is to examine the confluence of these themes in Jewish life and sources. Genesis 3:16, for example—"Your desire shall be for your husband and he shall rule over you"—offers a succinct condensation and coupling of compulsory heterosexuality and women's subordination. In these words of God punishing Eve for her role in eating the fruit of the tree of knowledge, her (heterosexual) desire for her husband is clearly linked to her subservience to him.

The few biblical passages dealing directly with homosexuality need to be read in the context of the critique of compulsory heterosexuality. In a situation in which intense political debate over the scanty references to homosexuality has shaped the framework for their interpretation, we need to ask how these texts represent important moments in the construction of heterosexuality. For example, Gary Comstock places the sexual injunctions of Leviticus in the context of a broader program of social control carried on by the priesthood after the exile. Allowed to return to Judah only as dependents on Persian rule, Israel's ruling elites could hope to exercise power only in the religious sphere. Comstock suggests that the whole range of Levitical rules tightly regulating personal behavior and emphasizing divine threats and punishments may have represented an effort on the part of these elites to hold onto power in the one area where they still had some influence.[32] While such a reading does not address the specific import of the prohibition of sex between men, it does draw attention to the relationship between cultural change and anxiety and the effort to maintain boundaries in the sexual arena.

Whatever the original purpose of the biblical condemnations of homosexual behavior, appeals to these passages constitute a major strategy in *contemporary* efforts to enforce compulsory heterosexuality. The whole controversy over the proper interpretation and use of these biblical texts serves to reinforce gay and lesbian marginality and to increase the pressure toward heterosexual dating and marriage. Religious appeals to traditional prohibitions validate and contribute to negative and discriminatory attitudes and behaviors in the larger society.

Broadening the Sources

The second dimension of a gay-centered encounter with tradition involves broadening the sources considered in relation to homosexuality so that the existence of homosexual activity in Jewish history begins to become visible.[33] The purpose of such an approach is not to deny the weight of tradition against homosexuality, but to begin to uncover the more complex reality masked by official opprobrium. It is striking that, until now, those on both sides of the religious debate on homosexuality have generally been satisfied with arguing over a limited number of texts. Even those who seek to show that biblical prohibitions no longer apply rarely consider the possibility of a positive witness to homoeroticism in the stories about David and Jonathan or Naomi and Ruth.[34] It is as if the desire to extend rights to contemporary gays and lesbians does not confer the ability to imagine heroes of the past engaging in same-sex relationships. The tradition is still read through the lenses of presumed heterosexuality, and the mutually exclusive categories of our own society—either homosexual or heterosexual; if homosexual, then not married—make it very difficult to imagine a different past.

The narrowness of the view of Jewish practices that flows from this perspective becomes very clear in relation to later materials. A number of prominent medieval poets, thinkers, and liturgists wrote, among their other works, love poems to young boys. Not only is this material simply unknown to most Jews but also many interpreters have gone to great lengths to deny that the poems are based on actual experience. But even if some of the homoerotic imagery does simply reflect literary convention, the willingness of prominent teachers and poets to use such tropes indicates a greater elasticity in the Jewish sexual ethos than is generally acknowledged.[35] Moreover, the existence of man-boy relationships among Jews is attested in a range of medieval sources, Jewish and non-Jewish. They suggest that in a number of cases in which Jewish men were accused of having sex with boys, the rabbis responded leniently or turned their backs on the evidence.[36] Perhaps, then, the sparseness of halakhic condemnations of homosexuality testifies not so much to the absence of such behavior as to the fact that it was not viewed with much severity. Such recovery of the complexities and contradictions of Jewish sexual attitudes and behaviors is linked to the critique of compulsory heterosexuality, in that naming heterosexuality as an institution is crucial to perceiving the data that might challenge or undermine it.

Creating a New Ethic

The third dimension of encounter with tradition is the creation of a new Jewish sexual ethic. A narrow focus on the issue of homosexual rights, by singling out the behavior of a vulnerable minority, serves to distract attention from the larger crisis in Jewish sexual ethics and the need for a fundamental rethinking of Jewish sexual values. Shifting attention from the acceptability of homosexuality to the constraints and deformations of the traditional ethical system makes it possible and necessary to open up thinking about sexual ethics in at least two ways. First, it becomes possible to articulate a sexual ethic that applies across differences in sexual orientation without advocating some version of heterosexual marriage as a universal norm. And second, it becomes necessary to place sexual values in the context of a larger ethical system. Although those involved in the debate about the appropriate interpretation of normative texts often seem to imply that an adequate sexual ethic must be sought only in those sources that deal directly with sexuality, I maintain that sexual ethics does not constitute a discrete realm.[37] The norms that guide our sexual behavior ought simply to be an extension of those we seek to realize in all relationships with others. The values that might guide our thinking about an inclusive sexual ethic are drawn partly from Jewish tradition, but also represent a counter to tradition and its ethic of domination. These values include justice, mutuality, an expanded notion of generativity, and the value of integrity in sexual expression.

Justice is a central Jewish value, and one that must be reinterpreted and extended in the context of sexual ethics. The importance of justice as a norm is that it pertains not simply to the quality of interpersonal relationships but also to the social system in which they are embedded. As I have argued elsewhere, what takes place in the bedroom can never be separated from the larger social setting of which the bedroom is part.[38] Patterns of domination and injustice in the larger society are both taught and repeated in the family and in intimate relationships, which are often the first schoolhouses for learning domination. While the interdependence of the so-called public and private spheres has ramifications for many dimensions of sexual interaction, it affects gays and lesbians in particular ways. Religious and social condemnation serve to keep people closeted to themselves and to others. They induce people to marry who never should marry. They generate self-doubt and self-contempt that can make healthy relationships difficult or impossible. A common argument against the acceptance of gays and lesbians is that they have difficulty forming enduring relationships. To the distinctly limited extent that this criticism is valid, it does not take account of the complete absence of social supports for gay and lesbian partnerships, and thus the connection of interpersonal difficulties to larger structures of injustice. Insofar as emotional and sexual intimacy are basic human goods, the demands of justice require that the social preconditions for achieving and sustaining intimacy are available to all persons.

Mutuality as a value is connected to justice in that it seeks the equalization of power in relationships, serving as a counter to the ethic of domination that characterizes compulsory heterosexuality. Privileging marriage as the only legitimate avenue of sexual expression makes it difficult to see the extent to which it is bound up with gendered inequalities in power or to evaluate the quality of sexual interactions within the institution of marriage. When two people marry, it is as if a curtain falls on their relationship behind which all behavior is assumed to be unobjectionable. Rising rates of sexual and domestic violence are seldom mentioned in discussions of the sanctity of marriage, nor are religious understandings of marriage examined in terms of their role in the origins of abuse.[39] Gay and lesbian relationships, lacking social and religious legitimacy, less easily fall into preestablished patterns; they must continually invent and reinvent themselves. While this certainly does not mean that all such relationships are models of mutuality, still mutuality is more possible in gay and lesbian relationships than in those that are rooted in socially sanctioned unequal roles. In breaking the links between marriage, gender roles, and the constraint of women's sexuality, gay and lesbian relationships point in the direction of greater mutuality in our intimacy constellations.

Generativity and intergenerational continuity are important Jewish values that are often invoked in condemning homosexuality. A central argument against accepting gay and lesbian relationships is that they are not procreative and thus cannot contribute to ensuring the Jewish future. Since this claim is empirically false, in that many lesbians and gay men do have or seek to have children, a Jewish community worried about the next generation should want to support *all* adults concerned with raising Jewish children. At the same time, however, the growing number of actively involved Jews not living in traditional family constellations argues for a broadening of the concept of generativity.[40] As the tradition has often acknowledged, Jews can contribute in many ways to nurturing the next generation. In fact, a persistent theme in rabbinic texts is the tension between commitment to procreation and family and a total engagement with Torah. The fact that the rabbis were vitally concerned with the reproduction of Torah learning and the raising up of disciples points to the diversity of ways in which Jews have expressed their concern for the future.[41] However generativity is understood, loving sexual relationships can enhance and foster it. By contributing to individual creativity and a general sense of well-being, they strengthen the capacity to make commitments to the next generation, whether these take the form of engaging in larger communal projects or bearing and raising children.[42]

A final value, integrity, may serve to integrate the personal and communal dimensions of sexual ethics. Many years ago, I suggested "integrity" to Hershel Matt as a key third term between his poles of arbitrary choice and constitutional determinism. In using the word, I was groping toward a way of describing gay and lesbian identity that sidestepped the question of causes and origins in favor of the significance and appropriateness of sexual decision making. Mary Hunt has recently advocated the same term as a way beyond the fruitless debates about whether homosexuality is chosen. "Does it make an *ethical* difference," she asks, "if... good things flow from the relationship—people are nurtured, the world is a safer, happier place, energies for justice are harnessed?"[43] Her understanding of integrity is important because, in providing criteria for recognizing ethical sexual choices, it situates the individual firmly in community. Integrity includes both what is synchronous for the individual—"I had to do it for myself"—*and* what spills over into creative involvement in the larger collectivity. I suggest that it is precisely the recognition of this integrity in many Jewishly active and involved gays and lesbians that has precipitated the crisis over homosexuality in the Jewish community and led to the current debates. Perhaps if we focused less on the justification of gay and lesbian existence in relation to certain texts and more on the fruits of sexual relationships for self and community, we would be better able to address the real problems of domination and abuse that characterize all too many sexual relationships, and at the same time encourage the intimacy and mutuality that distinguish holy sexuality.

Authority, Resistance, and Transformation

Jewish Feminist Reflections on Good Sex

This essay was originally written as part of an interreligious, intercultural project on feminist perspectives on good sex in the world religions.

The effort to develop feminist accounts of good sex within the context of patriarchal religious traditions raises a host of methodological problems. The very formulation of the project recognizes the tensions between feminism as a social movement committed to the liberation of women from all forms of oppression, and the direction and intention of traditions that have contributed directly and indirectly to women's subordination and marginalization in religion and society. The Good Sex project begins from the reality that women have rarely participated in the formulation of sexual norms and values in the major world religions, and that religious sexual values have seldom been conducive to the health or well-being of women.[1] In bringing together a group of women connected to different traditions, the project seeks to create a space in which the participants can "think new thoughts," reflecting on sexuality from the perspective of the concerns and experiences of women in our cultures. But at the same time, it assumes that these new thoughts will somehow remain in relation to the religions being transformed and will possibly authenticate themselves through connection to neglected or dissident strands within those religions.[2] The project thus immediately becomes entangled in fundamental questions about how feminists argue for and make change, especially when the changes envisioned may radically challenge central elements of tradition.

Defining the Questions

My interest in this essay is not so much in defining good sex from a Jewish feminist perspective as in thinking about how to think about the issue. As a

Jewish feminist theologian, I find that the task of transforming Jewish sexual norms raises questions about authority that I must sort out before I can begin to think substantively about the characteristics of good sex. The Jewish feminist movement in the United States has flourished in the context of a decentralized, remarkably diverse Jewish community, in which there are many competing visions of the nature of Judaism and many opportunities to shape Jewish life in new directions. In a situation in which the great majority of U.S. Jews have rejected or are redefining elements of traditional Jewish belief and practice, the issue of authority is crucial and has implications well beyond the area of sexuality.[3] The question of how to ground and argue for criticisms or constructive reworkings of religious tradition is pressing for any theology or group that does not simply assume the validity of traditional sources of authority, such as Scripture, revelation, or centralized religious leadership.[4] Yet, because sexual control of women is such a key element in broader patriarchal control, the topic of sexuality raises the issue of authority with particular vividness and urgency. On what basis can feminists advocate particular visions of sexuality in ways that will prove intelligible and convincing to others?

The problem of authority arises for feminists as soon as we begin to challenge any aspect of the status and role of women. Once we acknowledge the possibility of deeply questioning any element of tradition, we seem to undermine the hope of religious certainty at a level that goes far beyond the specific issue at hand. However narrow the grounds for a particular criticism—and feminist criticisms of the treatment of women and religious sexual values are in fact deep and wide-ranging—rejecting any element of tradition throws all the rest into question. This is because, however much feminists still may value certain insights and perspectives we glean from our traditions, we no longer value them simply because they are there. Rather, we are confronted with having to self-consciously appropriate and reappropriate from the conflicted strands within each tradition those that make sense and bear fruit in our own lives, finding ways to explain our choices that make sense both to ourselves and to others. Logically, we cannot have it both ways. We cannot both deny the authority of religious tradition where it negates our feminist values and, at the same time, build on that authority where it seems to support those values.

A lot of recent scholarship on Jewish attitudes toward sexuality intensifies this issue of authority in that it highlights the tensions and disagreements within Jewish tradition, denying the reality of any unitary perspective.[5] Such a move is enormously helpful in deconstructing fundamentalist appeals to religious authority, in that it makes clear that all claims to authority involve selectivity, that Jewish tradition by no means speaks on sexuality with a self-evident, unambiguous voice. This scholarship is also useful to feminist re-constructions of religion, in that it surfaces minority or dissident viewpoints in the Jewish past that may counter dominant perspectives on issues of sexual values. At the same time, however, in dissolving the purported unity of Jew-ish tradition into a series of dissonant and ever-shifting strands, it increases the difficulty of arguing for the priority or authority of one strand over any other. Jewish tradition—like all religious traditions—is characterized by continual contesting of key issues, issues which are in turn continually redefined in different geographic locations and different historical contexts. Notions of authority are also continually reinterpreted in accordance with the outcome of such contests. Claiming the authority of a specific strand, then, is not a matter of identifying the essential and authentic voice of *the* Jewish tradition. Rather, it is part of a contest in our own time over which voices claiming to speak for tradition will prove compelling to a significant proportion of the Jewish people.

The complex and contradictory nature of Jewish teachings on sexuality, moreover, points to another problem in privileging neglected, positive themes within Jewish tradition. All too often in feminist discussion, high-lighting the liberating elements of a tradition as its authoritative voice in-volves disregarding the strands that have been oppressive. The troublesome aspects of a tradition do not disappear, however, simply because we ignore them, but are left to shape consciousness and affect hearts and minds. Thus, appealing to the first creation story, in which male and female are made in God's image, and ignoring the second, in which woman is made from man, leaves intact the latter account to be used by others as a continuing justifica-tion for the subordination of women. Similarly, appealing to those elements in Judaism that honor the importance of married sex as a value in its own right apart from procreation, while neglecting the ways in which even mar-ried sex is restricted and controlled, allows the sexual control of women to continue unexamined as part of the fabric of Jewish marriage. But if one does acknowledge and attempt to grapple with the oppressive aspects of a tradition, the question inevitably arises as to the grounds on which its nonoppressive elements can be considered more fundamental.

A final problem relating to authority concerns the sources that are relevant in thinking about the subject of sexuality. Given that any reconstruction of tradition necessarily selects from the conflicting voices on a particular issue, still, what texts are even germane to a consideration of this topic? It is striking that, when issues of sexuality are discussed in religious contexts, a handful of texts are often cited and argued about over and over, as if they were the only sources relevant to shaping norms around sexual behavior. In the Jewish community, debates around homosexuality have often revolved around two verses in Leviticus and rabbinic commentary on them, while Christians add to the scanty resources in the Hebrew Bible a third verse in Romans. This approach ignores the host of other injunctions in the Bible and rabbinic tradition about forming ethical relationships, creating community, and ensuring social justice. It fails to view sexuality as just one dimension of human relationship, embedded in a constellation of familial, interpersonal, and communal connections that shape, support, or deform it. Instead, sexuality is seen as a peculiar problem for ethics, a discrete and troublesome domain requiring unique regulation. In addition to confronting problems around grounding sexual values, therefore, feminist accounts of sexuality also need to locate the issue in a larger social context. Building on the early feminist insight that the personal is the political, feminists need to insist that good sex on the interpersonal level is possible only in the context of just social, political, and economic relations.[6]

Thinking about Compulsory Heterosexuality

I would like to illustrate the ways in which some of these issues concerning authority come into play in relation to a particular dimension of sexuality, by reflecting on compulsory heterosexuality within the Jewish tradition as a barrier to good sex. I choose to focus on a central oppressive element in my tradition rather than on some emancipatory theme, because I believe that it is the negative aspects of tradition that most profoundly shape women's current sexual situation, and that most require attention and transformation. In my view, the starting point for feminists in thinking about good sex must be resistance. Feminists must begin by examining and dismantling the institutions that stand in the way of women even imagining fully our needs and desires.

The concept of "compulsory heterosexuality," which Adrienne Rich placed on the U.S. feminist agenda through her well-known essay on the topic, refers to the complex social and political processes through which people learn how and are made to be heterosexual.[7] The first and simplest way in which heterosexuality is made compulsory is that other modes of sexual expression are forbidden on pain of punishment or death. Such a prohibition on male/male anal intercourse appears in Leviticus 18:22 and 20:13 and forms the starting point for all Jewish discussion of homosexuality—as well as Jewish gay and lesbian resistance to traditional attitudes toward homosexuality. Although lesbianism is not mentioned explicitly in the Bible, the rabbis find a reference to it in Leviticus 18:3: "You shall not copy the practices of the land of Egypt...or the land of Canaan." They interpret the practices in question as a man marrying a man and a woman marrying a woman. Both the Palestinian and Babylonian Talmuds also contain brief discussions of whether women who " 'rub' with each other" are considered to have committed an illicit sexual act and are therefore forbidden to marry a priest.[8] The rabbis' consensus that such acts are "mere licentiousness," that is, not real sex, and therefore not disqualifying, reveals another weapon in the arsenal of compulsory heterosexuality: rendering sex between women invisible by defining it as impossible.[9]

While contemporary Jewish debates about homosexuality generally revolve rather narrowly around these verses in Leviticus and the few rabbinic sources interpreting them, I find this material less useful for understanding heterosexuality as an institution than the pervasive assumption in biblical and rabbinic texts that heterosexual marriage is the norm for adult life. In getting at this larger context of Jewish attitudes toward marriage and family relations, Genesis 3:16—"Your desire shall be for your husband and he shall rule over you"—is far more revealing than Leviticus 18 and 20, because it names the connection between gender complementarity, compulsory heterosexuality, and the subordination of women. Gayle Rubin, in her classic essay "The Traffic in Women," argues that, in traditional societies, the social organization of sex is built on the links between "gender roles, obligatory heterosexuality and the constraint of female sexuality."[10] Gender roles guarantee that the smallest viable social unit will consist of one man and one woman whose desire must be directed toward each other, at the same time that men have rights to exchange their female kin and control their wives in marriage that women do not have either in themselves or in men.

Genesis 3:16–19, which describes God's punishments of Adam and Eve for eating the fruit of the tree of knowledge, offers a remarkably condensed and powerful statement of the connections laid out by Rubin. In increasing Eve's pain in childbearing and punishing Adam with having to sweat and toil to gain his bread, God assumes or ordains differentiated gender roles and, at the same time, defines them asymmetrically. Eve's (heterosexual) desire for her husband will keep her tied to childbearing, despite its painfulness, and will allow him to "rule over" her. My point is not that compulsory heterosexuality as a Jewish institution is rooted in this story, but rather that this myth of origins provides a lens for examining interrelationships that are spelled out at length in Jewish narrative and law. In the Jewish case, as in the traditional societies Rubin discusses, rigid gender roles support the channeling of sex in marriage. A man who is not married (the texts speak from a male perspective) is seen as less than whole, for only a man and woman together constitute the image of God. The extensive laws regulating women's sexuality and placing it under the control of fathers or husbands ensure that women will be available for marriage to men who can be fairly certain that their wife's sexuality belongs only to them.

In a context in which good sex is defined as sex that is under male control, the question of what constitutes good sex from women's perspectives simply cannot be asked within the framework of the system. For the Bible and for the rabbis, good sex is sex that supports and serves a patriarchal social order. The so-called divinely ordained laws concerning marriage and divorce, adultery, rape, and so on, allow for the regular and orderly transfer of women from the homes of fathers to the homes of husbands, or, if need be, from one husband to another. Women's fears, desires, and preferences, their efforts to find meaning in or to resist this legislation, are nonissues and "nondata" that are also nonsense in the context of the rabbinic worldview.[11] As Rachel Adler points out in a powerful article about women's role in the Jewish covenant community, the categories of a system of thought determine the questions it can ask, allowing it to pile up huge amounts of information on certain questions while rendering others invisible. The problems that receive extensive attention in Jewish law are the "status problems of marriage, desertion, divorce and *chalitzah* [levirate marriage] which the tradition itself created and from whose consequences it now seeks to 'protect' women, since by its own rules they can never protect themselves."[12] Insofar as the rabbis do attempt to "protect" women—by trying to find ways to get a husband to divorce his wife if she so desires, for example—they indicate some awareness of the limits and injustices of the system they have created and, in this sense, offer some resources for criticism. But insofar as they are willing to address these injustices only within the framework of the system that gives rise to them, they close off any possibility of women entering as subjects and reframing the issues in genuinely new terms.

As Rubin's analysis suggests, however, control of women's sexuality is just one dimension of the institution of compulsory heterosexuality, which is also spelled out in halakhah (Jewish law) in terms of property rights, work roles, and religious obligations and exemptions. In her book on the construction of gender in Roman-period Judaism, Miriam Peskowitz examines a Mishnaic passage that shows the rabbis in the act of extending a husband's power over the property his wife acquired before marriage, so that, while the wife may continue to own property, the husband controls it and is entitled to the profits that flow from it.[13] In their ensuing debate about the validity of this legal innovation, the rabbis presuppose that a man has authority over his wife. What they need to determine is the extent of that authority in the sphere of property ownership, much as in other contexts they will discuss a husband's power over his wife's sexuality. The conversation, Peskowitz argues, reveals that there are many nodes "in the construction of sexual difference," sexual control constituting only one area in which marriage allows a man to "rule over" his wife.[14]

The Jewish division of religious labor also presupposes and helps construct a social structure in which heterosexual marriage is the norm. The exemption of women from positive time-bound commandments—in particular, set times for daily prayer—assumes that they are involved in household obligations that are their first responsibility and priority. In caring for small children, observing the rules of *kashrut* (dietary laws), and preparing for holy days by cooking special foods and making their homes ready, women free men for their own prayer and Torah study and enable them to observe the dietary laws and the Sabbath and holidays fully. For their part, women need men to take the ritual roles in the home that they themselves are neither obligated nor educated to assume. In other words, the whole series of laws that exclude women from public religious life, laws that Jewish feminists have analyzed and criticized from the perspective of women's spiritual disempowerment, are also part of the system of compulsory heterosexuality. That system is not just about sex, but also about the organization of daily life around gender-role differentiation and the power of men over women.

Because compulsory heterosexuality is interstructured with a whole network of sexual, social, economic, and religious relations in Jewish law, creating the preconditions for good sex cannot end with questioning the few biblical and rabbinic passages on same-sex relationships. The material on such relationships is scanty and specific, so that those advocating expanded rights for gays and lesbians have been able to challenge it from a number of directions. Are other forms of male sexual interaction, other than anal intercourse, forbidden by Leviticus?[15] Did the Torah or the rabbis have any concept of homosexuality as an orientation, or were they condemning homosexual acts performed by heterosexuals?[16] While such critical questions are important and useful in trying to gain acceptance for gays and lesbians within the framework of Jewish law, they never step outside that framework to confront the broader system of compulsory heterosexuality. That system controls and marginalizes all women, whether or not they are heterosexual, and whether or not they are married. It also makes illegitimate any sexual or life choice outside of heterosexual marriage, so that self-pleasuring, celibacy, singleness, cohabitation without marriage, et cetera, all constitute forms of resistance to compulsory heterosexuality.[17]

Once one begins to see the relationship between compulsory heterosexuality and sexism in its myriad forms, however, the questions about authority that I raised in the first part of this essay return in all their power. How does one question this central aspect of Jewish tradition and still remain in relation to the tradition? Are there voices in traditional Jewish texts that dissent from or reveal fractures in this system, and on what basis can they be mobilized? Where do I, where does any contemporary feminist critic, stand in even raising these questions?

Starting Points

I would argue that the feminist critic must begin, not by allying herself with dissenting voices within her tradition, but by questioning the authority of tradition, resisting any framework that leaves no room for women's agency, and then proceeding to transform tradition by placing women at the center.[18] Feminism begins in resistance and vision, a resistance and vision that are not simply personal but that are rooted in "communities of resistance and solidarity" that are challenging specific forms of oppression out of concrete experiences of alternative ways of being in the world.[19] Thus, the feminist and the lesbian, gay, and bisexual movements have allowed women to feel the power and potential of bonds between women; to experience an intimacy, sexual and otherwise, that often has been trivialized or undermined; and to claim our power as agents to participate fully in society and religious communities on terms that we define. This experience of the power of being, as Mary Daly described it early on, over against the institutions that have consigned women to nonbeing, does not of itself threaten these institutions or render them harmless, but it does provide starting points for imagining a different future and criticizing the forces that stand in its way.[20] To my mind, this experience, rather than any dissident strands within patriarchal religion, is the authoritative foundation of resistance and transformation. Given the conflicting voices within any normative text, the decision to claim such strands must come out of some experience of their greater power to support fullness of life for a larger group of people. Out of participation in a community of resistance and transformation, one then looks for and consciously claims the resistive elements in a particular tradition, in order to mobilize them toward a different future.[21]

What does this mean and not mean in relation to compulsory heterosexuality? Beyond the dimension of critique, which I see as central to a feminist appropriation of tradition, there are several ways in which feminists can find resources for resistance and transformation within our religious traditions. One is by deliberately allying ourselves with the self-critical strands in texts that have been understood as normative. In her early and influential reinterpretation of Genesis 2–3, Phyllis Trible pointed out that the explicit statement in Genesis 3:16 that a woman's "desire shall be for her husband, and he shall rule over [her]" occurs in the context of divine punishment for disobedience. Remarkably for a patriarchal society, the story does not depict women's subordination as natural and divinely ordained, but as a perversion of the created order that is a result of sin. Trible thus reads this story not as *pre*scribing male supremacy but as *de*scribing it, not as legitimating but as condemning it.[22] For her, the insight that male supremacy is a distortion of creation constitutes the true meaning of the biblical text, which thus stands over against patriarchy.

Given that the description of compulsory heterosexuality is part of the same passage, one could make a similar move, arguing that this aspect of social life too appears under the sign and judgment of sinfulness. But aside from the fact that such an approach would ignore Genesis 1, in which male and female together constitute the image of God, there are deeper problems with claiming to have found the true meaning of any biblical text. Just as every text was written in a specific historical, social, and religious context, so texts are interpreted in particular contexts that give rise to particular exegetical needs.

The current desire to find an underlying nonsexist or nonheterosexist vision in Scripture comes out of a political and religious situation in which various forms of fundamentalism are on the rise all over the globe and are attempting to tighten control over every area of women's lives. In the United States, the Christian Right has claimed the mantle of Christian authenticity, equating authenticity with control of sexuality and women, and the same dynamic is taking place within Judaism. As contemporary Judaism has become increasingly diverse and fragmented, issues of sexuality and women's roles have become battlegrounds for arguments about Jewish legitimacy. In a religious context in which the reactionary side of an increasingly heated debate claims divine authority for its position, it is tempting to argue that the essence or fundamental core of the tradition supports a progressive stance. But this is finally to get into an irresolvable shouting match in which each party claims God on its side. It also means that feminists accept in principle the authority of texts that are at many points antithetical to women's power and agency, and that can be used against the feminist cause as easily as for it.

Although the difference may be subtle, I see the claim to have discovered the authentic meaning of a tradition as different from self-consciously drawing on the dissident voices within it, while grounding oneself in a community that is actively working to create a Jewish future in which women are full Jews and full persons. For the purposes of resistance, it can be strategically useful to point to the contradictions or moments of self-criticism within normative texts, showing how opposing positions can be justified on the basis of the same sources. Yet it is not useful to argue about which position is finally more authentic. From the perspective of the texts, the question of authenticity has no meaning; the texts encompass genuine disagreements. The argument over texts is in reality an argument over competing social visions. Whose version of the future will hold sway? Who will have the right to determine the distribution of society's goods and resources, to say whether a given social or religious system meets basic human needs? Precisely because this is the real issue in question, however, it is important to highlight the dissident strands within a sacred text in order to crack open or challenge dominant religious and social perspectives and thus enlarge the space for change. From this point of view, it is useful to notice that women's subordination is conjoined with heterosexuality in the context of punishment for sin, not because this renders invalid two thousand years of sexist and heterosexist readings, but because it helps us to imagine an alternative future.

A second way to mobilize resources for resistance and change is to look at Jewish sources with an eye to the historical possibilities that they simultaneously conceal and reveal, so that one can make visible the existence of "forbidden" sexual practices or transgressive gender relations.[23] Thus, for example, the same rabbinic passages that can be read as denying the possibility of sexual activity between women can also be seen as acknowledging the existence of such activity, but regarding it as inconsequential. When the rabbis discussed the question of whether a woman who "rubs" with another woman is permitted to marry a priest, they may have been aware of the female ho-

moeroticism amply attested in Roman sources but seen it as not worth punishing.[24] From this perspective, the relative silence of Jewish tradition regarding both female and male homoerotic behavior may be construed as a form
of permission. To take this view is not to deny the importance of heterosexuality as an ideology and an institution, but it is to suggest that behavior that
did not threaten heterosexual marriage may not have been regarded with
much severity.[25] Reading Jewish texts in light of what we know of cultural attitudes and practices at the time they were written begins to uncover the complex historical reality masked by an exclusive focus on official prohibitions. It
also broadens the sense of historical possibilities on which feminists can draw
in seeking to transform the tradition in the present.

Still a third strategy of resistance and transformation that is especially
important in dealing with issues of sexuality involves broadening the context
of teachings on sexuality by looking at them through the lens of attitudes toward social justice. Rabbi Lisa Edwards, in a sermon on the Torah portions
that contain Leviticus 18 and 20, argued as follows:

> We are your gay and lesbian children: "You must not seek vengeance,
> nor bear a grudge against the children of your people" (Lev. 19:18);
> we are your lesbian mothers and gay fathers: "Revere your mother
> and your father, each of you" (19:3)...; we are the stranger: "You
> must not oppress the stranger. You shall love the stranger as yourself
> for you were strangers in the land of Egypt" (19:34).[26]

In reading the prohibitions against male/male sex in the context of surrounding injunctions about just social relations, Edwards risks getting drawn
into arguments about which is the more fundamental or essential dimension
of the tradition. But by focusing on broader social justice themes, she also
makes the critical point that any choice of sources in a debate about the
meaning and intent of tradition always involves selecting from conflicting
perspectives. Moreover, she places the biblical passages on homosexuality in
the context of gay and lesbian communities of resistance, focusing on the in-
terconnections between sexual ideologies and social injustice, rather than on
private sexual behavior.

Resistance and Transformation

I began this essay by raising issues of authority and tradition, and the authority of tradition in thinking about good sex. To what extent can we ground ourselves in the positive resources in our traditions in thinking about good sex? How do we justify the choices that we make in lifting up certain strands within Jewish tradition and repudiating others? I have argued that the authority for singling out the self-critical and dissident elements in our textual traditions comes not from the traditions themselves, but rather from the new possibilities envisioned and created by the particular communities of solidarity and resistance in which we participate. As I reflect on the Good Sex group itself as one such community, I am struck by the extent to which our initial work together provides us with methodological clues for approaching our common project. Brought together to think constructively about good sex from our perspectives as women, we found ourselves focusing again and again on the ideologies and institutions that stand in the way of good sex in our different cultures. We began, in other words, from a stance of resistance, realizing that the first task in creating a space for good sex is addressing the many injustices that make good sex unimaginable for many of the women in the world. We also, however, spoke of resources in our own experiences, in our cultures, and, occasionally, in our religious traditions that provide us with glimpses of a sexuality and sensuality that we would like to make more possible, both in our own lives and the lives of others. We repeatedly returned to these glimpses to authorize ourselves as we sought to find our way between most women's current sexual reality, and what we hope will someday be. Struggling with this gulf, both in our social institutions and our religious traditions, we look for energy and insight not only, and not primarily, in the positive strands of our religious traditions, but in our communities of resistance and transformation.

Speaking of Sex

Authority and the Denominational Documents

Beginning in the early 1990s, the Reform, Reconstructionist, and Conservative movements within Judaism began creating a series of documents on questions of sexual ethics. Varying in specificity and scope, the documents all seek to guide U.S. Jews as they negotiate between the traditional Jewish expectation that heterosexual marriage is the only appropriate model for adult life and the norms and practices of a sexually diverse and permissive contemporary culture. While the statements' substantive teachings about sex are interesting and worthy of careful examination, the documents are also significant for the ways in which they negotiate the vexed relationship between tradition and modernity. In this essay, I use the denominational statements to explore the problem of authority, examining the ways in which the documents both address and repeatedly sidestep this crucial issue.

The Issue of Authority

Questions of sexuality pose in an especially clear and vivid way a pervasive issue in contemporary Jewish life—namely that of authority. The great majority of Jews in the United States, including those for whom Jewish texts, practices, and values have significant meaning, inhabit multiple worlds and define themselves in relation to a variety of communities. At once Jews and Americans, they are also shaped by work and political commitments, class and national origin, sexual choices, and particular cultural tastes. In the arena of sexuality, they are subjected to a wide range of competing voices, from the sexual laws of Leviticus that form an important part of the Jewish liturgical cycle to the pervasive depiction of casual sex in advertisements, films, and television. These different messages and aspects of identity can be difficult to reconcile. Why should one accept the traditional Jewish insistence on the importance of marriage and family in a world in which sexual and interpersonal values are rapidly changing? Should one marry relatively young and have children in conformity with traditional Jewish norms or enact some of the many possibilities available in the culture—launching a career, traveling, or exploring a variety of relationships? Is it possible to spend many years of one's adult life as a single person—as is the case with many Jews and other Americans—and find a place in a community still often oriented around the model of the heterosexual nuclear family? Can lesbian, gay, bisexual, and transgendered Jews find a comfortable place in a Jewish community in which nontraditional sexual choices are often either rejected or rendered invisible?

The abyss between traditional sexual norms and contemporary sexual behaviors poses the problem of authority with particular urgency, but the issue underlies every religious accommodation to modernity.[1] As individual Jews modify traditional Sabbath observance, they need to wrestle with how to justify holding onto elements of Jewish law that enhance their experience of rest while jettisoning others that feel irrelevant or not doable. Or in relation to the dietary laws, they may find themselves uncomfortable with the seeming arbitrariness of keeping a kosher home but eating *treif* (nonkosher food) out, or ordering French fries but not meat cooked in a restaurant. No longer able simply to assume the validity of traditional sources of authority such as Scripture, revelation, or centralized religious leadership, Jews today need repeatedly to balance full citizenship in the contemporary world with loyalty to Jewish tradition. To what extent are the Jewish people bound by the values of the past? How can Jews know what values are too fundamental to be surrendered? What gives any Jew the right to criticize a religious tradition that claims a divine origin, and that, at the minimum, represents the accumulated wisdom of many centuries? What do Jews do when, as often happens, Jewish tradition itself speaks with many voices on a particular subject? What weight should Jews give to our own contemporary experiences? What happens when aspects of contemporary experience seem to offer a richer moral vision than that found in Jewish tradition?

The need to make decisions among competing values can be uncomfortable and unsettling, precisely because there are no absolute and universal guidelines for deciding what parts of tradition continue to be meaningful and which belong to earlier eras. I have often had students complain that the notion of selecting practices and values from the complex mix of tradition feels capricious and arbitrary. To be consistent, they argue, one should either fully embrace a traditional Jewish life or renounce Jewish practice completely. Yet much in Jewish tradition adds richness and depth to human existence. Why should Jews turn our backs on tradition if we cannot accept it whole? Rather than set up false choices, we need to ask where the tradition continues to be meaningful and where it fails to speak to the realities of contemporary life or makes demands that are undoable or unethical. Constructing a life means making difficult decisions, appropriating and reappropriating from the conflicted strands within tradition those that make sense and bear fruit individually and communally. Communal and individual identities are partly constituted by the ways in which we explain our choices, making sense of them for ourselves and others.

I would contend that the process of selecting from and recreating tradition is central to the way in which Judaism evolves. *Individuals* can escape the necessity of making choices by accepting once and for all the interpretative structures of particular communities. This does not make the process of meaning-making any less human, however. It just entails surrendering the power of decision to communal authorities who maintain the right to ongoing interpretation. When, in the aftermath of the destruction of the second Temple, the rabbis became the founders of a new Judaism based on prayer and study, they traced their authority back to Moses on Mount Sinai. "Moses received the Torah from Sinai," they said, "and transmitted it to Joshua, and Joshua to the Elders, and the Elders to the Prophets, and the Prophets handed it down to the members of the Great Assembly," the immediate predecessors of the rabbis.[2] Subsequent interpreters linked themselves to this same chain of transmission, locating their authority in earlier generations, who were always seen as more creditable than those who came later.

These claims to authority grounded a coherent and self-sustaining system whose legitimacy seemed self-evident when viewed from within. Studies of early rabbinic Judaism, however, suggest the incomplete and fragmentary nature of rabbinic authority and the diversity of beliefs and practices existing in the ancient Jewish world. It is not clear who sought and submitted to rabbinic rulings or how large the rabbis' circle of authority was beyond themselves. When the rabbis offered new interpretations of the rules governing sexuality, sacrifices, or the Sabbath, they were as much attempting to develop and consolidate their authority and worldview as legislating for people who accepted these things in advance. The rabbinic recitation of a direct lineage back to Sinai constituted their foundational claim to authority, but it was then tested and put into practice in hundreds of small decisions in which the rabbis created new forms of Jewish practice and belief and attempted to make rulings that would be recognized by (at least some segment of) the Jewish community. As the rabbis discussed the distribution of marital property, for example, strengthening the husband's power over his wife's possessions, or as they created elaborate rules for modest female sexual behavior, they created facts on the ground that were ultimately accepted as authoritative components of the rabbinic system.[3] Sexual legislation was one vehicle for claiming authority not yet fully achieved. Over and over again, the rabbis selected certain potentialities within a complex tradition and then legitimized their choices by depicting them as flowing from a tradition speaking in an unambiguous voice. In this way, Jewish tradition is continually sifted and redefined through appeals to sources of authority that are simultaneously created and consolidated in every individual moment of decision.

The idea that all claims to authority involve picking and choosing, and, through that process, producing new interpretations, has important implications for sexual ethics. It suggests that shaping a sexual ethic is not simply a matter of identifying the essential and authentic voice of "the" Jewish tradition. It is also, and more importantly, an imaginative project that incorporates individual and communal choices. It involves bringing contemporary questions and concerns into engagement with Jewish texts, traditions, laws, and practices, and selecting and reconfiguring elements of tradition so as to address those current concerns. The notion of imagination does not do away with the need to explain and justify criteria of selection, but it does make it impossible to avoid a circular relationship between the substance of particular arguments and the concepts of authority in which they are grounded. When the rabbis expanded husbands' rights over their wives' property, for example, they strengthened notions of male control that they already took for granted. When non-Orthodox Jews appeal to the authority of Leviticus in rejecting gay and lesbian commitment ceremonies but ignore its injunctions in other areas, they already determine the outcome of their deliberations through the ways they invoke authority. To claim the authority of specific strands of Jewish tradition on issues of sexuality is not to settle matters of truth but to enter into passionate arguments over who has the right to speak for tradition and how tradition is defined. It is part of making a case that will prove compelling to a significant proportion of the Jewish people and thus help to shape future Jewish behaviors and values.

The Denominational Documents

The necessity of continually constructing and reconstructing tradition through particular ethical choices is well illustrated by the denominational documents on sexuality, which both explicitly address the issue of authority and repeatedly obfuscate and evade it. On the one hand, the authors of the documents are acutely aware that any attempt to formulate sexual norms in the contemporary situation involves taking a stand on the questions of the authority of Torah and the nature of Jewish loyalty to received traditions.[4] The debate about sexual values is at its very heart a debate about authority. On the other hand, at crucial points, the documents make assumptions about the nature of Judaism and Jewish attitudes toward sex that conceal or finesse the choices of the authors and the ways in which they invoke the authority of tradition, and that thus depict certain ethical judgments as Jewishly inevitable. Examining these documents will allow me to elaborate on the significance and difficulty of the issue of authority and the importance of confronting it directly.

The reports prepared by the Conservative, Reconstructionist, and Reform movements on the subject of sexuality fall into two basic groups: those that deal specifically with homosexuality and those that address a variety of sexual questions. As increasing numbers of Jewishly involved gays and lesbians have come out within their congregations, schools, and summer camps over the past three decades, the liberal movements have begun to reexamine traditional teachings on homosexuality and to ask whether they are still authoritative. While the issue of homosexuality has in many ways served as a lightening rod deflecting attention from the larger breakdown of traditional sexual values, it has also provided an entry point for more far-reaching re-consideration of issues concerning sexuality. The Reform and Conservative movements, after extensive debate about homosexuality within their law committees, went on to issue general statements on sexual ethics. In the context of the Conservative debate in 1991–92, for example, Eliot Dorff called for a movement-wide discussion of sexual norms as they affect all Jews.[5] The Conservative rabbinical school and the synagogue arm of the movement declined to participate in such a conversation, but the rabbinical association set up a commission, and Dorff drafted a substantial statement on sexuality that was released in 1996.[6] At roughly the same time, the Central Conference of American Rabbis (CCAR; the Reform rabbinic organization) established an Ad Hoc Committee on Human Sexuality that gave a brief report to the CCAR convention in 1998.[7] The Reconstructionist movement wrote a report on "Homosexuality and Judaism" in 1993 that located the movement's stance in the context of a general consideration of Jewish and contemporary ethical values, addressing broader issues of sexual norms at the same time that it focused on homosexuality.[8] I will examine these general statements, including the Reconstructionist report, looking at how they grapple with and avoid problems of authority.

In seeking to provide guidance to contemporary Jews as they think about sexual questions, all the documents locate sexual ethics in the context of an ethics of relationship. They begin by laying out basic Jewish values that should be present in all human interactions and only then proceed to particular sexual issues. The Reform Ad Hoc Committee report, for example, opens by acknowledging that the value system of many liberal Jews is based on secular norms. But it argues that Judaism can speak meaningfully to many areas of life, including intimate relationships, and it offers *shleimut*—"wholeness, completeness, unity and peace"—as the overarching value to be realized in sexual relationships. This value entails a number of others: the dignity of humans as creatures made in the image of God, truth, health, covenant, holiness, and so on.[9] The Reconstructionist report lays out fifteen enduring Jewish and Western values ranging from human dignity and equality to democracy, in the light of which specific teachings on sexuality are to be examined and assessed.[10] And Eliot Dorff, writing for the Conservative Commission, discusses nine central Jewish values, including the notion of human beings as integrated wholes, creation in the image of God, respect for others, honesty, and holiness.[11]

Once they have laid out these overarching values, the reports proceed very differently. Discussion of "Reform Jewish sexual values" constitutes virtually the whole of the Reform document, which has just a brief conclusion stating that these values can be present in same-gender relationships. The Reconstructionist statement moves from discussion of fundamental values to an examination of Jewish sources on homosexuality, using the overarching values to evaluate the moral authority of traditional teachings on same-gender relationships. The Conservative letter, after its treatment of basic values, offers a detailed discussion of marital and nonmarital sex, as well as a summary of the movement's statements on homosexuality. The internal structure of the documents and their relationship to each other raise a number of interesting questions about how one decides what values are Jewish and which Jewish values are authoritative in the contemporary context. Partly because the documents are necessarily selective in the issues they consider, the complexities of the problem of authority emerge sharply.

To begin with, it is not clear how the statements choose from all "Jewish values" precisely those that should shape contemporary sexual ethics. Because only some of the discrepancies among the three lists seem to reflect denominational differences, it appears that the movements are guided in their choice of values by assumptions that they never discuss or name. When, for example, the Reconstructionist report talks about equality, personal freedom, Jewish continuity and adaptability, and democracy, it is obviously expressing the movement's commitment to incorporate what it sees as positive contemporary values into the Jewish people's evolving self-understanding. This approach is very different from that of the Conservative movement, which explicitly describes itself as trying to "present the thrust of the Jewish tradition . . . in a way which is as open and contemporary as possible."[12] Since it is not trying to break new ground, the Conservative document affirms only those values that it sees as firmly rooted in traditional Jewish sources. But even focusing on traditional values leaves a lot of room for selectivity. All the documents espouse the values of human dignity and integrity as created in the image of God, love, health and safety, holiness, and, in somewhat different contexts, family and childrearing. The Reform and Conservative statements, however—but not the Reconstructionist—list modesty and truth or honesty, while the Reform and Reconstructionist statements—but not the Conservative—list justice and joy. Since *all* of these values can be found in Jewish sources, however, one can only guess at why each movement lifts up some and not others. Is modesty too old-fashioned a value for the Reconstructionists? Is joy at odds with the tone of moderation that characterizes the Conservative letter? The selection of values that are to be perceived as valuable is a defining ethical moment for each statement, yet none of them is forthcoming about how this selection was made.

A second set of important questions concerning authority is whether broad statements of value provide sufficient guidance in thinking about sexuality, and how they are related to more specific norms. In general, the values proposed by the denominational documents are difficult to fault. Few people are against love, or human dignity, or holiness, or family. But such basic values are shared by individuals and groups who would disagree deeply on what it might mean actually to live them out in relationships, or on where and to whom they apply. The real judgments about what values take priority in concrete situations become clear only in relation to particular questions. And while the Reconstructionists explicitly assign basic values priority over legal rulings that they see as out of tune with the modern temper, the Reform and Conservative movements are inconsistent in the extent to which they choose between general values and material norms.

The report of the Reform movement's Ad Hoc Committee on Human Sexuality, for example, entirely contradicts an earlier decision of the same organization's law committee about lesbian and gay commitment ceremonies because the two groups appeal to different Jewish norms. The Ad Hoc Committee document consists of little besides a statement of values, but it concludes with the observation that the presence of core Jewish values in committed, same-gender relationships means that such relationships between two Jews are worthy of ritual recognition.[13] The majority of the Responsa Committee, on the other hand, finds it impossible to extend the concept of marriage to gays and lesbians because such relationships plainly violate the biblically prescribed boundaries of permitted and forbidden intercourse. For the Responsa Committee, specific sexual norms override abstract values because such values take on meaning only within the context of particular historical traditions.[14] Not surprisingly, the Conservative rabbinic letter, reflecting the movement's commitment to Jewish law, moves directly from a description of general Jewish values to a consideration of norms for marriage, which it considers the only appropriate context for sexual intercourse.[15] Appeals to the authority of specific teachings play a stronger and more direct role in the Conservative letter than in the documents of the other movements. But even here, there are inconsistencies, in that the authority of Torah teaching is not invoked as strictly in relation to the laws of family purity, as it is in relation to adultery, incest, or the value of marital sex.[16] While the letter sees these latter values as nonnegotiable, it simply summarizes the arguments for and against refraining from sex during a woman's menstrual period, leaving it up to readers to form their own judgments. The methodological contradictions evident in the documents suggest that their authors are being guided by a priori commitments to certain conclusions that are not fully analyzed and discussed.

The existence of such commitments becomes especially clear in relation to a third set of issues raised by the documents: namely their striking unwillingness to grapple with what I might call the negative values within Jewish tradition. All the statements assume that *values* are necessarily positive, and that once a value has been named as Jewish, it has been endorsed as an ideal toward which Jews should strive. In making this assumption, the documents fit into a well-established American Jewish pattern of depicting Judaism as a model of erotic health that, at least within the bonds of marriage, affirms the holiness of sexual pleasure for both partners.[17] But there are many values found in the Jewish tradition that are not sex-affirming or egalitarian and are either uncomfortable or antithetical to contemporary sensibilities. Much recent Jewish scholarship on sexuality points out, for example, that asceticism has been a stronger strain in Jewish attitudes toward sex than most Jews today like to acknowledge. Sex-positive perspectives certainly exist within the Jewish tradition, but they constitute one side of a persistent ambivalence that finds expression both in explicit debates about the value of pleasure and abstinence, and in fundamentally different attitudes toward the goodness or dangers of desire.[18] Male dominance is another profoundly important Jewish value historically, and one that shapes every aspect of sexual relations from the basic structures of marriage, to the expectations surrounding sexual relations within it, to the regulation of sexual interactions outside the marital bond. Yet one would never know from these documents that sex is *gendered*. Apart from some brief nods to the inequality of traditional Jewish marriage, they talk about sexual norms as if they had identical meaning for women and men.[19] It seems that as values not shared by most contemporary Jews, asceticism and sexism are unworthy of discussion.

This silence—especially the silence about gender—is very problematic, and not simply because it further evades the question of how particular values are chosen as authoritative. Treating sexual values as if they existed in some ideal sphere outside the power relations created and maintained by Jewish sexual norms serves to reinforce existing inequalities by rendering them invisible. The Conservative letter, for example, talks in gender-neutral terms about the *mitzvah* (commandment) of procreation, the importance of children, and the need for a proper balance between work and family. In treating these issues as if they affected women and men in the same ways, the letter probably imagines itself as egalitarian. But by ignoring the fact that women bear primary responsibility for childrearing within both the Jewish community and larger society, it obscures the ways in which women and men negotiate issues of family from different starting points and with very unequal access to power and resources.[20] It thus naturalizes the status quo by failing to raise it as a subject worthy of Jewish discussion. Similarly, when the documents talk abstractly about fundamental values, they fail to consider the meaning of these values in different periods of history. Can it be irrelevant to the dynamics of contemporary relationships that fidelity, for example, has long been defined only in terms of a wife's obligation not to have sex with anyone but her husband? Are, and how are, cultural expectations concerning faithfulness in marriage still different for women and men? Why is this not addressed in discussions of fidelity?

In failing to analyze or even acknowledge the power relations embedded in traditional norms, the documents miss an important opportunity to explore the ways in which power still operates and even contributes to abuses in sexual relationships that all the documents condemn as unjust. After roundly rejecting incest, rape, and other forms of victimization or abuse of power, for example, the Reform and Conservative statements do not mention them again, as if declaring them unacceptable were enough to banish them from the real world of human relationships. Sexual acts that are "adulterous, incestuous, or involuntary . . . [are] a gross violation of Jewish law" and of all the fundamental values discussed in the letter, says the Conservative document as the sum total of its treatment of the subject.[21] When the Conservative letter briefly acknowledges that, "Marriage is no guarantee that sexual relations will be respectful and non-coercive," it does not pause to explore the implications of this statement, but quickly adds that such respect is more likely within marriage than in a nonmarital relationship.[22] This optimistic understanding of marriage is supported by the letter's depiction of *kiddushin* (Jewish marriage) as a ceremony through which the bride and groom become "uniquely the marital partner of each other"—an interpretation echoed in the CCAR Responsa Committee's definition of *kiddushin* as the process though which "husband and wife set each other apart."[23] Neither document acknowledges that the traditional marriage ritual is about the groom's acquisition of exclusive access to his wife's sexuality in a nonreciprocal way, or that all rabbinic discussion of marital sex presupposes male headship and female subordination. The documents can thus sidestep the question of whether and how a framework of fundamental inequality might undermine respect and provide a basis for coercion. It is as if they wave a magic wand over the inequalities that shape Jewish attitudes toward sexuality and think by this act they can make them disappear. If these issues are not addressed, however—if the ideal is presented as already the real—then it is difficult to imagine moving from a sexual culture that is rife with inequalities to one that genuinely realizes the values propounded by these documents.

The inconsistencies and evasions that to varying degrees mark the denominational statements point to the impossibility of *not* choosing among a welter of competing values in constructing a sexual ethic. Whether in appealing to underlying values on certain issues and bringing in the authority of material norms on others, or in simply ignoring the aspects of tradition they find troubling or wrong, the documents repeatedly appeal to particular readings of tradition to make their case for particular ethical judgments. Only the Reconstructionist report, however, clearly acknowledges the inevitability of choice, stating forthrightly that it honors basic values such as human dignity and equality above the historically conditioned laws of Torah.

The other statements try—not always terribly successfully—to depict their conclusions as emerging from a straightforward reading of tradition. The Reform Ad Hoc Committee on Human Sexuality breezily expands the notion of family to include singles, gays, and lesbians without articulating the reasons that lead them to this significant reinterpretation. The Conservative movement letter presents the Torah's prohibition of incest and adultery as nonnegotiable but leaves open the question of whether Conservative Jews must refrain from sex during a woman's menstrual period as the Torah commands. It never discusses how the issues are different from each other. The documents are thus less than forthright about the outcomes to which they are committed, and about the relationship between the desire for certain outcomes and their understandings of authority.

Conclusions

These inconsistencies in appeals to authority suggest that there is no way to approach Jewish tradition from a neutral or disinterested place. Just as individuals attempting to construct a Jewish ethic that is coherent and meaningful always begin with certain prior commitments and understandings of tradition, the same is true of the authors of the denominational documents who are trying to articulate norms for a larger community. Since all Jews face the task of negotiating among competing values both within the tradition and between it and the larger culture, our choices will always be guided by certain basic assumptions and loyalties. There is nothing wrong with being invested in the outcome of one's religious and ethical deliberations. On the contrary, since the substance of specific decisions is supposed to reflect and affect the intimate lives of the decision makers, it only makes sense that there will always be perspectives at work shaping the path of argument in particular directions. The question is not *whether* there are interests at stake in the advocacy of particular guidelines but *what* those interests are and whether those who represent them are honest about their commitments.

There are at least two dimensions to forthrightly addressing the issue of authority. One is greater *transparency* or openness about the interests that motivate any particular approach to sexuality. It may be that the rabbis of the past had the luxury of claiming authority unselfconsciously and creating new norms by simply applying what they saw as the rules of a coherent and divinely ordained system. But contemporary Jews can no longer share their innocence. We are burdened by consciousness of our own choices and by awareness of the ideological commitments that inescapably shape our perspectives.

Secondly, transparency involves examining the *frameworks* within which choices are made. The long history of Jewish interpretation comprises a conversation across the centuries in which each generation brings its insights and questions to earlier materials. Because the first generations of rabbis established the rules within which all conversation takes place, however, the imagination of later generations is always to some extent constrained by those preceding it. As historical circumstances change, and new groups enter the discussion that played no part in establishing its framework, they often find themselves forced to contort or deny aspects of their experience to fit into preestablished categories. They discover that the questions they can ask are often preselected, and not necessarily those they find most urgent and central. The texts concerning sexuality with which contemporary Jews engage were formulated by an overwhelmingly married, male, rabbinic elite who worked to normalize certain understandings of sexuality and gender and to expand their own authority in the process. The current leadership of the liberal Jewish community is far more diverse and has rejected certain assumptions about gender that were central to the rabbinic paradigm. Yet, trained in the methods and worldviews of normative texts, those who speak for the community often approach issues of sexuality from within already established legal and institutional frameworks, so that they have difficulty finding a place for contemporary ethical questions and insights that might challenge those frameworks in fundamental ways.

This is why the problem of authority is so important—indeed, as important as the specifics of sexual legislation. Facing the issue of authority allows us to ask, *Who is speaking? Who decides? Who has the power to participate in this conversation? What interests do the participants likely reflect? From whom do they not want to hear? Who is the "we" of the Jewish community and those who have the power of decision making within it—both for the denominational documents and for the authors of the traditional sources in which these docu-*

ments are to varying degrees grounded? Who is left out when discussions of sexuality begin from the authority of traditional texts? Raising these questions opens up the possibility of consciously renegotiating the ground rules of conversation in ways that allow for rupture with and reframing of the assumptions of the past.[24]

Today, there are many groups of Jews who find themselves at odds with a one-size-fits-all model of adult sexual life. Single people; those who are divorced or widowed; Jews who marry late, who cohabit, or who decide not to have children; Jewish women seeking to redefine their roles in the synagogue, work world, and family; Jews who have been the victims of sexual or domestic violence; lesbians, gay men, bisexuals, and transgendered Jews—all often wonder how the rules apply to them or whether there is a place for them in the Jewish community. If the perspectives of large groups within the Jewish people are systematically excluded from rabbinic discourses about sexuality, then accepting the authority of these discourses—even where they are liberally reinterpreted—will continue to exclude those who historically have been silenced.

This is why it is important to extend authority to perspectives that have been erased or marginalized by traditional Jewish texts and that are often excluded from mainstream conversations. As those whose experiences have not been heard add their words to Torah and enter fully into the process of interpretation, they will expand and shift our understandings of tradition.[25] For some, this expansion evokes anxieties that can be quieted by appeals to traditional authority—or by ignoring the issue of authority altogether. But to posit the existence of *a* Jewish sexual ethic that emerges seamlessly from the past is to lock Jews into an idealized and imaginary history that forever excludes large segments of the Jewish people. Acknowledging that authority is always rooted in a community of contemporary interpreters opens a space for full inclusion of previously neglected voices and opts for Judaism as a living and evolving tradition.

Notes

Intersections: An Introduction

1. Valerie Saiving, "The Human Situation: A Feminine View," in *Journal of Religion* 40 (April 1960): 100–112, and in *Womanspirit Rising: A Feminist Reader in Religion,* ed. Carol P. Christ and Judith Plaskow (San Francisco: Harper & Row, 1979).

2. Judith Plaskow, *Sex, Sin, and Grace: Women's Experience and the Theologies of Reinhold Niebuhr and Paul Tillich* (Lanham, MD: University Press of America, 1980).

3. See "The Jewish Feminist: Conflict in Identities," p. 35 in this volume.

4. My essay "Appropriation, Reciprocity, and Issues of Power," *Journal of Feminist Studies in Religion* 8 (Fall 1992): 105–110, which was part of a panel on "Appropriation and Reciprocity in Womanist/ Mujerista/Feminist Work" at the 1991 Annual Meeting of the American Academy of Religion, is more typical of my work on the complexity of oppression in that it requires the larger context of the panel to make sense.

I: Formulating a Feminist Theology

The Coming of Lilith:
Toward a Feminist Theology

1. For discussion of the term *feminist theology,* see question 2 at the end of this essay.

2. The group met at the Conference of Women Exploring Theology at Grailville, Loveland, Ohio, June 18–25, 1972. The other women in the group were Karen Bloomquist, Sister Margaret Early, and Elizabeth Farians.

3. See question 1 at the end of this essay for a consideration of this process.

4. For further reflection on the effects of consciousness-raising on women, see Nelle Morton, "The Rising Woman Consciousness in a Male Language Structure," *Andover Newton Quarterly* 12, no. 4 (1972): 179.

5. Mary Daly, "The Spiritual Revolution: Women's Liberation as Theological Re-Education," *Andover Newton Quarterly* 12, no. 4 (1972): 163–176.

6. The "click" is part of this experience. See Jane O'Reilly, "The Housewife's Moment of Truth," *Ms.,* Spring 1972, 54–55, 57–59.

7. Morton, "The Rising Woman Consciousness," 180.

8. Stephen Crites, "Five Philosophical Points on the Nonphilosophical Truth of Theology," *Soundings* 53, no. 2 (1970): 191.

9. Crites, "Five Philosophical Points," 192, 198.

The Jewish Feminist: Conflict in Identities

1. Mary Daly, "After the Demise of God the Father: A Call for the Castration of Sexist Religion," in *Women and Religion: 1972,* ed. Judith Plaskow (Missoula, MT: American Academy of Religion, 1973).

2. Elizabeth Farians, "Phallic Worship: The Ultimate Idolatry," in *Women and Religion: 1972.*

3. Interestingly, since this speech was delivered, some Jewish leaders have resorted to exactly this argument against ordaining women as rabbis. See Mortimer Ostow's comments in "Women and Change in Jewish Law," *Conservative Judaism* 29, no. 1 (Fall 1974): 5–12.

4. See my "The Coming of Lilith: Toward a Feminist Theology," pp. 23–34 in this volume, for a discussion of the origins of this story.

Male Theology and Women's Experience

1. See Elizabeth Janeway, *Man's World, Woman's Place* (New York: William Morrow, 1972), for a thorough and insightful analysis of this polarity.

2. Simone de Beauvoir, *The Second Sex* (New York: Bantam Books, 1961), xv.

3. Inge K. Broverman et al., "Sex-Role Stereotypes and Clinical Judgments of Mental Health," *Journal of Consulting and Clinical Psychology* 34, no. 1 (1970): 1–7.

4. For a fuller development of this theme and other issues discussed here, see my dissertation *Sex, Sin, and Grace: Women's Experience and the Theologies of Reinhold Niebuhr and Paul Tillich* (Lanham, MD: University Press of America, 1980).

5. See, for example, Rosemary Radford Ruether, ed., *Religion and Sexism* (New York: Simon & Schuster, 1974); Mary Daly, *Beyond God the Father* (Boston: Beacon Press, 1973). For further bibliography, see Ann Driver, "Religion," *Signs: Journal of Women in Culture and Society* 2, no. 2 (Winter 1976): 434–442.

6. Dietrich Bonhoeffer, *Letters and Papers from Prison* (New York: Macmillan Company, 1967), 28, 29.

7. Karl Barth, *Church Dogmatics,* vol. 3, pt. 4 (Edinburgh: T&T Clark, 1961), 169, 171, 172.

8. See Joan Arnold (Romero), "The Protestant Principle: A Woman's Eye View of Barth and Tillich," in *Religion and Sexism.*

9. Bishop C. Kilmer Myers, "Statement on the Proposed Ordination of Women to the 122nd Diocesan Convention." Quoted by Elizabeth Farians in "Phallic Workshop: The Ultimate Idolatry," in *Women and Religion,* ed. Judith Plaskow and Joan Arnold (Missoula, MT: American Academy of Religion and Scholars Press, 1974), 84, 85.

10. Carol P. Christ noticed this several years ago. See her paper "A Question for Investigation," in *Notes, Conference of Women Theologians* (Milwaukee, WI: Alverno College Research Center on Women, June 1971).

11. Barth, *Church Dogmatics,* 173–175.

12. Ibid., 155.

13. Erich Neumann, "The Psychological Stages of Feminine Development," *Spring* (1959): 70–74.

14. Elaine Pagels, "What Became of God the Mother? Conflicting Images of God in Early Christianity," *Signs: Journal of Women in Culture and Society* 2, no. 2 (Winter 1976): 293–303.

15. Valerie Saiving [Goldstein], "The Human Situation: A Feminine View," *Journal of Religion* 40 (April 1960): 110–112.

16. Reinhold Niebuhr, *The Nature and Destiny of Man,* 2 vols. (New York: Charles Scribner's Sons, 1964), 1:178–186.

17. Ibid., 1:186, 228–240.

18. Saiving [Goldstein], "The Human Situation," 109.

19. Niebuhr, *The Nature and Destiny of Man,* 1:188–203.

20. Ibid., 2:108. Niebuhr says, "The Christian doctrine of grace stands in juxtaposition to the Christian doctrine of original sin and has meaning only if the latter is an accurate description of the actual facts of human experience."

21. Ibid., 2:108–110.

22. Mary Daly, *Beyond God the Father,* 100.

23. Doris Lessing, *The Summer Before the Dark* (New York: Bantam Books, 1974), 92, 93.

24. Niebuhr, *The Nature and Destiny of Man,* 2:110.

25. Lessing, *The Summer Before the Dark,* 93.

26. Juan Luis Segundo, "Seminar-Introduction" (paper circulated to the theology colloquium, Harvard Divinity School, May 1974).

27. This paragraph and parts of the next are drawn from my paper "The Feminist Transformation of Theology," in *Beyond Androcentrism,* ed. Rita Gross (Missoula, MT: Scholars Press, 1978).

The Right Question Is Theological

1. Cynthia Ozick, "Notes Toward Finding the Right Question," *Lilith* 6 (1979): 19–29.

2. Judith Hole and Ellen Levine, *Rebirth of Feminism* (New York: Quadrangle Books, 1971), ix–x.

3. Simone de Beauvoir describes woman as the Other in *The Second Sex* (New York: Bantam Books, 1961). Rachel Adler ("The Jew Who Wasn't There: *Halakhah* and the Jewish Woman," *Response* 18 (Summer 1973): 77–82) and Ozick ("Finding the Right Question," 21) make use of this basic concept but without understanding its implications for halakhic change.

4. Ozick, "Finding the Right Question," 27, 29.

5. Jacob Neusner, "Mishnah on Women: Thematic or Systemic Description," *Marxist Perspectives* 2 (Spring 1980): 94–95.

6. See, for example, Moshe Meiselman, *Jewish Woman in Jewish Law* (New York: KTAV Publishing House and Yeshivah University Press, 1978), 43–44.

7. There are, of course, important differences between Judaism and Christianity on this issue.

8. Neusner, "Mishnah on Women," 96.

9. Ber. 152a; Louis Epstein, *Sex Laws and Customs in Judaism* (New York: KTAV Publishing House, 1967), 114.

10. See also Paula Hyman, "The Other Half: Women in the Jewish Tradition," *Response* 18 (Summer 1973), 67–75.

11. This applies to Adler and Ozick. Hyman calls for changes in "attitude" as well as law.

12. Dorothy Sayers uses the phrase "The Human-Not-Quite-Human" in *Are Women Human?* (Grand Rapids, MI: Eerdmans Publishing, 1971). Rosemary Radford Ruether has dealt extensively with the issue of projection as it affects women, Jews, blacks, and other oppressed groups. See, for example, her *New Woman/New Earth* (New York: Seabury Press, 1975), esp. 89–114.

13. Ozick, "Finding the Right Question," 20.

14. Clifford Geertz, "Religion as a Cultural System," in *Reader in Comparative Religion: An Anthropological Approach,* ed. William Lessa and Evon Vogt (New York: Harper & Row, 1965), 205, 207, 213. See also *Womanspirit Rising: A Feminist Reader in Religion,* ed. Carol P. Christ and Judith Plaskow (San Francisco: Harper & Row, 1979), 2–3.

15. Mortimer Ostow, "Women and Change in Jewish Law," *Conservative Judaism* 29, no. 1 (Fall 1974): 5–12.

16. For example, Ozick, "Finding the Right Question," 20; Ostow, "Women and Change." Ozick is obviously not a general critic of Jewish feminism, but Ostow gives the impression that women are intrinsically pagan and that justice for women necessarily means the paganization of Judaism.

17. Rita Gross, "Female God-language in a Jewish Context," *Womanspirit Rising,* 170–171.

18. Raphael Patai documents both the persistence of Goddess worship in Israel and the fact that suppression of the Goddess was never complete. *The Hebrew Goddess* (New York: KTAV Publishing House, 1967).

19. Ozick, "Finding the Right Question," 24–25.

Jewish Theology in Feminist Perspective

1. These sentiments are more often expressed orally—or even institutionally—than in writing. For example, when I was a graduate student at Yale, Judah Golden frequently insisted that there was no Jewish theology, so there was no possibility of our having a course on the subject. More revealing, when I began graduate work in theology in 1968, I had to study Christian theology be-

cause there was simply no place in the country to study Jewish theology. Other Jews before me had found themselves in the same situation.

2. Arthur A. Cohen and Paul Mendes-Flohr, *Contemporary Jewish Religious Thought* (New York: Scribner, 1987), xiii.

3. For examples of the body of feminist work on Christian theologians, see Rosemary Radford Ruether, "Misogynism and Virginal Feminism in the Fathers of the Church," and Eleanor Commo McLaughlin, "Equality of Souls, Inequality of Sexes: Woman in Medieval Theology," both in *Religion and Sexism: Images of Woman in the Jewish and Christian Traditions,* ed. Rosemary Radford Ruether (New York: Simon & Schuster, 1974); Valerie Saiving [Goldstein], "The Human Situation: A Feminine View," *Journal of Religion* 40 (April 1960): 100–112, and in *Womanspirit Rising,* ed. Carol Christ and Judith Plaskow (San Francisco: Harper & Row, 1979); and Judith Plaskow, *Sex, Sin, and Grace: Women's Experience and the Theologies of Reinhold Niebuhr and Paul Tillich* (Lanham, MD: University Press of America, 1980).

4. This paragraph is based on a conversation I had in May 1990 with Lauren Granite and also on her reflections, "Some Notes Toward a Feminist Critique of Buber's Work" (June 1990, available from L. Granite). Granite was a graduate student at Drew University, who, when she sat down to prepare a comprehensive exam on Buber, was startled to find that there was no feminist criticism of his work.

5. Granite, "Some Notes," 1–2, 10–11.

6. Martin Buber, *I and Thou,* trans. Walter Kaufmann (New York: Scribner, 1970), 76–80.

7. Granite, "Some Notes," 10–11.

8. See "The Right Question Is Theological," pp. 56–64 in this volume.

9. T. Drorah Setel, "Feminist Reflections on Separation and Unity in Jewish Theology," *Journal of Feminist Studies in Religion* 2 (Spring 1986): 113–118.

10. Plaskow, *Standing Again at Sinai: Judaism from a Feminist Perspective* (San Francisco: Harper & Row, 1990), 96; Setel, "Feminist Reflections," 116.

11. See Marcia Falk's response to Setel in the same issue of the *Journal of Feminist Studies in Religion* 2 (Spring 1986):121–125.

12. Rita Gross, "Female God Language in a Jewish Context," in *Womanspirit Rising: A Feminist Reader in Religion,* ed. Carol P. Christ and Judith Plaskow (San Francisco: Harper & Row, 1979), 168–171.

13. Setel, "Feminist Reflections," 117; Plaskow, *Standing Again at Sinai,* 123–135.

14. For example, Rita J. Burns, *Has the Lord Indeed Spoken Only Through Moses? A Study of the Biblical Portrait of Miriam,* Society of Biblical Literature Dissertation Series 84 (Atlanta: Scholars Press, 1987), chap. 2, esp. p. 40. For development of these themes, see my *Standing Again at Sinai,* 36–51.

15. David Goodblatt, "The Beruriah Traditions," *Journal of Jewish Studies* 26 (Spring–Autumn 1975): 68–85. For the "bad end" assigned this uppity woman by the rabbis, see Rachel Adler, "The Virgin in the Brothel and Other Anomalies: Character and Context in the Legend of Beruriah," *Tikkun* 3 (November–December 1988): 28–32, 101–106.

16. Chava Weissler, "The Traditional Piety of Ashkenazic Women," in *Jewish Spirituality from the Six-*

teenth Century Revival to the Present, ed. Arthur Green (New York: Crossroad, 1987); Chava Weissler, "The Religion of Traditional Ashkenazic Women: Some Methodological Issues," *AJS Review* (June–July 1987): 87–88; Chava Weissler, "Voices from the Heart: Women's Devotional Prayers," in *The Jewish Almanac,* ed. Richard Siegel and Carl Rheins (New York: Bantam Books, 1980), 544; Chava Weissler, "Women in Paradise," *Tikkun* 2 (April–May 1987): 43–46, 117–120.

17. Ellen M. Umansky, "Piety, Persuasion, and Friendship: Female Jewish Leadership in Modern Times," in *Embodied Love: Sensuality and Relationship as Feminist Values,* ed. Paula Cooey, Sharon Farmer, and Mary Ellen Ross (San Francisco: Harper & Row, 1987); Ellen M. Umansky, *Lily Montagu and the Advancement of Liberal Judaism: From Vision to Vocation,* Studies in Women and Religion 12 (New York: Edward Mellen, 1983), 205–206.

18. Ellen M. Umansky, "Matriarchs and Monotheism: A History of Jewish Women's Spirituality," in *Piety, Persuasion, and Friendship: A Sourcebook of Modern Jewish Women's Spirituality,* ed. Ellen Umansky and Dianne Ashton (Boston: Beacon Press, 1992), 15–18.

19. Plaskow, *Standing Again at Sinai,* 134–136.

20. Gluckel of Hameln, *The Memoirs of Gluckel of Hameln,* trans. Marvin Lowenthal (1932; repr., New York: Schocken, 1977).

21. Gross, "Female God Language," 165–173, esp. 172–173.

22. Naomi Janowitz and Maggie Wenig, *Siddur Nashim: A Sabbath Prayer Book for Women* (Providence: Privately published, 1976); short sections are reprinted in *Womanspirit Rising,* 174–178. Since Janowitz and Wenig, there have been many other prayer services using female language, many privately circulating for use in small groups. *Vetaher Libenu* (Sudbury, MA: Congregation Beth El, 1980) and *Or Chadash* (Philadelphia: P'nai Or Religious Fellowship, 1989) are two generally available prayer books that use female language, the latter in Hebrew as well as English.

23. Much of Lynn Gottlieb's work is unpublished, but see "Speaking into the Silence," *Response* 41–42 (Fall–Winter 1982): 19–32, esp. 21–22, 32.

24. Marcia Falk, "Notes on Composing New Blessings: Toward a Feminist Jewish Reconstruction of Prayer," *Journal of Feminist Studies in Religion* 3 (Spring 1987): 39–49. I discuss the new Jewish feminist God-language in *Standing Again at Sinai,* 136–143.

25. Gross, "Female God Language," 169; Falk, "Notes on Composing New Blessings," 44–45.

26. Falk, "Notes on Composing New Blessings," 41 (emphasis in original).

27. Plaskow, *Standing Again at Sinai,* 150–153.

28. Nelle Morton, *The Journey Is Home* (Boston: Beacon Press, 1985), 54–55.

29. Carol P. Christ, "Heretics and Outsiders," in her *Laughter of Aphrodite: Reflections on a Journey to the Goddess* (San Francisco: Harper & Row, 1987), 35–40; Bernadette Brooten, "Could Women Initiate Divorce in Ancient Judaism? The Implications for Mark 10:11–12 and 1 Corinthians 7:10–11" (Ernest Cadwell Colman Lecture, School of Theology at Claremont, April 14, 1981).

30. Plaskow, *Standing Again at Sinai,* 33. My explication of the phrase here depends on my discussion in the book, pp. 32–34.

31. Compare, for example, Tamar Frankiel, *The Voice of Sarah: Feminine Spirituality and Traditional*

Judaism (San Francisco: Harper & Row, 1990), with Sue Levi Elwell, "Texts and Transformation: Towards a Theology of Integrity" (Rabbinic thesis, Hebrew Union College-Jewish Institute of Religion, 1986).

32. I have in mind such things as the ancient inscriptions testifying to women's religious leadership studied by Bernadette Brooten (*Women Leaders in the Ancient Synagogue: Inscriptional Evidence and Background Issues,* Brown Judaic Studies 36 [Chico, CA: Scholars Press, 1982]); the New Testament as evidence for the right of Jewish women to initiate divorce (see note 29); the *tkhines;* novels like E. M. Broner's *A Weave of Women* (New York: Bantam Books, 1978); and midrash like Ellen Umansky's "Creating a Jewish Feminist Theology," in *Weaving the Visions: New Patterns in Feminist Spirituality,* ed. Judith Plaskow and Carol P. Christ (San Francisco: Harper & Row, 1989), 195–197.

Lilith Revisited

1. Rosemary Radford Ruether, ed., *Religion and Sexism: Images of Women in the Jewish and Christian Traditions* (New York: Simon & Schuster, 1974), 12.

2. See my "The Coming of Lilith: Toward a Feminist Theology," pp. 23–34 in this volume.

3. "Singleness/Community Group," *Women Exploring Theology at Grailville* (packet from Church Women United, 1972). See also my discussion in Judith Plaskow, *Standing Again at Sinai: Judaism from a Feminist Perspective* (San Francisco: Harper & Row, 1990), 86, 143–144.

4. Plaskow, *Standing Again at Sinai,* 79–81.

5. Plaskow, *Standing Again at Sinai,* 217–220.

6. See "The Coming of Lilith."

7. Louis Ginzberg's *Legends of the Jews* (Philadelphia: Jewish Publication Society of America, 1968), 1:65.

II: The Complexity of Interlocking Oppressions

Christian Feminism and Anti-Judaism

1. Sheila Collins has given this myth clearest form (*A Different Heaven and Earth* [Valley Forge: Judson Press, 1974], 25–30), but she is by no means the only writer who has made it an explicit or implicit presupposition of her/his work.

2. Rosemary Radford Ruether warns feminism against precisely this in *New Woman/New Earth* (New York: Seabury Press, 1975), 63. See also her *Faith and Fratricide* (New York: Seabury Press, 1974) for a history and analysis of Christian anti-Judaism. Christian feminism is by no means unique in the ways it perpetuates this history.

3. Leonard Swidler, "Jesus Was a Feminist," *Catholic World* 212 (January 1971): 177–183. Swidler was the first to suggest this argument, but others soon took it up. See, for example, Collins, *A Differ-*

ent Heaven and Earth, 128; Alicia Craig Faxon, *Women and Jesus* (Philadelphia: United Church Press, 1973), 11–12; Constance Parvey, "The Theology and Leadership of Women in the New Testament," in *Religion and Sexism*, ed. Rosemary Radford Ruether (New York: Simon & Schuster, 1974); Virginia Mollenkott, *Women, Men and the Bible* (Nashville: Abingdon Press, 1977). My observations are based on these writings (among others). More important, however, they are based on observation of what students learn and repeat when they study these materials and also on numerous conversations with Christian feminist colleagues.

4. See Swidler, "Jesus Was a Feminist," 178; Parvey, "The Theology and Leadership," 120; Mollenkott, *Women, Men and the Bible*, 10.

5. Mollenkott, *Women, Men and the Bible*, 12.

6. Collins, *A Different Heaven and Earth*, 75.

7. Swidler, "Jesus Was a Feminist," 178; Faxon, *Women and Jesus*, 12; Mollenkott, *Women, Men and the Bible*, 10.

8. Mollenkott, *Women, Men and the Bible*, 29.

9. B. Yevamot 62a; Baba Mezia 59a.

10. Krister Stendahl makes this point in *The Bible and the Role of Women* (Philadelphia: Fortress Press, 1966), 26.

11. Y. Sotah 1:4; Lev. Rabbah 9:9.

12. Mary Daly, *Beyond God the Father* (Boston: Beacon Press, 1973), 10.

13. H.R. Trevor-Roper, *The European Witch-Craze* (New York and Evanston: Harper & Row, 1969), 110. See also Ruether, *New Woman/New Earth*, 105–107.

Anti-Semitism: The Unacknowledged Racism

1. Rosemary Radford Ruether uses the concept of "interstructuring." See, for example, her *New Woman/New Earth* (New York: Seabury Press, 1975), particularly part 2.

2. Maurice D. Atkin, "United States of America," in *Encyclopedia Judaica* (Philadelphia: Coronet Books, 1972), 15:1636.

3. Robert Weisbord and Arthur Stein, *Bittersweet Encounter* (New York: Schocken Books, 1972), 15.

4. Weisbord and Stein stress this point.

5. Letty Cottin Pogrebin, "Anti-Semitism in the Women's Movement," *Ms.*, June 1982, 68, 69; Evelyn Torten Beck, ed., *Nice Jewish Girls* (Watertown, MA: Persephone Press, 1982), particularly the introduction and first section.

6. Ann Wilson Shaef makes this point for female and male culture in *Women's Reality* (Minneapolis: Winston Press, 1981), chap. 1.

7. The destruction of the Temple in Jerusalem in 70 CE necessitated a profound reorientation of Jewish religious life, a reorientation carried out under the auspices of the rabbis beginning at Yavneh around 70.

8. Both Pogrebin and Beck discuss this phenomenon.

9. Jean-Paul Sartre, *Anti-Semite and Jew* (New York: Schocken Books, 1965), 69.

10. Pogrebin, "Anti-Semitism in the Women's Movement," 66, and Beck, *Nice Jewish Girls,* particularly the introduction and first section.

11. See "Christian Feminism and Anti-Judaism," pp. 89–93 in this volume.

12. Alice Walker, "One Child of One's Own: An Essay on Creativity," *Ms.,* August 1979; reprinted in Alice Walker, *In Search of Our Mother's Gardens* (New York: Harcourt, Brace, Jovanovich, 1983).

13. Esther Ticktin, "A Modest Beginning," *Response* (Summer 1973), 83–88.

14. Quoted by Beck in *Nice Jewish Girls,* xxi.

Feminist Anti-Judaism and the Christian God

1. bell hooks, *Feminist Theory: From Margin to Center* (Boston: South End Press, 1984); Cherrie Moraga and Gloria Anzaldua, eds., *This Bridge Called My Back: Writings By Radical Women of Color* (1981; repr., Latham, NY: Kitchen Table: Women of Color Press, 1983); Gloria Hull, Patricia Bell Scott, and Barbara Smith, *All the Women Are White, All the Blacks Are Men, But Some of Us Are Brave* (Old Westbury, NY: Feminist Press, 1982); Elizabeth V. Spelman, *Inessential Woman: Problems of Exclusion in Feminist Theory* (Boston: Beacon Press, 1988).

2. Sheila Collins, *A Different Heaven and Earth* (Valley Forge, PA: Judson Press, 1974), 25–30; quotation, 28–29.

3. Rosemary Radford Ruether, *Sexism and God-Talk: Toward a Feminist Theology* (Boston: Beacon Press, 1983), 1–11, esp. 1, 5–6.

4. Ruether, *Sexism and God-Talk,* 3.

5. Collins, *A Different Heaven and Earth,* 27–28; Ruether, *Sexism and God-Talk,* 2.

6. Carol P. Christ, *Laughter of Aphrodite: Reflections on a Journey to the Goddess* (San Francisco: Harper & Row, 1987), 84.

7. See, for example, Mary Wakeman, "Ancient Sumer and the Women's Movement: The Process of Reaching Behind, Encompassing, and Going Beyond," *Journal of Feminist Studies in Religion* 1 (Fall 1985): 7–27.

8. Virginia Ramey Mollenkott, *Women, Men and the Bible* (Nashville: Abingdon, 1977), 10.

9. Judith Romney Wegner, *Chattel or Person? The Status of Women in the Mishnah* (New York and Oxford: Oxford University Press, 1988), esp. chap. 7.

10. Krister Stendahl, *The Bible and the Role of Women* (Philadelphia: Fortress Press, 1966), 40.

11. Carter Heyward, *Our Passion for Justice: Images of Power, Sexuality, and Liberation* (New York: Pilgrim Press, 1984), 17.

Dealing with the Hard Stuff

1. Rebecca T. Alpert, "In God's Image: Coming to Terms with Leviticus," in *Twice Blessed: On Being Lesbian or Gay and Jewish,* ed. Christie Balka and Andy Rose (Boston: Beacon Press, 1989), 69.

2. Rivkah Walton, "Proposal for Liturgical Changes After the Hebron Massacre" (written for Minyan Dorshei Derekh of Germantown Jewish Centre, Philadelphia, 1994).

III: Creating a Feminist Judaism

The Year of the Agunah

1. Although this article was written in 1992, the situation of *agunot* in the United States has not improved in the last twelve years.

Preaching Against the Text

1. Renita Weems, *Battered Love: Marriage, Sex, and Violence in the Hebrew Prophets* (Minneapolis: Fortress Press, 1995), 2, 16–17. This sermon is based on Weems's text. I refer to God as "him" because God is the husband in the metaphor.

2. Ibid., 23–25, 30, 42, 79.

3. Ibid., 19.

4. T. Drorah Setel, "Prophets and Pornography: Female Sexual Imagery in Hosea," in *Feminist Interpretation of the Bible,* ed. Letty M. Russell (Philadelphia: Westminster Press, 1985), 88, 87, respectively.

5. Weems, *Battered Love,* 32, 49, 93.

IV: Sexuality, Authority, and Tradition

Sexuality and Teshuvah: Leviticus 18

1. I first raised this issue in my short article "Sex and Yom Kippur," *Tikkun* 10, no. 5 (September–October 1995): 71–72, parts of which I repeat here.

2. Baruch A. Levine, *The JPS Torah Commentary: Leviticus* (Philadelphia: Jewish Publication Society, 1989), xiv, 110–111.

3. Biblical references are to the new JPS (Jewish Publication Society) translation.

4. Stephen F. Bigger, "The Family Laws of Leviticus 18 in Their Setting," *Journal of Biblical Literature* 98, no. 2 (June 1979): 195–196.

5. Mary Douglas, *Purity and Danger: An Analysis of the Concepts of Pollution and Taboo* (London and New York: Routledge, 1966), 3, 36, 133.

6. Bigger, "The Family Laws of Leviticus 18," 196–202.

7. Ibid., 188.

8. Ibid., 202.

9. Howard Eilberg-Schwartz, *The Savage in Judaism: An Anthropology of Israelite Religion and Ancient Judaism* (Bloomington and Indianapolis: Indiana University Press, 1990), 179–180.

10. Eilberg-Schwartz, *The Savage in Judaism*, 180–181; Rachel Adler, "In Your Blood, Live: Re-visions of a Theology of Purity," *Tikkun* 8, no. 1 (January–February 1993): 40.

11. Eilberg-Schwartz, *The Savage in Judaism*, 180. He is quoting Freud.

12. The translation is Saul Olyan's, "'And with a Male You Shall Not Lie Down the Lying Down of a Woman': On the Meaning and Significance of Leviticus 18:22 and 20:13," *Journal of the History of Sexuality* 5, no. 2 (1994).

13. Ibid., 200–203.

14. Rachel Adler, "Feminist Folktales of Justice: Robert Cover as a Resource for the Renewal of Halakhah," *Conservative Judaism* 45 (Spring 1993): 42; Rachel Adler, *Engendering Judaism* (Philadelphia: Jewish Publication Society, 1998), chap. 2.

15. Cf. Rebecca T. Alpert, "In God's Image: Coming to Terms with Leviticus," in *Twice Blessed: On Being Lesbian or Gay and Jewish*, ed. Christie Balka and Andy Rose (Boston: Beacon Press, 1989), 68–70.

16. Adler, *Engendering Judaism*, 132.

17. The members of Su Kasha were Sandy Abramson, Martha Ackelsberg, Joseph-Chaim Alpert, Victor Appell, David Bank, Ora Chaiken, Bob Christensen, Terry DeFiore, Marla Gayle, Colin Hogan, Larry Kay, Rosanne Leipzig, Betsy Leondar-Wright, Gail Leondar-Wright, Judith Plaskow, Irma Ross, Melanie Schneider, and Jason Stone. For the first year, the process was ably facilitated by Jason Stone.

18. What I have left out is the large area of sexual responsibilities to oneself.

Sexual Orientation and Human Rights: A Progressive Jewish Perspective

1. I move back and forth in this essay between using the term *gay* as a generic for gay, lesbian, and bisexual and using all three terms. Since the liberal religious discussion within Judaism (and Christianity) has deliberately not addressed the issue of bisexuality, however, I use only the terms *gay* and *lesbian* when referring to that discussion.

2. Steven Epstein makes this same point in "Gay Politics, Ethnic Identity: The Limits of Social Constructionism," in *Forms of Desire: Sexual Orientation and the Social Constructionist Controversy*, ed. Edward Stein (New York and London: Routledge, 1992), 243. While some bisexuals see bisexuality as fundamentally challenging assumptions about the immutability of sexual identity, others define bisexuality as a third inherent category.

3. For an earlier synopsis of my argument, see "Lesbian and Gay Rights: Asking the Right Questions," *Tikkun* 9, no. 2 (March–April 1994): 31–32.

4. For an excellent discussion of the issues from a gay perspective, see Gary David Comstock's book *Unrepentant, Self-Affirming, Practicing: Lesbian/Bisexual/Gay People Within Organized Religion* (New York: Continuum, 1996).

5. Maurice Lamm, *The Jewish Way in Love and Marriage* (San Francisco: Harper & Row, 1980), 65–66; Joel Roth, "Homosexuality," in *Papers on Issues Regarding Homosexuality* (The Committee on Jewish Law and Standards, The Rabbinical Assembly, 1992), 4, 8–9.

6. Rachel Biale, *Women and Jewish Law: An Exploration of Women's Issues in Halakhic Sources* (New York: Schocken Books, 1984), 195; Roth, "Homosexuality," 10–12.

7. Roth, "Homosexuality," 12–15, 25–35.

8. Lamm, *The Jewish Way,* 65, 66, citing B. Kiddushin 82a.

9. Hershel Matt, "Sin, Crime, Sickness, or Alternative Life Style? A Jewish Approach to Homosexuality," in *Walking Humbly with God: The Life and Writings of Rabbi Hershel Matt,* ed. Daniel Matt (Hoboken, NJ: KTAV Publishing House, 1993), 226. This article first appeared in *Judaism* in 1978.

10. Matt, "Sin, Crime, Sickness," 227.

11. Hershel Matt, "A Call for Compassion," in *Walking Humbly with God,* 237. This article originally appeared in *Judaism* in 1983.

12. Elliot Dorff, "Jewish Norms for Sexual Behavior: A Responsum Embodying a Proposal," in *Papers on Issues Regarding Homosexuality,* 7–15.

13. This is a standard distinction within the traditional psychoanalytic position. See, for example, Charles Socarides, "The Homosexualities: A Psychoanalytic Classification," in *The Homosexualities: Reality, Fantasy, and the Arts,* ed. Charles Socarides and Vamik Volkan (Madison, CT: International Universities Press, 1990), 11.

14. Matt, "Sin, Crime, Sickness," 228.

15. Matt, "A Call for Compassion," 237, 238; Hershel Matt, "Homosexual Rabbis?" in *Walking Humbly with God,* 241. The latter article initially appeared in *Conservative Judaism* in 1987.

16. Epstein, "Gay Politics," 239.

17. Matt, "Homosexual Rabbis?" 232.

18. Annabel Faraday, "Liberating Lesbian Research," in *The Making of the Modern Homosexual,* ed. Kenneth Plummer (Totowa, NJ: Barnes and Noble Books, 1981), 114–115.

19. William Byne, "The Biological Evidence Challenged," *Scientific American,* May 1994, 50.

20. Barbara Ponse, *Identities in the Lesbian World: The Social Construction of Self* (Westport, CT: Greenwood Press, 1978), 140, 159–161; Carla Golden, "Diversity and Variability in Women's Sexual Identities," in *Lesbian Psychologies: Explorations and Challenges,* ed. The Boston Lesbian Psychologies Collective (Urbana and Chicago: University of Illinois Press), 25–26.

21. Ponse, *Identities in the Lesbian World,* 173–192; Golden, "Diversity and Variability," 27–29, 31.

22. Golden, "Diversity and Variability," 32.

23. A. P. McDonald, "Some Comments on Research and Theory," *Journal of Homosexuality* 6, no. 3 (Spring 1981): 21.

24. Marilyn Frye, *The Politics of Reality: Essays in Feminist Theory* (Trumansburg, NY: Crossing Press, 1983), 152–173.

25. Biale, *Women and Jewish Law*, 194–195; cf. Frye, *The Politics of Reality*.

26. Diana Fuss, *Essentially Speaking: Feminism, Nature and Difference* (New York and London: Routledge, 1989), 45–49.

27. John P. DeCecco and John P. Elia, "A Critique and Synthesis of Biological Essentialism and Social Constructionist Views of Sexuality and Gender," in *If You Seduce a Straight Person, Can You Make Them Gay?: Issues in Biological Essentialism Versus Social Constructionism in Gay and Lesbian Identities,* ed. John P. DeCecco and John P. Elia (Binghamton, NY: Haworth Press, 1993), 13; Epstein, "Gay Politics," 260; Eve Kosofsky Sedgwick, *Epistemology of the Closet* (Berkeley and Los Angeles: University of California Press, 1990), 40–41; Carole Vance, "Social Construction Theory: Problems in the History of Sexuality," in *Homosexuality, Which Homosexuality?* ed. Dennis Altman, Carole Vance, Martha Vicinus, Jeffrey Weeks, et al. (Amsterdam: Schorer and London: GMP, 1989), 16–17.

28. Shane Phelan, "(Be)Coming Out: Lesbian Identity and Politics," *Signs: Journal of Women in Culture and Society* 18, no. 4 (Summer 1993): 771.

29. I think, for example, of the battle over a gay rights ordinance in Wichita, Kansas, in 1977–78, during which it turned out that the organist in the largest Baptist church in the city—a church firmly against the ordinance—was a gay man who had been a lifelong member of the church.

30. Judith Plaskow, *Standing Again at Sinai: Judaism from a Feminist Perspective* (San Francisco: Harper & Row, 1990), chap. 5.

31. Adrienne Rich, "Compulsory Heterosexuality and Lesbian Existence," in *Signs: Journal of Women in Culture and Society* 5, no. 4 (1980): 631–660, and in *Powers of Desire: The Politics of Sexuality,* ed. Christine Stansell and Sharon Thompson (New York: Monthly Review Press, 1983); Gayle Rubin, "The Traffic in Women: Notes on the 'Political Economy of Sex,'" in *Toward an Anthropology of Women,* ed. Rayna Reiter (New York: Monthly Review Press, 1975); Jonathan Ned Katz, *The Invention of Heterosexuality* (New York: A Dutton Book, 1995).

32. Gary David Comstock, *Gay Theology Without Apology* (Cleveland, OH: Pilgrim Press, 1993), 63–68; cf. David Greenberg, *The Construction of Homosexuality* (Chicago: University of Chicago Press, 1988), 193–195.

33. See, for example, Arthur Waskow, *Down-to-Earth Judaism: Food, Money, Sex, and the Rest of Life* (New York: William Morrow, 1995), 296–300.

34. But gay and lesbian writers have explored this possibility. See, for example, Rebecca Alpert, *Like Bread on the Seder Plate: Jewish Lesbians and the Transformation of Tradition* (New York: Columbia University Press, 1997), chap. 3; Faith Rogow, "Speaking the Unspeakable: Gays, Jews and Historical Inquiry," in *Twice Blessed: On Being Lesbian or Gay and Jewish,* ed. Christie Balka and Andy Rose (Boston: Beacon Press, 1989), 75–76; Tom Horner, *Jonathan Loved David: Homosexuality in Biblical Times* (Philadelphia: Fortress Press, 1978), esp. chaps. 2, 3.

35. Raymond Scheindlin, *Wine, Women, and Death: Medieval Hebrew Poems on the Good Life* (Philadelphia: The Jewish Publication Society, 1986), 82, 86–88.

36. Norman Roth, " 'Fawn of My Delights': Boy-Love in Hebrew and Arabic Verse," in *Sex in the Mid-*

dle Ages, ed. Joyce E. Salisbury (New York and London: Garland, 1991), 162–164; Norman Roth, "'Deal Gently With the Young Man': Love of Boys in Medieval Hebrew Poetry in Spain," *Speculum* 57 (1982): 22–23.

37. Margaret Farley, "An Ethic for Same-Sex Relations," in *A Challenge to Love: Gay and Lesbian Catholics in the Church*, ed. Robert Nugent (New York: Crossroad, 1983).

38. Plaskow, *Standing Again at Sinai*, 198.

39. On the latter issue, see Renita Weems, *Battered Love: Marriage, Sex, and Violence in the Hebrew Prophets* (Minneapolis: Fortress Press, 1995).

40. Martha Ackelsberg, "Families and the Jewish Community: A Feminist Perspective," *Response* 14 (Spring 1985): 15–16; Martha Ackelsberg, "Redefining Family: Models for the Jewish Future," in *Twice Blessed*, 115.

41. Howard Eilberg-Schwartz, *The Savage in Judaism: An Anthropology of Israelite Religion and Ancient Judaism* (Bloomington and Indianapolis: Indiana University Press, 1990), 229–234; and Daniel Boyarin, *Carnal Israel: Reading Sex in Talmudic Culture* (Berkeley and Los Angeles: University of California Press, 1993), chap. 5.

42. Plaskow, *Standing Again at Sinai*, 209–210.

43. Mary E. Hunt, "Sexual Integrity," *Waterwheel* 7, no. 3 (Fall 1994): 3.

Authority, Resistance, and Transformation: Jewish Feminist Reflections on Good Sex

1. Mary E. Hunt, "Good Sex: Women's Religious Wisdom on Sexuality," *Reproductive Health Matters* 8 (November 1996): 97–103.

2. Ibid., 97.

3. Only 50 percent of U.S. Jews are affiliated with any particular religious movement within Judaism. Of that 50 percent, 80 percent are non-Orthodox. This means that, to varying degrees, they accept the notion of Judaism as an evolving tradition that must adapt itself to changing historical and social circumstances.

4. Judith Plaskow, *Standing Again at Sinai: Judaism from a Feminist Perspective* (San Francisco: Harper & Row, 1990), 18–21.

5. I have in mind such works as Daniel Boyarin, *Carnal Israel: Reading Sex in Talmudic Culture* (Berkeley and Los Angeles: University of California Press, 1993) and *Unheroic Conduct: The Rise of Heterosexuality and the Invention of the Jewish Man* (Berkeley and Los Angeles: University of California Press, 1997); Howard Eilberg-Schwartz, *People of the Body: Jews and Judaism from an Embodied Perspective* (Albany, NY: State University of New York Press, 1992); David Biale, *Eros and the Jews: From Biblical Israel to Contemporary America* (New York: Basic Books, 1992); and Michael Satlow, *Tasting the Dish: Rabbinic Rhetorics of Sexuality*, Brown Judaic Studies 303 (Atlanta: Scholars Press, 1995).

6. This was a central and recurrent theme in all our Good Sex conversations.

7. Adrienne Rich, "Compulsory Heterosexuality and Lesbian Existence," *Signs: Journal of Women in*

Culture and Society 5, no. 4 (1980): 631–660, and in *Powers of Desire: The Politics of Sexuality*, ed. Christine Stansell and Sharon Thompson (New York: Monthly Review Press, 1983).

8. The Talmud is a compendium of Jewish law and lore, taking the form of a commentary on the Mishnah, a second-century code of Jewish law. Since the Mishnah was the center of study at rabbinic academies in both Palestine and Babylonia, there are two Talmuds. The Babylonian Talmud is fuller and is considered the masterwork of rabbinic Judaism.

9. For some introductory material on these issues, see Rachel Biale, *Women and Jewish Law* (New York: Schocken, 1984), 192–197; and Rebecca Alpert, *Like Bread on the Seder Plate: Jewish Lesbians and the Transformation of Tradition* (New York: Columbia University Press, 1997), 25–34.

10. Gayle Rubin, "The Traffic in Women: Notes on the 'Political Economy' of Sex," in *Toward an Anthropology of Women*, ed. Rayna R. Reiter (New York: Monthly Review, 1975), 179–180.

11. Mary Daly, *Beyond God the Father* (Boston: Beacon Press, 1973), 12.

12. Rachel Adler, "I've Had Nothing Yet So I Can't Take More," *Moment* 8, no. 8 (September 1983): 24.

13. On the Mishnah, see note 8.

14. Miriam B. Peskowitz, *Spinning Fantasies: Rabbis, Gender, and History* (Berkeley and Los Angeles: University of California Press, 1997), 35.

15. Saul Olyan, "'And with a Male You Shall Not Lie the Lying Down of a Woman': On the Meaning and Significance of Leviticus 18:22 and 20:13," *Journal of the History of Sexuality* 5, no. 2 (1994): 185.

16. Bradley Artson, "Gay and Lesbian Jews: An Innovative Jewish Legal Position," *Jewish Spectator* 55 (Winter 1990–1991): 11.

17. It is remarkable how little has been written criticizing the Jewish insistence on marriage from other than gay and lesbian perspectives. See Laura Geller and Elizabeth Koltun, "Single and Jewish: Toward a New Definition of Completeness," in the first anthology of Jewish feminist work, *The Jewish Woman: New Perspectives,* ed. Elizabeth Koltun (New York: Schocken, 1976), 43–49. Also see the section "Being Single" in Debra Orenstein, ed., *Lifecycles: Jewish Women on Life Passages and Personal Milestones* (Woodstock, VT: Jewish Lights, 1994), 99–116.

18. I am very grateful to the group conversation at the Good Sex meeting in Amsterdam for pushing me to be clearer about the ways in which Jewish feminists have moved beyond simply resisting women's traditional roles to creating new forms of practice, identity, and community.

19. Sharon D. Welch, *Communities of Resistance and Solidarity* (Maryknoll, NY: Orbis, 1985).

20. Daly, *Beyond God the Father,* chap. 1.

21. See Daniel Boyarin, "Justify My Love," in *Judaism Since Gender,* ed. Miriam Peskowitz and Laura Levitt (New York: Routledge, 1997).

22. Phyllis Trible, "Eve and Adam: Genesis 2–3 Reread," in *Womanspirit Rising,* ed. Carol P. Christ and Judith Plaskow (San Francisco: Harper & Row, 1979), 80.

23. This theme of concealment and revelation kept coming up in our Good Sex conversations, in relation to recovering women's history and experiences in many traditions.

24. Alpert, *Like Bread on the Seder Plate,* 29–34; Bernadette Brooten, *Love Between Women: Early Christian Responses to Female Homoeroticism* (Chicago: University of Chicago Press, 1996).

25. Alpert, *Like Bread on the Seder Plate*, 33.

26. Lisa A. Edwards, "A Simple Matter of Justice" (sermon, April 29, 1993).

Speaking of Sex: Authority and the Denominational Documents

1. See my discussion of method and authority in *Standing Again at Sinai: Judaism from a Feminist Perspective* (San Francisco: Harper & Row, 1990), 13–21.

2. Mishnah Avot, 1.1.

3. Daniel Boyarin, "Women's Bodies and the Rise of the Rabbis: The Case of Sotah," in *Jews and Gender: The Challenge to Hierarchy*, Studies in Contemporary Jewry 16, ed. Jonathan Frankel (Oxford: Oxford University Press, 2000), 92–95.

4. Rabbi Avram Reisner, "On Homosexuality and Biblical Imperatives: A Concurrence," in *Papers on Issues Regarding Homosexuality* (The Committee on Jewish Law and Standards, The Rabbinical Assembly, 1992), 3.

5. Elliot Dorff, "Jewish Norms for Sexual Behavior: A Responsum Embodying a Proposal," in *Papers on Issues Regarding Homosexuality*, 4–6, 7–15.

6. Elliot Dorff and the Commission on Human Sexuality of the Rabbinical Assembly, *"This Is My Beloved, This Is My Friend": A Rabbinic Letter on Intimate Relations* (New York: The Rabbinical Assembly, 1996).

7. CCAR Ad Hoc Committee on Human Sexuality, "Report to the CCAR Convention, June 1998" (unpublished document).

8. Report of the Reconstructionist Commission on Homosexuality, *Homosexuality and Judaism: The Reconstructionist Position* (Wyncote, PA: Federation of Reconstructionist Congregations and Havurot and the Reconstructionist Rabbinical Association, 1993).

9. CCAR Ad Hoc Committee, "Report to the CCAR Convention," 2–5.

10. Reconstructionist Commission on Homosexuality, *Homosexuality and Judaism*, 9–17.

11. Dorff and the Commission on Human Sexuality, *"This Is My Beloved*," 6–8.

12. Ibid., 6.

13. CCAR Ad Hoc Committee, "Report to the CCAR Convention," 5. This conclusion was partially affirmed by the CCAR when it voted at its 2000 convention to support the decision of rabbis who choose to officiate at same-sex ceremonies as well as those who do not.

14. CCAR Responsa Committee, "On Homosexual Marriage," *CCAR Journal* 45 (Winter 1998): 36, 16, respectively.

15. Dorff and the Commission on Human Sexuality, *"This Is My Beloved*," 30.

16. Ibid. Cf., for example, pp. 19 and 24–25.

17. David Biale, *Eros and the Jews: From Biblical Israel to Contemporary America* (New York: Basic Books, 1992), 210.

18. This ambivalence is the major theme of David Biale's *Eros and the Jews*. Cf. Boyarin, *Carnal Israel: Reading Sex in Talmudic Culture* (Berkeley, Los Angeles, and Oxford: University of California Press, 1993), 47–57.

19. Reconstructionist Commission on Homosexuality, *Homosexuality and Judaism,* 12; CCAR Responsa Committee, "On Homosexual Marriage," 22. The Conservative letter seems to go out of its way to paper over this inequality (see, for example, pp. 13 and 14), acknowledging it only in relation to the laws concerning bodily emissions (note 36, pp. 53–54).

20. Dorff and the Commission on Human Sexuality, *"This Is My Beloved,"* 15–18.

21. CCAR Ad Hoc Committee, "Report to the CCAR," 3; Dorff and the Commission on Human Sexuality, *"This Is My Beloved,"* 19–20, 30.

22. Dorff and the Commission on Human Sexuality, *"This Is My Beloved,"* 32.

23. CCAR Responsa Committee, "On Homosexual Marriage," 19.

24. Rachel Adler uses Robert Cover's term "jurisgenesis" to describe this process as it applies to halakhah. See *Engendering Judaism: An Inclusive Theology and Ethics* (Philadelphia and Jerusalem: The Jewish Publication Society, 1998), 34. I am talking about renegotiating ground rules in all aspects of Jewish life.

25. Most of the essays in this volume provide concrete examples of the kinds of substantive changes that might emerge from the inclusion of new voices.

Works by Judith Plaskow

Entries are listed in ascending order by year of first publication. Those marked with an asterisk (*) are included in this volume.

Books

Women and Religion: 1972. Editor. Missoula, MT: American Academy of Religion, 1972. Also *Women and Religion,* revised edition. Joan Arnold Romero, coeditor. Missoula, MT: American Academy of Religion and Scholars Press, 1974.

Womanspirit Rising: A Feminist Reader in Religion. Carol P. Christ, coeditor. San Francisco: Harper & Row, 1979. Japanese edition, 1982.

Sex, Sin, and Grace: Women's Experience and the Theologies of Reinhold Niebuhr and Paul Tillich. Lanham, MD: University Press of America, 1980.

Weaving the Visions: New Patterns in Feminist Spirituality. Carol P. Christ, coeditor. San Francisco: Harper & Row, 1989.

Standing Again at Sinai: Judaism from a Feminist Perspective. San Francisco: Harper & Row, 1990. German edition, 1992; Dutch edition, 1992.

Scholarly Articles

* "The Coming of Lilith: Toward a Feminist Theology." In *Women Exploring Theology at Grail-ville.* Church Women United, 1972. Reprinted in *Womanspirit Rising: A Feminist Reader in Religion,* edited by Carol P. Christ and Judith Plaskow. San Francisco: Harper & Row, 1979. Also in *Frauen in der Mannerkirche,* edited by Bernadette Brooten and Norbert Greinacher. München and Mainz: Kaiser Grunewald, 1982.

"Carol Christ on Margaret Atwood: Some Theological Reflections." *Signs: Journal of Women in Culture and Society* 2 (Winter 1976): 331–339.

"The Feminist Transformation of Theology." In *Beyond Androcentrism,* edited by Rita Gross. Missoula, MT: Scholars Press, 1978.

* "Christian Feminism and Anti-Judaism." *CrossCurrents* 33 (Fall 1978): 306–309. Reprinted in *Lilith* 7 (1980) and in *Nice Jewish Girls,* edited by Evelyn Torten Beck. Boston: Persephone Press, 1982.

* "Teologia maschile ed esperienza femminile" ("Male Theology and the Experience of Women"). In *La sfida del femminismo alla teologia,* edited by Mary Hunt and Rosino Gibellini. Brescia: Queriniana, 1980. Reprinted in English in this volume.

"Women as Body: Motherhood and Dualism." *Anima* 8 (Winter 1981–1982): 56–67.

* "The Right Question Is Theological." In *On Being a Jewish Feminist: A Reader,* edited by Susannah Heschel. New York: Schocken Books, 1983. Preprinted as "God and Feminism" in *Menorah: Sparks of Jewish Renewal* (February 1982).

"Language, God, and Liturgy: A Feminist Perspective." *Response* 44 (Spring 1983): 3–14.

* "Anti-Semitism: The Unacknowledged Racism." In *Women's Spirit Bonding,* edited by Janet Kalven and Mary Buckley. New York: Pilgrim Press, 1984. Reprinted in a slightly different form in *Women's Consciousness, Women's Conscience: A Reader in Feminist Ethics,* edited by Barbara Hilkert Andolsen, Christine E. Gudorf, and Mary D. Pellauer. Minneapolis: Winston Press, 1985.

"In Memory of Her: A Symposium on an Important Book." Contributor. *Anima* 10 (Spring 1984): 98–102.

"The Wife/Sister Stories: Dilemmas of a Jewish Feminist." In *Speaking of Faith: Global Perspectives on Women, Religion, and Social Change,* edited by Diana Eck and Devaki Jain. Delhi: Kali Press and Philadelphia: New Society Press, 1986.

"Standing Again at Sinai: Jewish Memory From a Feminist Perspective." *Tikkun* 1 (November–December 1986): 28–34. Reprinted in *Weaving the Visions: New Patterns in Feminist Spirituality,* edited by Judith Plaskow and Carol P. Christ. San Francisco: Harper & Row, 1989.

"Christian Feminist Anti-Judaism: Some New Considerations." *New Conversations* 9 (Spring 1987): 23–26.

"*Halakha* as a Feminist Issue." *The Melton Journal* 22 (Fall 1987): 3–5, 25.

"Religion and Gender: The Critical and Constructive Tasks." *The Iliff Review* 45 (Fall 1988): 3–13.

"Toward a New Theology of Sexuality." In *Twice Blessed: On Being Lesbian, Gay, and Jewish,* edited by Christie Balka and Andy Rose. Boston: Beacon Press, 1989. Reprinted in *Redefining Sexual Ethics,* edited by Susan Davies and Eleanor Haney. Cleveland: Pilgrim Press, 1991.

"Divine Conversations." *Tikkun* 4 (November–December 1989): 18–20, 85.

* "Feministischer Antijudaismus und der christliche Gott." *Neukirchener Theologische Zeitschrift: Kirche und Israel* 5 (January 1990): 9–25. Reprinted in the *Journal of Feminist Studies in Religion* 7 (Fall 1991) as "Feminist Anti-Judaism and the Christian God."

"Feminist Reflections on the State of Israel." In *Beyond Occupation: American Jewish, Christian, and Palestinian Voices for Peace,* edited by Rosemary Radford Ruether and Marc Ellis. Boston: Beacon Press, 1990.

"Transforming the Nature of Community: Toward a Feminist People of Israel." In *After Patriarchy: Feminist Transformations of the World Religions,* edited by P. Cooey, W. Eakin, and J. McDaniel. Maryknoll, NY: Orbis Books, 1991.

"Appropriation, Reciprocity, and Issues of Power." *Journal of Feminist Studies in Religion* 8 (Fall 1992): 105–110.

"Feminist Judaism and Repair of the World." In *Ecofeminism and the Sacred*, edited by Carol J. Adams. New York: Continuum, 1993. Reprinted in Spanish in *Del Cielo a la Tierra: Una Antologia de Teologia Feminista*, edited by Mary Judith Ress, et al. Santiago, Chile: Sello Azul, 1994.

"We Are Also Your Sisters: The Development of Women's Studies in Religion." *Women's Studies Quarterly* 21 (Spring–Summer 1993): 9–21. Reprinted in "Looking Back, Moving Forward: 25 Years of Women's Studies History." Special issue, *Women's Studies Quarterly* 25 (Spring–Summer 1997).

"Anti-Judaism in Feminist Christian Interpretation." In *Searching the Scriptures: A Feminist Introduction*, edited by Elisabeth Schüssler Fiorenza. New York: Crossroad, 1993.

* "Jewish Theology in Feminist Perspective." In *Feminist Perspectives on Jewish Studies*, edited by Lynn Davidman and Shelly Tenenbaum. New Haven: Yale University Press, 1994.

"What's in a Name? Exploring the Dimensions of What 'Feminist Studies in Religion' Means." Contributor. *Journal of Feminist Studies in Religion* 11 (Spring 1995): 132–136. Reprinted in *Feminism in the Study of Religion: A Reader*, edited by Darlene Juschka. London and New York: Continuum, 2001.

"Embodiment and Ambivalence: A Jewish Feminist Perspective." In *Embodiment, Morality, and Medicine,* edited by Lisa Sowle Cahill and Margaret Farley. Dordrecht, Netherlands: Kluwer Academic Publishers, 1995.

"Jewish Feminist Thought." In *History of Jewish Philosophy,* edited by Daniel H. Frank and Oliver Leaman. London and New York: Routledge, 1997.

* "Sexuality and *Teshuva:* Leviticus 18." In *Beginning Anew: A Woman's Companion to the High Holy Days,* edited by Judith Kates and Gail Reimer. New York: Simon & Schuster, 1997.

"Feminist Theology." In *The Sh'ma and Its Blessings.* Vol. 1, *My People's Prayerbook: Traditional Prayers, Modern Commentaries,* edited by Lawrence Hoffman. Woodstock, VT: Jewish Lights Publishing, 1997.

* "Sexual Orientation and Human Rights: A Progressive Jewish Perspective." In *Sexual Orientation and Human Rights in American Religious Discourse,* edited by Saul M. Olyan and Martha C. Nussbaum. New York and Oxford: Oxford University Press, 1998.

* "Lilith Revisited." In *Eve & Adam: Jewish, Christian, and Muslim Readings on Genesis and Gender,* edited by Kristen E. Kvam, Linda S. Schearing, and Valerie H. Ziegler. Bloomington and Indianapolis: Indiana University Press, 1999.

"The Academy as Real Life: New Participants and Paradigms in the Study of Religion." *Journal of the American Academy of Religion* 67 (September 1999): 521–538.

"Decentering Sex: Rethinking Jewish Sexual Ethics." In *God Forbid: Religion and Sex in American Public Life,* edited by Kathleen Sands. New York: Oxford University Press, 2000.

* "Authority, Resistance and Transformation: Jewish Feminist Reflections on Good Sex." In *Good Sex: Feminist Perspectives from the World's Religions,* edited by Patricia Jung, Mary Hunt, and Radhika Balakrishnan. New Brunswick, NJ: Rutgers University Press, 2001. Reprinted in *Body and Soul: Rethinking Sexuality as Justice Love,* edited by Marvin Ellison and Sylvia Thorson-Smith. Cleveland: Pilgrim Press, 2003; and in a slightly different form in *Best Jewish Writing 2002,* edited by Michael Lerner. Somerset, NJ: Jossey-Bass, 2002.

"Whose Initiative? Whose Faith?" *Journal of the American Academy of Religion* 70 (December 2002): 864–867.

"Dealing with Difference Without and Within." *Journal of Feminist Studies in Religion* 19 (Spring 2003): 91–95.

"Critical Theology and Jewish Sexual Ethics." In *Toward a New Heaven and a New Earth: Essays in Honor of Elisabeth Schüssler Fiorenza,* edited by Fernando Segovia. Maryknoll, NY: Orbis Press, 2003.

"Judith Plaskow: Jewish Feminist Theologian." In *Transforming the Faiths of Our Fathers: Women Who Changed American Religion,* edited by Ann Braude. New York: Palgrave Macmillan, 2004.

"Womanist/Jewish Feminist Dialogue." *The Union Seminary Quarterly Review* 58, nos. 3–4 (2004): 216–218.

Roundtable Discussion on Same-Sex Marriage, "Response." Martha Ackelsberg, coauthor. *Journal of Feminist Studies in Religion* 20 (Fall 2004): 107–112.

Entries in Reference Works

"Covenant" and "Feminist Theologies, Jewish." In *Dictionary of Feminist Theologies,* edited by Letty Russell and Sharon Clarkson. Louisville, KY: Westminster John Knox Press, 1996.

"Spirituality." In *Jewish Women in America: An Historical Encyclopedia,* edited by Paula Hyman and Deborah Dash Moore. New York and London: Routledge, 1997.

"Judaism and Feminism." In *Encyclopedia of Feminist Theories,* edited by Lorraine Code. London and New York: Routledge, 2000.

"Gott/Gottin aus judisch-feministischer Perspektive" (God/Goddess in Jewish Feminist Perspective). In *Worterbuch der Feministischen Theologie,* edited by Elisabeth Gossmann, et al. Gutersloh: Gutersloher Verlagshaus, 2002.

Popular Articles

* "The Jewish Feminist: Conflict in Identities." *Response* 18 (Summer 1973): 11–18. Reprinted in *The Jewish Woman: New Perspectives,* edited by Elizabeth Koltun. New York: Schocken Books, 1976. Also in *The Ethnic American Woman,* edited by Edith Blicksilver. Dubuque, IA: Kendall/Hunt, 1978.

* "The Coming of Lilith." In *Religion and Sexism: Images of Women in the Jewish and Christian Traditions,* edited by Rosemary Radford Ruether. New York: Simon & Schuster, 1974. Reprinted in *Womanguides: Readings Toward a Feminist Theology,* edited by Rosemary Radford Ruether. Boston: Beacon Press, 1985. Also in *Four Centuries of Jewish Women's Spirituality,* ed. Ellen Umansky and Dianne Ashton. Boston: Beacon Press, 1992.

"Bringing a Daughter into the Covenant." In *Womanspirit Rising,* edited by Carol P. Christ and Judith Plaskow. San Francisco: Harper & Row, 1979.

* "God: Some Feminist Questions." *Sh'ma* 17 (January 9, 1987): 38–40.

* " 'It Is Not in Heaven': Feminism and Religious Authority." *Tikkun* 5 (March–April 1990): 39–40.

"Up Against the Wall." *Tikkun* 5 (July–August 1990): 25–26.

* "Beyond Egalitarianism." *Tikkun* 5 (November–December 1990): 79–80. Reprinted in *The Jewish Philosophy Reader,* edited by Daniel Frank, Oliver Leaman, and Charles Manekin. London and New York: Routledge, 2000. Also in *Tikkun: An Anthology,* edited by Michael Lerner. Oakland and Jerusalem: Tikkun Books, 1992.

* "Jewish Anti-Paganism." *Tikkun* 6 (March–April 1991): 66–67.

* "Facing the Ambiguity of God." *Tikkun* 6 (September–October 1991): 70, 96. Reprinted in *The Jewish Philosophy Reader.*

* "What's Wrong with Hierarchy?" *Tikkun* 7 (January–February 1992): 65–66.

"The Problem of Evil." *Reconstructionist* 57 (Spring 1992): 17–19.

* "About Men." *Tikkun* 7 (July–August 1992): 51, 76.

"Creating a Feminist Judaism." *Manna* 37 (Autumn 1992), supplement.

"First Year Faculty" and "Promotion and Tenure." In *Guide to the Perplexing: A Survival Manual for Women in Religious Studies.* Atlanta: Scholars Press, 1992.

"Burning in Hell Conservative Movement Style." *Tikkun* 8 (May–June 1993): 49–50.

* "The Year of the Agunah." *Tikkun* 8 (September–October 1993): 52–53.

"Lesbian and Gay Rights: Asking the Right Questions." *Tikkun* 9 (March–April 1994): 31–32.

* "Dealing with the Hard Stuff." *Tikkun* 9 (September–October 1994): 57–58.

"Im and B'li: Women in the Conservative Movement." *Tikkun* 10 (January–February 1995): 55–56.

"Spirituality and Politics: Lessons from B'not Esh." *Tikkun* 10 (June–July 1995): 31–32, 85.

"Sex and Yom Kippur." *Tikkun* 10 (September–October 1995): 71–72.

"Progressive Homophobia." *Tikkun* 11 (March–April 1996): 65–67.

"Critique and Transformation: A Jewish Feminist Journey." In *Lifecycles: Jewish Women on Biblical Themes in Contemporary Life,* edited by Rabbi Debra Orenstein and Rabbi Jane Litman. Woodstock, VT: Jewish Lights Publishing, 1997.

* "Expanding the Jewish Feminist Agenda." *Sh'ma* 30, no. 586 (January 2000): 12.

* "The Continuing Value of Separatism." In *The Women's Passover Companion: Women's Reflections on the Festival of Freedom,* edited by Rabbi Sharon Cohen Anisfeld, Tara Mohr, and Catherine Spector. Woodstock, VT: Jewish Lights Publishing, 2003.

"Why We're Not Getting Married." Martha Ackelsberg, coauthor. *Lilith* 29 (Fall 2004): 48.

Credits